THE BARRISTER'S WORLD

And the nature of law

JOHN MORISON and PHILIP LEITH

OPEN UNIVERSITY PRESS
Milton Keynes · Philadelphia

Open University Press
Celtic Court
22 Ballmoor
Buckingham
MK18 1XW

and
1900 Frost Road, Suite 101
Bristol, PA 19007, USA

First Published 1992

British Library Cataloguing in Publication Data

Morison, John
  The barrister's world: And the nature of law.
  I. Title   II. Leith, Philip
  347.41

  ISBN 0–335–09396–5
  ISBN 0–335–09395–7 pbk

Library of Congress Cataloging-in-Publication Data

Morison, John, 1958–
    The barrister's world – and the nature of law/John Morison &
  Philip Leith.
      p.   cm.
    Includes bibliographical references (p.   ) and index.
    ISBN 0–335–09396–5 (hb) – ISBN 0–335–09395–7 (pb)
    1. Lawyers – Great Britain.   2. Practice of law – Great Britain.
  I. Leith, Philip, 1954–   .   II. Title.
  KD463.M67   1991
  349.41–dc20   91–12943
  [344.1]   CIP

Typeset by Redwood Press Limited
Printed in Great Britain by St Edmundsbury Press Limited
Bury St Edmunds, Suffolk

For Sue, Rachel, Hannah, Christine and Annie

'Whatever else you say tell them it's a wonderful life.'
(A barrister)

'You mustn't believe everything that barristers tell you:
barristers are always the heroes of their own stories, they're
all about how brilliantly they conducted their cases.'
(A barrister)

CONTENTS

PREFACE AND ACKNOWLEDGEMENTS

The printed word has held lawyers and legal academics in its spell for too long. Mostly, when we think about 'law' or 'Law', we think of it as a body of clear printed texts which open themselves up to close textual analysis and which then 'tell us' what to do. Yet the printed word has blinded us to the fact that much of what happens in law is not textual at all – it is to do with advocacy and persuasion. This blindness has been particularly apparent as it relates to what solicitors and barristers actually do: the research in this area is very limited. If only one percent of the time spent in textual analysis had been spent on analysing law in practice, we would have a completely different view of the nature of law.

In this book, we look to the non-textual nature of law and try to present a view of law which is more accurate, and which better describes the nature of law. Such a view is important for lawyers, academics and the public – for we move from accepting ideologically based pictures of the grandeur of law, to seeing law as a necessarily flawed human process.

The researches which led us to take this view of law were funded by the Queen's University of Belfast. We thank our colleagues in the School of Law for diverting these moneys in our direction. We are grateful to those barristers and advocates who allowed themselves to be interviewed. We also thank all those who helped us by providing contacts and in other related ways – Douglas Taylor, Ernest Ryder, Niall O'Shea, Norman Doe, John Edgar and the Council of Legal Education, Inns of Court School of Law.

The interviews conducted were given on the understanding that anonymity would be guaranteed. Apart from slight editing, the quotations are as they were recorded by us.

Our interview methodology was not as crudely empirical as some might have wished, since our target was the 'style of thinking' of advocates and barristers, rather than a mapping and measuring exercise in some neo-scientific manner. However, we feel that our chosen procedure has produced perspectives which the crude empiricists have not managed to produce in the past, and has thus been highly successful. We thank Professor Alan Paterson of Strathclyde University Law School, author of *The Law Lords*, for early discussion on these methods and providing helpful contacts and comments. Professor Paterson's comments upon drafts of this text were also very helpful.

In this book – unless specifically stated – we use the terms 'advocate' and 'barrister' interchangeably. Also in our interviews, a male-oriented flavour was apparent even when interviewing female barristers. This is reflected in the quotations, if not – hopefully – in the text.

Finally, we must acknowledge that the idea for the project began in informal discussions with some of our colleagues who have part-time practices at the bar. Without those early insights which they provided, we might never have began our researches at all. We also thank these colleagues for their useful comments upon earlier drafts of the manuscript.

PART I

THE PROBLEM OF LEGAL THEORY AND LEGAL PRACTICE

1

THE IMPORTANCE OF ADVOCACY

INTRODUCTION

We have lived through a century where, in the teaching and discussion of academic law, the role of the advocate has mostly been downplayed. As the training of the lawyer has moved from an apprenticeship system over to a university-based system (Abel, 1988), intending lawyers have found themselves more remote from the practice of law than ever before. In opposition to this, various forces and schools of thought (legal realism, clinical legal education and, most recently, Critical Legal Studies) have tried to bring the horse of legal education to the water of practice. Unfortunately, the typical teacher of law has drunk elsewhere.

Law, for most who teach law, has been seen to have life only in the law books on the library shelf, and to have authority only from the gradations of the printed word: case notes, legislation, law reports. It has been a century where the teaching of law has been remote from the practice of law, so much so that Roscoe Pound very early on asked why law in the law books was so different from law in practice (Pound, 1910). Since Pound's discussion of the divergence of law and practice, the situation may have got even worse. There now exists an embarrassed silence between the academic lawyer and the practitioner, marred only by the slight jarring sound of socio-legal research heard in the background.

We can see this silence by the fact that the advocate is the one actor in the legal process who has escaped the scalpel of the investigative researcher. Few studies have tried to explicate and understand the role of the barrister in the UK legal system. Yet, as we shall argue, the advocate and advocacy are central to the very notion of the nature of law and legal practice. A legal theory which ignores the art and science of advocacy is limited and blinkered by bottle-end spectacles.

Our study began through casual conversation with colleagues who carried out part-time practices at the bar. These colleagues, as skilled at teaching substantive law rules as anyone else, seemed to take on a different mask when describing law in action. Here there was little of the dry, technical analysis and commentary upon legal texts. It was replaced by discussion of the art of persuasion – persuading judges, juries, solicitors, clients – and the art of strategy – minimizing sentences, maximizing awards. There was a richness of description of the world of the barrister where obstacles had constantly to be side-stepped – the awkward judge, the unhelpful solicitor, the client who wished to plead not guilty to a strong prosecution. Our immersion in this was a baptism to Pound's law in practice.

We looked to the written materials on the barrister and the techniques of advocacy and found that it did not help us make the connection between practical and theoretical law. There was a tension which effectively pulled them apart. The writings of the barrister him or herself were generally of the sort which explained how Smith was saved from the gallows, or how – unluckily – Jones was lost to those same gallows. These were the writings of law as a game – winning some and losing others, the cut-and-thrust of life in the courtroom. The writings of the barrister turned academic gave no hint of the complexity of life in the courtroom. Herbert Hart, transformed from barrister to pivotal position in academic legal theory as Professor of Jurisprudence at Oxford, sets aside any knowledge he might have had about law in practice and talks about law as it ought to be – clear and safe for the middle classes (Morison, 1988: 138).

One form of writing spoke of strategy, eloquence and the testimony which saved or lost the day, and the other talked about dry rules, even though both were supposedly about the same institutional fact.

Even those who had written vade-mecums describing the barristerial role, had, it seemed to us, missed the mark. Those like Du Cann (1980) provided a picture of the barrister as an upstanding figure with strict moral codes but did not mention the tactics and less sightly behaviour which we heard of from our colleagues. On the other hand, a writer like Evans (1985) emphasized the strategic but gave no hint as to how law related to the task of advocacy. Indeed, to Evans, the much discussed (in academic circles) law of evidence could be reduced to several simple rules and, in criminal advocacy, it seemed that this was all the law that was required. Neither of these told us anything about how law and advocacy were related.

Those few academics who have considered the bar have mainly been interested in carrying out a social geography – mapping and measuring the social structure and familial relationships of barristers and solicitors. Foremost among these, of course, is Abel (1988), with his dense tabular argument for the Weberian progression of the legal profession from individual agent to corporate intermediary. For all the undoubted usefulness of this kind of research, it does not tell us what barristers do, nor how advocacy relates to the ideology of law and of justice. It simply continues the emphasis upon the legal profession as an upper-middle-class occupation. But this is not profoundly insightful: many other professions (e.g. academia) are essentially middle class, but studies which concentrate only on the schooling or back-ground of law teachers tell us little about their interests or what they do as academics.

We were thus left confused about what being a barrister was, what advocacy was and how much it related to legal education, and how law in practice related to law in books. We decided, therefore, to undertake our own investigation. The rest of this book is an attempt to explain what we found, and how we began to think about the relationship between written law and advocacy.

Perhaps the main theoretical point which we arrived at, and which we describe in Part III, is to do with rhetoric, a subject which is most commonly (and, we argue, errantly) seen as simply speechifying, or in St Augustine's words, as 'so much wind and noise'. Mostly, when rhetoric is described, it is considered a low form of persuasion, using subtle techniques to sell untruths, or half-truths. Even those authors who have shown an interest in the relationship of rhetoric to law have been cast under this shadow, which was described by Socrates as simply flattery:

> I sum up its substance in the name *flattery*. This practice, as I view it, has many branches, and one of them is cookery, which appears indeed to be an art [but is only] a habitude or knack . . . rhetoric [is] another branch of it, as also personal adornment and sophistry (quoted in I. F. Stone, 1988: 91).

Researchers have thus felt obliged, once having made the link between rhetoric and law, to try to make the link between rhetoric and justice as a counter to the Socratic charge of sophistry. We look to this later in the text where we suggest that this is a cul-de-sac in thinking. However, we can briefly outline our view here, that we see one of the main opponents of 'justice' as being the time-dependent nature of the legal process, i.e. the fact that a timetable exists to which the advocate, judge and litigants all have to accord. Justice, in its ideal form, would allow the continual replay of each and every case until the final truth (or death of the parties) was arrived at. The legal process cannot, of course, allow this (now the system even relies on the fact that most cases are not fought through). Since litigants, defendants and prosecutors do not have this time, they are left to marshal their facts, evidence and persuasion as best they can.

Our view is that law is essentially rhetorical, rather than logical as many would have it. But rhetoric, exemplified and practised by the advocate, is about the dual facets of persuasion and information. Those who look to rhetoric as speechifying do not see that legal information and legal knowledge are as intimately connected to the rhetorical arts as is persuasion. Later in the book, we will try to present a more flattering view of rhetoric. For now, we might suggest that our position is rather like that of Cicero who suggested that rhetoric is the first step in the civilizing process: no longer is force dominant, rather discussion, persuasion and the presentation of evidence become the necessary acts. This less critical view of rhetoric is why we have come to see advocacy as being of central importance in the understanding of legal theory and legal practice.

In the remaining sections of this chapter, we shall give a brief introduction to the history of advocacy and the bar, and outline our research method.

LEGAL RHETORIC IN THE ANCIENT WORLD

It is frequently asserted that there were no professional advocates in ancient Athens, for each and every citizen had the right and obligation to both act as judge and to present his own case should this be necessary. No doubt many of the political trials – including that of Socrates – were marked by the fact that those accused were capable of defending themselves through a high degree of oratory. However, this could not have been the case with every citizen. As Bonner (1979: 11) tells us:

> With the object of making each citizen take his full share in public life, and of preserving equality . . . in the citizen body, litigants, if citizens, were required to take their own cases in court. But this was an ideal beyond the possibility of achievement even in the Athens of Pericles. And so there were a class of men whose business it was to write speeches for those who were unequal to the task of pleading their own cases. These . . . did to a certain degree constitute a professional class, but they were not lawyers in our sense of the word. A knowledge of rhetoric was quite as essential as a knowledge of law. Moreover, the necessity of fitting the speech to the character of his client tended to keep the speech-writer in the background. Indeed, every artifice was resorted to in order to keep up the delusion that the litigant had prepared his own speech.

Athens was, of course, a highly rhetorical culture. Unlike today, where it is possible to carve a successful career in many areas without great powers of speech and oratory, it was not so in this Athenian world. The written word was not printed, and writing itself was nowhere near so common as we might imagine. We shall come back to this point later when we consider the nature of 'legal information', but the general point – expressed, for example, by Havelock (1963) and Kennedy (1963) – is that Athenian society at its height was primarily an oral society. Reading matter was limited, reading was taught at a much later age than would be expected today, and most information was passed on through oral techniques. Thus Homer's *Iliad* is now commonly seen as having been designed for public performance rather than private reading. It is now perceived as a social encyclopaedia which was told by storytellers, and was written down by, rather than written by, Homer (Parry, 1971; Kirk, 1976).

In this kind of oral culture, it was important for the citizen to have a command of the necessary techniques for putting his own case, and debating and arguing with fellow citizens. Even the rules of law were based in custom (which was oral, not written) rather than the formalized legislation of our times. The *Iliad*, as Parry has argued, was a social encyclopaedia which acted in part as a resource for customary and magisterial law. But, as Bonner's quotation tells us, the problem with such cultures is that even though so much of the educational process was directed towards teaching rhetoric, not everyone has the same rhetorical skill. As in a written culture, not everyone's writing is as persuasive as that of others. It became necessary to have a class of people who would help in the preparation of arguments to be put before the Athenian court. The divergence between individual oratorical skills was as problematic for Athenians as it is now for us. For, if we believe that the purpose of a court is to get to the truth of a matter, might it not be the case that a good orator can hide the truth from the court and free the guilty or convict the innocent? As Cicero was later to say (in private) to someone he had spoken for, 'Let me tell you it was I who produced the necessary darkness in court to prevent your guilt from being visible to everyone.'

There were even some suggestions that it was poor strategy to let it be known that one's speech had been written by particularly good orators. Antiphon was a case in point:

> Antiphon's reputation for rhetorical skill and subtlety aroused so much popular prejudice against him that his open advocacy for a cause would have been more harmful than helpful. Consequently, as Thucydides points out, he refrained from speaking in public (Bonner, 1927: 8).

Though it should also be said that Antiphon's oligarchic views and his later execution for being involved in undermining Athenian democracy might have had as much to do with his unpopularity as his rhetorical skills. It is Socrates who we recognize as the main opponent of the primacy of rhetoric, decrying it as sophistry, a word which is now read as a term of abuse. Stone has suggested that Socrates was both opposed to the Sophist's philosophical position as well as their (lower) position in the social order, and that:

> The antagonism between Socrates and the Sophists, as portrayed in Xenephon and Plato, has blackened their name.
> Until then the term sophiste denoted a skill of any kind. The word sophistes came to mean a skilled workman or artist and was soon also applied to diviners, poets and musicians. The legendary Seven Wise Men of Greece were called *sophistai*, as were the pre-Socratic philosophers. It became an honorable appellation again in the Roman empire for teachers of Greek rhetoric and philosophy (I. F. Stone, 1988: 41).

Since so much of our contemporary thinking about law and advocacy is related to this very idea about the ability of rhetoric to act for ill causes – is it sophistry or is it not – we shall return to discuss this point later. For example, in Part III, when we look to the evidence we have from barristers, we shall see that the relationship between 'speechifying' and 'facts' is another representation of this problem.

With the decline of Athenian culture and the rise of the Roman Republic, there was no concomitant rise or fall in the value of rhetoric and legal advocacy: in Rome, it remained every bit as important as in Athens. However, it now became more common for legal advocacy to be handled by a third party to the affair, even though payment was not supposed to be made for these lawyering services. As described by a spokesman in Tacitus' *Dialogue on Orators*, legal rhetoric was something apart:

> You cannot imagine any profession in the whole country more productive of practical benefits, or that carries with it a sweeter sense of satisfaction, or that does more to enhance a man's personal standing, or that brings more honour and renown here in Rome, or that secures a more brilliant reputation throughout the Empire and in the world at large. . . . Can there be any safer line to take than the practice of an art which gives you an ever-ready weapon with which to protect your friends, to succour those to whom you are a stranger, to bring deliverance to persons in jeopardy, and even to strike fear and terror into the hearts of malignant foes – while you yourself have no anxiety, entrenched as you are behind a rampart of inalienable authority and power? (Tacitus, 1970: 239–40)

As we know from studies of Roman Law, there was much more formal law than had been in the Greek model. Yet, the transcripts of speeches made of legal advocacy refer little to the rules of law. Most use the techniques of persuasion rather than the techniques of textual interpretation. Quintilian, whose rediscovery so radically changed the medieval educational world (Ong, 1958), is perhaps the prime example of the legal rhetorician. His *Institutio Oratoria* provides a detailed introduction to the many technical aspects of rhetoric and advocacy: speech production (a loud voice was essential), physical movement, rhetorical figures or tropes, and so on. Of the charge of sophistry ('It is eloquence that snatches criminals from the penalties of the law'), he replied that oratory did have the power to act both for the good and bad, and thus was or could be problematic. However, he attempted to divorce oratory from rhetoric, the latter being the 'science of speaking':

> These problems, however, may be left to those who hold that rhetoric is the power to persuade. If our definition of rhetoric as the science of speaking well implies that an orator must be a good man, there can be no doubt about its usefulness (Quintilian, Book II, 1921: xvi).

And the 'science of speaking' was the way in which we give voice to reason:

> But reason by itself would help us but little and would be far less evident in us, had we not the power to express our thoughts in speech; for it is the lack of this power rather than thought and understanding, which they do to a certain extent possess, that is the great defect in other living things (Quintilian, Book II, 1921: xvi).

The notion of 'giving voice' to reason (particularly legal/factual reason) is one which we today find expressed by barristers and advocates.

The role of rhetoric has been of enormous philosophical and historical significance, and nowhere has the role of rhetoric been more obvious than in the court of law. For it was here that politics were acted out: the trial of Socrates; the various trials where Quintilian himself prepared the defence or prosecution, etc. We can clearly see that the forensic aspect of rhetoric was of vital import to both Athenian and Roman societies. We shall see later that the problems which busied the ancients still philosophically and practically busy us.

THE INNS OF COURT, FACULTY OF ADVOCATES AND THE BAR LIBRARIES

The legal system in the British Isles consists of four main jurisdictions, each of which is structured in a slightly different way. Generally, though, barristers have rights of audience – that is, rights to appear in courts – which far exceed those granted to the other side of the legal profession, solicitors. Currently, the legal profession in the UK is going through a period of enforced change where there are attempts to break down this traditional distinction between the two sides of the profession. The Scottish legal system has taken to this more readily, perhaps, than the English or Northern Ireland jurisdictions. As we shall see later, this is perhaps because the relationship between solicitor and advocate (which is what the 'barrister' in Scotland is called) differs in Scotland from the other jurisdictions. However, this re-lationship seems to have altered only recently. Wilson (1965) asserts that the taboo of advocates mixing with solicitors (which now seems to happen frequently) existed in Scotland (as it does now in England and Northern and Southern Ireland) when she carried out her fieldwork. Scotland is, it appears, at the very forefront of changes in both sides of the profession and perhaps needs a fuller study than we could give it – particularly a study looking at structural aspects, rather than the nature of advocacy, as is the concern of this text.

The structure of the legal profession, though, has never been completely set in concrete and the current changes being forced by government, while radical in intent, are not changing a profession which has existed unchanged for a millennium. However, the profession has been relatively static in terms of occupational role since the middle of the eighteenth century. By this time, English barristers were a clearly definable section of the profession, whose primary task was advocacy. Prior to this period, barristers were not regarded as full advocates until they became benchers:

> The majority [of barristers] did not appear again in the records of the Inn and were not practitioners of any note at Westminster. For these, as for the non-practising barrister of today, call to the bar was a mark of intellectual attainment and of gentle (or professional) status, but not an occupational description (Baker, 1981: 30).

In Scotland, the titular role of advocate as full participant in the court has had a longer history than that of the barrister in England. It was in the sixteenth century that the Faculty of Advocates was initiated in Edinburgh. However,

> It was not until the seventeenth century that advocates began to act exclusively as pleaders before the supreme courts, a role all members of the Faculty adopted by the end of the eighteenth century (Murdoch, 1981: 151).

Essentially, then, the modern structure of the barrister/advocate as pleader rather than as someone who 'solicits' began in the seventeenth and eighteenth centuries. But from about the end of the fifteenth century, there was a clear profession of lawyer, albeit existing in a different professional structure. This does not mean that advocacy was not important prior to this time in the legal histories of England, Scotland and Ireland.

The reader of Bede's *A History of the English Church and People* is able to follow the move from the tribal, warring society which was the situation left after the Roman occupation ended in Britain. As Christianity gradually came to prominence, the tensions between the Celtic and Roman versions of Catholicism led to the dominance of the latter (and its particular ecclesiastical legal orientation). With Viking and Norman attentions, the political/legal system of the British Isles began the move from the patchwork of tribal leaders into the medieval world, a world we know to have been highly influenced by rhetoric. Though we have no history of legal advocacy in these times, we know that speech was by far the most important form of communication – the level of literacy among the population was low, and, as many have asserted, the medieval mind was much more like that of the Ancient Greek than of today's scientific culture. Even reading was different from today – the ability to read a manuscript in silence was such a novelty that a monk who could do it was hailed as a marvel (Hadas, 1954). It was not to be until the invention of the printing press that the medieval mind subsided (Huizinga, 1924) and the modern visually oriented mind took prominence.

Walter Ong, in his writings on orality and literacy, has concentrated upon the manner in which knowledge is held and transmitted in these sorts of oral, manuscript and print cultures (see e.g. Ong, 1981). He suggests that in pre-print cultures, for example, this is done by the continual use of proverbs. If we sat beside someone from an oral or medieval culture, Ong asserts, the speaker would not use the same speech techniques as we would – his or her talk would be full of proverbs and aphorisms. Indeed, he or she would not be able to converse without these. We have much evidence that this aspect of oral culture existed right up to Elizabethan times: there is, for example, the text of an MP's speech in Parliament which is almost a serial recitation of proverbs (Wilson, 1941), and we know that one of Erasmus' first tasks after the invention of printing was to collect lists of proverbs and have them printed (Erasmus, 1530).

The point of this diversion into medievalism is to emphasize that, in the pre-medieval and medieval world where there was little of today's noise, the sound of the human voice and the continual oral recitation of knowledge was paramount. Law, when written, could not have been the same creature it is in our current legal culture, for it was used and understood with a completely different mental outlook. This was a more oral mental outlook than we have now.

The rise of the lawyer, and particularly the barrister/advocate as a professional class of pleader, can thus be seen to be linked to the decline of this orally inclined mentality. Exactly what sort of a linking this is is difficult to judge. We might say that as British society become more modern in outlook because it had broken the barrier of manuscript culture, law too became more modern and complex and required a professional class to interpret it. Or, alternatively, it might be maintained that the rise of printing, which was so decisive in initiating the Reformation, gave the impetus to make law more secular and less oriented to ecclesiastical power. (The bible, and therefore interpretation of religious and legal-religious truth, was kept in the hands of the priest until the Reformation, when it became readily available to non-clergy through printing.) Or, again, it could be said that printing turned law into a commodity which could be processed and handled by this newly required and important occupational class.

These are the sorts of problems concerning the history of law and lawyers which have received scant attention. Most historians seem implicitly to argue for the continuity of legal experience from Athens (or perhaps Rome) to today. Yet the differences between medieval and post-medieval law seem to us to be connected to the problem of rhetoric and law which we mentioned above – that is, how much is law rhetorical and how much is law positivist (i.e. rule- and fact-oriented). We shall return to this matter later. For now, though, it is important to set a marker in place to highlight the fact that the barrister/advocate did not simply come into existence by magical forces of spontaneous creation: something changed in the world which made the barrister an essential element of the legal process. The same, of course, has to be said for the solicitor and his historical predecessors.

Max Weber, whose work has moved many studies into the legal profession, was of the opinion that lawyers themselves were a major cause of the rise of the legal-rational society. But this, in our view, seems to give too large a degree of power to one small group of actors to change society. Larger forces must have been at work than that of the legal profession.

The rise of this new class of professional advocate was structured by their educational and business environment. It has only been in the twentieth century that universities have become major agents for legal education. Until this period, most legal training was by an apprenticeship system – one learned the law in the company of lawyers rather than academic lawyers. This legal education was carried out in England in the Inns of Court, and in Scotland by the Faculty of Advocates.

Today, these institutions have changed from being guild associations concerned with education as much as self-support, to being largely professional societies which are a mix between businesses and cooperatives. This strange mix is due to the fact that, in the UK, the barrister and advocate are almost always self-employed. As we shall see, any coming together of barristers into a working group that shares resources is still constrained by the fact that they are self-employed.

The Inns of Court are located in central London. They are essentially late medieval guilds of lawyers which function in the present day as an organizational focus for the profession. Around the Inns of Court, there are a whole series of sets of chambers – groups of barristers who share offices, clerks and (sometimes) secretarial support. The physical conditions are generally agreed to be intolerable, e.g. senior barristers who earn six-figure sums often have to share office space. Yet little has been done to improve the situation. Chambers are usually served by a barristers' clerk, an administrator who serves as an intermediary between barristers and solicitors in the taking of briefs (i.e. cases) and the agreement of financial terms. These clerks usually earn a percentage of the income generated by their chambers. Given the large income which some clerks do earn, there has been a recent tendency to turn the position into a salaried post. Flood's (1983) *Barristers' Clerks* paints the picture of the social status and the importance of the clerk to the barrister.

In the English provinces, sets of chambers are to be found in many cities. Here, frequently, the pattern of large incomes being supported by an inadequate physical environment is often the norm. It is the exceptional chambers which have moved into modern office accommodation.

Chambers are composed of a well-rounded body of barristers – there might be several Queen's Counsel, i.e. barristers who have 'taken silk' and moved up the legal hierarchy, together with more senior barristers all the way down to raw recruits straight from pupillage. We look in Chapter 2 in more detail at the career path of the barrister. Some chambers will offer a mixed practice of both criminal and civil work (the latter covering divorce, business and other non-criminal litigation) and some will be more specialized. As barristers leave a chambers (to become judges, or to set up their own chambers perhaps) and others join, the character of that chambers may change, e.g. moving from civil to criminal work.

Chambers are cooperative ventures. The costs of running these are met from the income of barristers as individuals: their earnings are their own, rather than that of the chambers.

In Scotland, there is no chambers system, although there are clerks (some six in number). Advocates frequently work from their homes where they meet clients, or from the Faculty of Advocates in Edinburgh. This is situated in the old Scottish Parliament buildings, and consultations with clients take place in Parliament Hall. The latter often evidences the unusual habit of pacing up and down (with a firm turn at each end) a historic hall filled with oil paintings of past and distinguished lawyers while discussing a case with a solicitor or client. Although there are no chambers, there are clerks, who are centrally located in Parliament House and who look after the diaries and such like of the advocates. The Faculty of Advocates is a combination of a business centre (based on the clerks) and a law library. Since much litigation in Scotland takes place in Edinburgh (where the supreme courts are), most advocates are resident in Edinburgh. We are told that some resentment exists among Glaswegian solicitors for having to brief advocates from Edinburgh. Our interviews in Edinburgh were small in number; however, it seems from Wilson's (1965) study that the clerks in the Faculty of Advocates mirror closely those of the English clerks. The Scottish system thus seems to be closer to that of England than to Northern Ireland or the Republic of Ireland with their clerk-free system.

In Northern Ireland, barristers use the Bar Library, and have neither chambers nor clerks. Barristers in Northern Ireland thus have to make contacts with solicitors themselves, and are more individually organized even than in Scotland. In the Republic of Ireland, the set-up is similar, with barristers working out of a law library situated within the Four Courts building in the centre of Dublin.

In all four situations, it is important to realize that barristers and advocates operate professionally in courts, particularly if they undertake criminal work. This means that they are not completely office-bound, unless they are civil barristers who are primarily concerned with handling paper. There are, therefore, many opportunities to meet with colleagues in a collegiate atmosphere and discuss the various happenings in the courts and such like. They are, particularly outside of London, small worlds where most practitioners know many of their barristerial colleagues, having met them both socially and in court.

The picture painted is one of the individual practitioner in a relatively static structure – chambers, Faculty of Advocates or Bar Libraries. In this situation, the individual barrister or advocate needs to be a competitive animal. There is only a certain amount of work available at any point in time, and there are frequently periods when there is a surfeit of barristers.

The competitive element ensures that not all barristers earn six-figure salaries. Certainly, those at the top of the profession can make such salaries – in many cases, higher than the managing directors of the companies who use their services. But, at the bottom of the hierarchy – where newly called barristers spend much time in magistrates' courts, etc. – work is often difficult to come by, and payment is (as all barristers complain) delayed by solicitors. Many drop out from practice simply because of the financial problems they are experiencing.

Finally, a word should be said about the 'Weberization' of the legal profession, which means basically the progression suggested by Max Weber that lawyers will become more employed than self-employed. Some evidence of this has been reported, where barristers are being employed as salaried employees rather than operating in the structure described above. An overview is given of this in Mackie's (1989) *Lawyers in Business*. However, the numbers presently seem not to be large.

THE RESEARCH

As with the beginning of most research, we were unsure about exactly what we would find. Our initial plan had been to concentrate upon the Bar Library in Belfast, since it was convenient and we already had relatively good contacts there. We also felt that 'The Troubles' – that euphemism for para-military activity – might highlight aspects of the bar which were hidden in the other jurisdictions. Thus, we began by interviewing a relatively random sample of barristers, at all stages of their careers.

Early comments from academic lawyers suggested that we should con-strain ourselves more according to the various types of court, i.e. we should have samples of barristers who usually appeared in magistrates' courts, county courts, etc. This approach accords with the more traditional view of legal education – teaching about the legal process as relatively structured units of adjudication. We did not take this approach because we felt that our interest was advocacy rather than the courts. Anyway, our findings agreed with our hunch, i.e. there was a commonality in technique and philosophy among all the barristers we originally spoke to. But this is not surprising, for barristers will frequently appear in different courts, even in one day. They transcend the individual courts, rather than are limited by them.

As we discovered this commonality, we began to wonder whether this transferred over to the other jurisdictions, which we had only intended to look at briefly. We therefore carried out more interviews than originally planned in England and Wales, and some in Scotland. (The Republic of Ireland, too, provided informants.) There too, despite some clear differences between the Scottish advocate and the barrister in England and Wales, we discovered this commonality of technique and philosophy. After our initial interviews in Scotland, we made reference to Nan Wilson's (1965) excellent, but unpublished, PhD thesis. However, it should be noted that in the past 25 years, much has changed in Scottish legal circles which requires updating in Wilson's work. In many respects, though, we find her analysis comple-mentary to our own.

There are – as the literature of the social sciences attest – many problems with fact gathering from interviewing. It is frequently difficult for people to give truthful and frank answers to interviewers for multiple reasons. For example, they might wish to express (and, perhaps, believe in) the pro-fessional ideology; they might be suspicious of our intentions; they might simply misinterpret the questions asked of them. All of these problems were evident, but we still feel that – given the limitations of interview time and the ever-turning tape-recorder – our interviewees tried their best to answer our questions. However, it was often apparent that, the more experienced the barrister, the more difficult it was to achieve any sort of interview rapport; the less experienced the barrister, the more quickly could we get useful information. This, of course, is easy to understand: barristers generally are used to choosing their words with care, and not giving hostages to fortune. We did, anyhow, have sources who were prepared to provide us with less ideologically sound pictures of life at the bar: this was particularly the case when the behaviour being described was not approved of.

We are aware that we have not provided the final and full picture of the barrister's world. However, we are confident that our perspective is reasonably close to life. There are any number of ways in which our study could have been enlarged, e.g. by interviewing more solicitors about barristers, judges about barristers, etc. However, any research project has to constrain itself somehow, and we hope that our future research, as well as that of others, will take these multivariates into account.

In the chapters in Part II, we look to the different aspects of the barrister's world. We look to the ever present need to find work, where this comes from, the decisions which have to be made about career paths, relationships with the client, solicitor and the judge, and so on. These can all be seen to be obstacles which the advocate has to surmount and evade in his or her professional career. But we also look to the element of persuasion which advocates repeatedly emphasized to us: the control over the unfolding drama in the court, and the loss of control when things go wrong.

Our interest in advocacy was never simply the outcome of a desire to classify and describe. More important to us was the already mentioned 'embarrassed silence' between the academic lawyer and the practitioner. To the academic lawyer, law exists in the textbooks of a law library; to the practitioner, law seems to be something different and more strategic. Rather than try to bring these two views together, the silence is brought in to cover up the differences: barristers consider that academics don't know what 'it's really like', and academics frequently think that barristers rarely bother with 'the law'.

Our questions to barristers frequently mirrored the concern of academics, and dealt with subjects such as rules, the manipulation of these rules, etc. And we met the recurrent reply that most advocacy is not about rules, but about 'facts'. Since we had been involved in an earlier project to argue against a rule-based approach to law (Leith and Ingram, 1988), we were none too keen to accept a fact-based one in its place. It seemed to us that these were simply the two sides of the practitioner/advocate dichotomy.

As we continued to interview and consider our results, it became apparent to us that there was a truth between these two opposing perspectives. It was that 'law' is a confusing mix of rhetoric and information. The former was not simply speechifying about factual situations, and the latter was not simply, for example, about rules culled from legislation or case reports. In Part III, we will look in more detail at this problem and compare our interpretation of our findings with that discussed in the book *Reconstructing Reality in the Court-Room* by Bennett and Feldman (1981), a text which is seen as being important in the context of understanding legal language and the relationship of rhetoric to law. Simply put, the authors argue that advocacy in a criminal trial is primarily a task of storytelling. We will argue that it is too simplistic a thesis which these authors argue, and that, for example, they ignore the relationship between the courtroom and the written texts of law. Our thesis is that advocacy is much more than storytelling techniques.

CONCLUSION

Although our central concern is the role of the barrister, it should not be forgotten that our broader aim is to try to shed light on the nature of law. It would have been easy to have been side-tracked into analysing the differences between the three jurisdictions of the British legal system, but this measuring and mapping exercise would have told us little about 'law' and more about the social structure of society. Our tendency, therefore, has been to gloss over some of the differences that we found between the different juris-dictions. No doubt such differences are interesting, and do highlight aspects of the cultural nature of legal systems, but in a book which attempts to provide an overview and an introduction to advocacy and the study of advocacy, such evidence would have hidden the trees in the forest. We have therefore tried to give the necessary flavour without the pedantry.

Some of the literature which we consult in Part III is of North American origin, and it is useful to consider the discrepancies between the sorts of research which are frequently carried out in that jurisdiction than those carried on in the UK. It seems to us that it is much more readily accepted in the USA that, for example, the result of any trial can be affected by the participating judge or lawyers. This has led to much research into many areas of legal life in the USA. For example, one early study of the ethnomethodol-ogist school of sociology involved taping a jury deliberation room to ascer-tain the sorts of aspects discussed and the strategies used to reach a conclusion (Turner, 1974: 15). Such research would not be possible in the current UK climate.

The problem seems to be that, for whatever reason, there is a commitment to keeping up the British ideological picture of justice, and a fear of the actuality becoming reported. We do not, of course, support this view. It seems to us that law and the legal process are so central to the operation of society, that it is healthier to accept the warts than to hide them with make-up that will crack with time. Too high a commitment to the heightened, ideological view can cause serious miscarriages of justice, since the system is seen as more important than the bit players. Jerome Frank's very last book (written with his daughter), *Not Guilty* (1957), emphasizes our point that the timetable of law and the rhetorical nature of advocacy should not allow us to believe that judgements, once made, should be inviolate.

In Part II, we look to the evidence and materials which we gained from our interviews with barristers, and begin to suggest the complexity of what we describe as legal information.

PART II

THE PRACTICE OF LAW

Introduction to Part II

THE BARRISTER'S WORLD

One popular image of the barrister – both as the figure in literature and the ideal to which many law students gravitate – is of someone very learned in the texts of law: someone in a wig and gown who spends time immersed in ancient books searching for arcane points of law emerging only to triumph in the courtroom by outwitting the opposition. The printed word, according to this view, is the very life source of the barrister, whether in the form of legislation, reported court decision, or in the briefs (tied in pink ribbon) which follow the barrister from library or chambers to court and back.

The emphasis upon the text-based nature of advocacy (which mirrors the text-based view of law) suggests that the barrister is a specialist in textual interpretation. Solicitors, therefore, consult barristers on difficult points of law.

Taken to extremes, this view of advocates suggests that they may be men (usually) of affairs. But this is generally in a somewhat donnish sense and the trappings of chambers and clerks, libraries and robing rooms serve only to reinforce the impression that the barrister is the conduit between the wisdom of the law in books and its application in the world.

Our view is that such an image gives a skewed picture of the barrister's world and thus of the legal universe. We will, in this Part, argue that most barristers are involved in very much more than a simple hunt for a precedent or point of procedure that will save the case. Their world is a complex, often hostile one, where scholarship and oratory are not necessarily among the necessary or essential survival skills.

While our own interest is the barrister, it is useful to note that a limited amount of work has been done in investigating the solicitor's world. As will be seen, the barrister's world links closely with that of the solicitor; therefore, it is important to understand the pressures upon the solicitor, and in what light this latter profession is best seen. The research that has been carried out tends to point to the fact that solicitors are *small businessmen*, rather than interpreters of law. For example, Campbell (1976) found that a sample of solicitors spent only about an hour a week on legal research, the rest of their time being taken up with client management, negotiation, routine procedure etc. Even the time spent on legal research was more akin to revising old knowledge, rather than learning new legal knowledge. The solicitor works in an environment where telephones ring, clients appear and many clients' files are in action or awaiting action. It is not an atmosphere that encourages legal research.

This might suggest that, if solicitors do not undertake legal research, then barristers must do so. However, this was not our finding. One reason for this is that the career of the barrister is so dependent upon the active assistance of many other people. Given the lack of independence, barristers must be ever careful to succeed in interpersonal relationships: failure to do so could result in lost work, and could mitigate against future advancement.

In the early stages, the barrister must find a senior barrister who is prepared to act as *pupil master*, and, in those jurisdictions which operate a chambers system, a tenancy must still generally be won. At every stage, barristers are dependent on solicitors in private practice, business or government, not only to give them work of the right kind and on the correct scale but to pay them promptly. The advocate is always dependent on those others involved in the preparation and presentation of his or her case. The solicitor must process the raw information properly and provide sufficient information. The witnesses must perform as expected. The opposing counsel (and, if they exist, one's senior or junior partner) must play not only according to the rules, but in line with the common expectations and understandings which can make life so much easier and predictable. There is, or may be, a jury of twelve ordinary citizens, perhaps of fixed opinion or perhaps simply resentful of having to attend, who must be persuaded. Above all, there is the judge who becomes, in the words of one advocate we spoke to, the 'centre of the barrister's universe'.

After the case, whether successfully or unsuccessfully run, there may still be a solicitor and client that need to be satisfied. There is also the wider audience beyond the particular case in hand: other solicitors who must be satisfied enough in order that one secures future work and one's peers. Elevation in the profession – securing better work, attaining senior counsel status or being appointed to the bench – depends on the good opinion of one's colleagues and particularly on the judiciary. It is against this background that the strategy of each case must be planned using all the knowledge, insight and experience that one has, in addition to whatever information can be scrambled together in the time available.

It is this element of time that dictates much in the life of a barrister. There is not only the problem of finding time for preparation (including, if necessary, legal interpretation), but all sorts of problems caused by the difficulty of predicting how long other cases are to run. Will Smith's be a ten-minute affair, an hour, a morning? Can Jones' case be fitted in on the same day, too? These are important matters for the barrister. If he or she is able to make such predictions successfully, then he or she will be able to be in certain locations at certain times to cover enough cases so as to be busy and successful. It is perhaps revealing to note that among all the barristers we spoke to, most were late for their appointment with us. Many simply could not attend, having being held up elsewhere (sometimes in different cities).

Therefore, given the unfriendly environment in which we find the barrister immersed, we are able to paint a different picture from that traditionally presented of the barrister. Rather than seeing the barrister as a reflective, scholarly individual dividing his or her time between a book-lined study and the rarefied, debating chamber atmosphere of the court, we will argue for a different image of both our subject and his or her milieu. We see the barrister more accurately portrayed as a fully social individual who must satisfy all sorts of competing demands, while at the same time carving out a living from a not particularly welcoming environment.

At the same time, we suggest that the court, and indeed the whole legal process, can be understood only if we move away from the academically (and popularly) construed perception of law being about abstract rules and towards a fuller understanding of what goes on in the real world of the barrister.

2

THE BARRISTER'S ROLE
AND CAREER

INTRODUCTION

An idealized potted history of the successful barrister would begin with a degree, most frequently today a law degree. After this degree course, potential barristers undertake some postgraduate professional study encompassing the various procedural elements of being a barrister (which forms to use in various situations, etc.) that are not found in the undergraduate legal courses. Presentation in court and advocacy is also taught and discussed. Generally, these professional courses are not too intellectually demanding, but are more burdensome than the examinations for entry to the profession were in the past. Few who successfully gain a place on such a course fail.

On leaving professional training, the potential barrister enters *pupillage*, and he or she must find a *pupil master* and/or *chambers* (the latter in England) to whom/which he or she is attached for a period of some months. In Scotland and the Republic of Ireland, pupillage is referred to as 'devilling'. During the early part of pupillage, young barristers are not allowed to work on their own and thus have no earning power. Finding chambers or a pupil master is difficult, and some potential barristers fail at this point.

After the specified time as pupils, young barristers are allowed to take cases in their own right and thus have some earning power. The cases which are offered to them are in the lowest courts where their advocacy is tested. If they are successful in gaining work, they should be able to move gradually up the hierarchy, taking on more difficult and more remunerative cases. They might then begin to specialize in either criminal or civil law, but this will depend as much upon contacts, chambers, etc., as anything else.

A reasonably senior and successful barrister might then consider 'taking silk', that is, becoming a Senior or Queen's Counsel (QC). Or, as a barrister with a number of years' practice, his or her name might be put forward as a potential judicial appointment. Such an appointment is particularly welcome to a barrister approaching retirement, for a pension comes with a judicial post. A lower income as a judge might well be countered by a higher income during retirement.

At all these stages, of course, there is the possibility of failure or an alternative career move. Such a progression might not be successfully managed due to limited ability or (especially in the early stages) a lack of income. Many barristers have left the bar to pursue a career in politics (and some MPs still have active practices). Some become legal academics, and practise less frequently or not at all. However, the more successful the advocate, the more difficult it will be – as in any profession – to alter one's career path.

While this potted outline is perhaps familiar, it tells us nothing about the relationship between law and practice. What is less familiar are the rites of passage that begin after the call to the bar and the commencement of the period of pupillage, where begins the process that separates barristers from other lawyers and further again from the rest of the world.

The sort of practice-oriented education which begins after a first law degree is very different from anything that has gone before. Indeed, one writer of a textbook written for students at the Inns of Court School of Law goes so far as to suggest that as students prepare for professional practice, it might be necessary to ' "unlearn" some elements of the academic stage' (Blake, 1989: 2).

If the emergent barrister is not then simply putting into effect the law in books, what is he or she then learning to do? The course manuals for professional examinations are full of information about whether to sit or stand in a special appointment with the bankruptcy master and the correct form of address in the vocative case for a Recorder in Manchester ('My Lord/My Lady', but 'Your Honour' anywhere else) (Council of Legal Education, 1989: 306–309). Clearly, however, a mastery of such professional shibboleths does not by itself transform the former law student into an advocate. What does the job description of barrister involve?

For us, the centrally defining characteristic of a barrister's work is advocacy. Advocacy or persuasion is what the barrister does in looking for work, preparing for work and executing work. In asserting this, we realize that we may be going against a trend in the training of the profession which is increasingly emphasizing the broad front of practical skills. This trend can be seen in the weight given to the training of barristers in the Green Paper on *The Work and Organisation of the Legal Profession* (1989) and in the new bar vocational course which began in 1989. The redesigned course for bar students, with its identification of the skills a barrister actually uses and therefore needs to acquire, isolated seven areas:

- legal research,
- fact management,
- interviewing,

- opinion writing,
- drafting,
- negotiation,
- advocacy.

For those doing the job and those teaching others to do it, advocacy seems to be only a part of the picture. Why then, in the face of such authority, do we place advocacy in such a central position? Briefly, it is because we argue for a new and more general understanding of what advocacy is all about – both what is involved and who is persuaded. As this book progresses, it will become apparent that we see advocacy not just as one aspect of the barrister's job, but as the central and defining characteristic of the barrister's role.

It is not just judges and juries who are persuaded, but solicitors, lay clients, colleagues, witnesses and the general public. They are persuaded not just of the rightness of one or other side of an argument, but to a view of many issues that coincides with that of the barrister. Persuasion takes place orally but also in writing. We were reminded many times by barristers of the importance of paperwork in their lives. Even on paper their role is to persuade, to find out what is wanted via instructions and then advocate that thing using whatever arguments can be found. Legal aid boards are persuaded of the merits or otherwise of a case, solicitors and lay clients are persuaded to take up or drop various courses of action (and afterwards of the rightness of such decisions) and other barristers are persuaded to concede points or to settle. Only after success or failure here, does a barrister get an opportunity to persuade a judge or jury in the traditional sense.

Even in court, persuasion is not just a simple yes-or-no, take-it-or-leave-it affair: witnesses are persuaded that certain conclusions might be more consistent with their observations, nuances are urged, alternative scenarios at many levels are suggested and unsatisfactory interpretations and outcomes are mitigated. Many of the practitioners we spoke to referred to the difficulty of anticipating exactly which cases will go to court and which will settle. As a consequence, most barristers treat all cases in a similar fashion, as if they were going to have to argue them all the way. One result of this is that a barrister screens everything with a view to its usefulness or otherwise to the point of view that he or she will be putting forward. Bad points are as important as good ones in order to know what has to be done.

This court/persuasion focus is, of course, an obvious consequence of the adverserial system: partiality, although falling short of what in the USA is euphemistically termed *extreme client identification*, is what is required, and clearly the system is built around this. This wide view of advocacy is not without its adherents in the profession itself. David Latham QC, Chairman of the Bar's Working Party on Pupillage and Vice-Chairman of the Professional Standards Committee of the Bar Council, has written:

> There are specialist areas at the Bar in which court advocacy plays only a
> small part in the overall work of the barrister. But for the vast majority

of the Bar, even the paperwork is a form of advocacy, in the sense that it is either advice directly concerned with the client's chance of success in proceedings, or the drafting of pleadings and other documents which are, in effect, written advocacy, and can have a significant effect on the ultimate outcome of any proceedings. At the end of the day, however, the barrister is judged on his ability in court (Latham, 1990: 12).

In our view, advocacy starts well before the courtroom door and it involves very much more than simply deploying formal legal arguments in a purely rational process. Advocacy takes place in the context of the complex social world of the legal profession and the courts, and its successful practice involves mastery of this environment just as much, if not more, as it does purely legal skills. In this chapter, we will begin our analysis of what barristers actually do by looking at their career progression and what it is exactly that makes a barrister successful.

GETTING STARTED

The initial problem of finding work of any sort usually disappears for the successful barrister: if it does not, the unsuccessful barrister disappears. However, maintaining the correct level of work, and work of the right kind and at the right level of remuneration, remains a concern throughout a barrister's professional life. In our interviews, we were told that it was not uncommon for a solicitor to suddenly and inexplicably stop briefing a senior advocate who had for many years taken cases from that particular firm of solicitors.

In many ways, barristers seem independent. They are self-employed, freelance consultants and, other than the educational qualifications, there are only two formal hurdles to be overcome: first, finding a chambers or pupil master and, secondly, deciding whether to become a Senior Counsel. The first applies to everyone, but while the second applies in all jurisdictions, the decision whether to become a QC does not fall to everyone.

Despite the limited number of formal distinctions present in the profession, we found that in reality, however, there were an almost infinite number of gradations of success and failure within the profession and everyone was very alive to them.

The early struggles faced by barristers are well known and well documented. That genre of writing which deals with the life and times of the famous barrister seems to have a compulsory chapter about how the famous advocate nearly relinquished the unequal struggle to survive and prosper at the bar. Marshall Hall is reported not to have earned any money for a year and Lord Atkin was about to join a bank when his first client approached him. It seems to have been ever thus. One very senior counsel told us:

> . . . it was just as hard when I started . . . even in the fifties and sixties . . .
> before legal aid . . . there were far too many of us competing . . . not just
> for a chambers, etc., etc., . . . but for that very rare thing – the client
> with enough money to pay privately for legal action.

Even today, one source of advice for prospective barristers contains the
suggestion that life as a commercial solicitor in London can be more rewarding and less precarious (Semple, Piggot and Ramsey, 1990: 38). Our information is that in Scotland the supply/demand equation is more equally
balanced than in other parts of the UK. This has tended to mean that Scottish
advocates have an easier early career.

   This has always been a source of concern for those who have wished a more
socially representative group of barristers (e.g. Zander, 1978), since it is
obviously easier to survive while earning little or no money if you come from
a wealthy background. Stories of hardship were confirmed in our research.
One pupil barrister complained that:

> . . . at least solicitors don't have to find all their own expenses. I'm not
> from a well-to-do family and I'm not sure if I can afford to stay at the
> bar much longer. It's a very expensive business: it's not just a matter of
> bank loans, but it delays you doing other things – for example buying a
> house.

And it seems that things do not improve all that quickly. Apparently,
married men in their late twenties and early thirties are a source of concern for
barristers' clerks anxious to maximize the efficiency of their chambers. It is
felt that their accumulated commitments of wife, mortgage and other neces-
sities and luxuries of life, perhaps divert energies away from the law, the
chambers and the work necessary to build up a successful practice, while
simultaneously engendering a need for funds (Flood, 1983: 51).

   Seemingly, the conclusion urged by those who contribute to the mapping
and counting genre of literature on the bar is true even if a little obvious.
There *is* a financial hurdle. Although the Bar Council's efforts to secure for its
junior members a minimum award or guaranteed income during pupillage
will perhaps change the situation in the future, the bar remains a difficult road
on which to get started.

   There is, however, a more formidable challenge even than relative poverty
awaiting new barristers. Pupillage is where the profession begins – the real
job of being a barrister rather than a student. Although practice in one's own
right does not begin until towards the end of pupillage, pupils are immersed
in the real world of the barrister with courtroom and chambers politics and
with real clients expecting the real thing. There is a period of partial or
complete bemusment, perhaps even worse than that experienced in the first
few weeks and months of a law course. It was described to us as being akin to
being party to an animated conversation in French if your knowledge stops at
O-level: you can recognize bits and pieces but not quickly enough to form
into a coherent whole and certainly not to enable you to contribute.

There is, of course, the Council of Legal Education's short course on preparing for pupillage. However, this was described to us, perhaps a little unkindly, as amounting to little more than advice to bring a clean handkerchief and be polite. Certainly, much of what needs to be taken on board is not learned beforehand. One young English barrister put it this way:

> The bar school is renowned for not having a particularly good course, particularly if you have been there recently as I have you will remember it more clearly – it has to be said that . . . it just wasn't turning out members of the bar as it should have been – it was just an academic course. What was happening was they weren't teaching you properly in the skills of advocacy and paperwork. In fact, you have to have a crash course in it in your first six months' non-practising, just sitting watching your master churning out paperwork.

The first months of being 'on your feet' are perhaps challenging enough but there is the additional obstacle, at least in England and Wales, of being simultaneously measured up for a tenancy in a set of chambers. Not only are pupils learning an entirely new set of skills, but they are constantly being assessed as to whether their personality or competence fits. This aspect of the barrister's rite of passage has provoked particular criticism from the radical bar as represented by the *Bar on Trial* group (Hazell, 1978: 95–8). One recently qualified barrister told us how, among her contemporaries in England, the provinces were a more popular career choice than London for those who sought at least a modicum of job security. Outside London, chambers tend to take on only two or three pupils rather than five or more, which means that competition for any vacancies in the *set* (of chambers) is less intense. There 'the hurdle is to get in in the first place. If you perform well and don't antagonize anyone you should get taken on – although I didn't in my last set.'

Of course, this does not apply in the bar library systems of Northern Ireland, the Republic of Ireland and Scotland where a seat is allocated to all practising barristers at their time of call. These seats, which are usually notional rather than actual, give barristers access to the law library and consultation rooms and a receptionist and telephone facilities. For an annual fee of a few hundred pounds (as opposed to maybe twice or three times as much in some London chambers), new barristers are able to begin to practise. Maurice Healy, in his enchanting account of the *Old Munster Circuit*, is misty eyed about this system in the context of the Dublin bar in the earlier part of the century. He says of the library system, that it 'not only enabled us all to practise cheaply, but gave every neophyte three hundred tutors to knock the corners off him . . . it was a corporate body' (Healy, 1939: 272).

Looking later at the relationship between barristers, we will see that a library system does radically affect the way that work is allocated when compared to a chambers system.

One of the basic, ice-breaking questions in our interviews with barristers was about what sort of work they did and how they ended up in that area of practice. Most of our interviewees, in common with most of the bar, are generalists with interests defined broadly in terms of civil or criminal, commercial or family, etc., but always within the limits of maintaining a general common law practice. There are, of course, specialists, but these are in a minority and are based mainly in London. The opportunity to specialize in one or two areas comes to very few barristers and only then after a good many years knocking on the door. The reasons for a barrister's career taking whatever general path it had were most commonly expressed as being a result of chance: the type of chambers entered, the sort of practice conducted by a pupil master and, of course, at least in the early days, the role of the clerk. Personal aptitude or interest were cited much less often than might be supposed (see also Johnston and Shapland, 1990). These fairly unconsidered responses to our very general question in fact belie a very much more complex social interaction surrounding the getting and keeping of work. On this issue, as with most others in the barrister's world, there is a social dimension – explained only in part in terms of the professional organization of the bar and its relationship with the solicitor's profession – that needs to be taken into account before we make any assumptions about what barristers are actually doing as they argue in court.

When young barristers begin to earn money, hopefully during the final months of their pupillage, they are normally dependent upon work that is too lowly and unrewarding to attract anyone more established. This is reasonably well accepted. As one barrister who has just survived the early struggle commented: 'when you start out you have to do anything that comes along. That's just the way it is and often you're glad to get it – whatever it is.'

Briefs – the name refers to both the cases and documents – normally come directly from solicitors. However, briefs may be passed on from colleagues in a bar library or from other members of a chambers because they are overcommitted or because the fee is simply not worthwhile to them. In the bar library in Belfast, it is common for young barristers to wait around all day knowing that sometimes, often in the late afternoon, there will be someone seeking to pass on a brief. This is often a case that the barrister making the offer is anxious to pass on. A cry of 'Anyone going to Ballymena tomorrow?' more often than not signals the start of a process whereby an unprofitable or poorly prepared case begins its descent to the lower echelons of the local profession. We heard tales of briefs being preferred as 'a windfall', passing from hand to hand as their true nature is discovered until, at last, a difficult, unprofitable or poorly prepared case finds its way to a new barrister too lowly to pass it any further. In Northern Ireland, this practice of passing briefs downwards has been institutionalized for the benefit of solicitors. There is a large book which is kept at the reception desk in the bar library into which a young barrister can enter his or her availability to conduct cases in various courts across the province. A solicitor who is stuck for counsel can then consult the book and find a champion for whatever case is on offer.

However, the passing of briefs in the library system is not invariably a case
of the desperate taking the despicable. Many pupil masters make introduc-
tions and channel excess work in the direction of their protégés. One advocate told us:

> . . . a lot depends on who your master is. You tend to follow into his line
> of work because you tend to meet the same solicitors that he works for
> and the masters, after you have done your six months pupillage,
> genuinely feel obliged to ask their solicitors 'would you give a little bit
> of work to so and so – the pupil – just to get them started off?'

The gratitude that was expressed to pupil masters by a fairly large number of
now well-established practitioners makes one wonder what happened to
those who were not so lucky with their master.

It is at this early point in a career at the bar that contacts can perhaps be most
useful. Connections through family, politics or church are, in Northern
Ireland, regularly exploited to produce work.[1]* This is probably the same
everywhere. We could not ascertain how widespread this was, although
most barristers we talked to were accepting of this as a reality of life and
comforted themselves with the belief that now the professional nature of
the bar is such that contacts alone cannot overcome the grossest absence of
talent.

Those without contacts must shift for themselves. Without even a clerk to
offer protection there are hazards. One barrister who had just successfully
negotiated the shoals and shallows of the early years told us:

> . . . there are the known solicitors who use people for the first year
> because they won't pay them and they just keep using that first year
> every year. . . . Obviously because you're not 'in' enough, you don't
> know the name of the solicitors or you forget the name of the solicitors
> [and] you accept the work. . . . You soon learn and you just don't accept
> it, or the only time you would accept it was if you had money upfront
> which is totally unethical and totally illegal [sic] and we're not allowed
> to do that, but that's the only way you would do it.

Poor cases, bad or non-existent instructions and difficulties with payment
do not go away completely during a career at the bar, but their effects are
perhaps hardest at the start. We shall look later in more detail at the problems
within the solicitor–barrister relationship, but since the relationship is essentially one of providing and taking work, it cannot be glossed over here. This
relationship is the most important for the successful career of a barrister, for
without solicitors who are prepared to pass work on, there can be no career at
all.

In a chambers system, most colleagues, while unlikely to take the bread out
of their own mouths, are perhaps less indifferent to the fate of their junior
colleagues. And there is, of course, the intercession of the clerk.

* Superscript numerals refer to numbered notes at the end of each chapter.

THE CLERK

In a chambers system, newly qualified barristers are to a considerable extent dependent on the good offices of barristers' clerks. The occupation of barristers' clerk is in some ways a relic of the past, something more in keeping with the time of Dickens' *Bleak House* where *Jarndyce* v *Jarndyce* wound its tortuous way through the Chancery Courts rather than the word-processors and litigation support systems of modern chambers. Nevertheless, and despite a recent tendency towards practice managers rather than old-fashioned clerks, there is a clerk in most chambers. In the best and most extensive study of the clerk that is currently available, Flood maintains that the role of clerk involves being a counsellor, negotiatior and fixer, with the most important function being that of fixer. He maintains that:

> . . . essentially the clerk is the middleman, or mediator, between the diverse interests of the legal system, namely those of barristers, solicitors, judges, list offices, and occasionally the client upon whom the system depends (Flood, 1983: 3).

Another commentator sees the clerk as 'a complicated cross between a theatrical agent, a business manager, an accountant and a trainer' (Megarry, 1962: 55).

All those who write about the clerk point to the low educational background, minimum training and archaic recruitment procedure from boy to junior and then senior that pertains in the occupation. Most then point to the (now declining) payment system, whereby remuneration is by way of percentage commission, which may be as much as ten percent of the barrister's fees. Several commentators, most notably Zander (1968), see this as a sinister aspect inasmuch as the clerk has a personal interest in extracting the largest possible fee. There is little doubt that clerks do exert some influence over barristers, particularly in the early stages of their careers.

After listing the nature of his practice, one young practitioner in South Wales seemed surprised to discover the clerk's role in the shaping of his professional life, although simultaneously he accepted it:

> I hadn't really thought about it. It's just the way you end up. The clerk decides exactly what they want us to do and of course from the feedback from solicitors they decide what we're best at and that's how it happens.

While more senior barristers do not have the same fatalistic attitude that their destinies are exclusively in the hands of the barristers' clerk, this is probably an accurate enough view of the relationship between the clerk and the young barrister. Traditional clerks, castigated by Zander as all-powerful, seem to be on the decline. Certainly in the early days of practice, however, clerks are of considerable importance even if they are not invariably a malign influence. Our findings echoed those of Flood, at least with respect to the influence that the traditional type of clerk has over young barristers.

One senior clerk with more than 40 years' experience in London and more recently in the provinces, took a very strongly paternalistic view of his young barristers and viewed his role as setting them on their way: 'For the first two years you do what you're given: you need the money, you need the expertise and you need to be seen around.' Barristers with less than the magic figure of two years' experience are given 'the rubbish – that's a term we use here – and told to bloody well get on with it'.

Accepting that the clerk has influence does not necessarily mean that the relationship between the clerk and barrister is one based simply on the patronage of the clerk as Abel-Smith and Stevens (1967: 110–11) see it, or further that the relationship is a 'disturbing one' as Zander (1968: 83) would have it. There is a rather more complex relationship involved here, and it is one that is only mediated by the clerk. As the clerk mentioned above explained it to us:

> . . . young members of chambers coming in, starting right at the bottom, getting them started, getting them work from the barristers above them. The barristers above them are all probably very busy. The time comes when they have more than one case in one day and despite the efforts of a senior clerk and his staff to try and arrange cases so that a barrister does not have a clash, we know that because of court avail-ability, judge availability, witness availability, it is not always possible. There comes a time when a barrister cannot do all his work and that is when the clerk then starts to 'feed' the young barrister coming in, to get him started.

Young barristers are to a certain extent dependent on the success of their chambers: in an upwardly mobile set with fairly large numbers of active barristers, there will be more work free-falling downwards as those higher up the ladder develop their careers. A clash in the timetable for a barrister on any given rung in the ladder, as a case is held over or rescheduled, brings into effect an often elaborate 'cover' system. This is where the clerk arranges and rearranges the diaries of the barristers in chambers to ensure that a case can be taken up by someone of roughly similar experience. Of course, because the more successful barristers are by definition busy barristers, it is not always possible to cover with a barrister of equal seniority. There is inevitably a slight downward pull in these covering exercises. The clerk often finds him or herself persuading the solicitor to take the next best alternative. This will have an effect further below as the more lucrative brief from above displaces poorer cases on the desk of the barrister immediately next in line. The net result of this process is that a quantity of fairly low-level work becomes available to the most junior members of chambers. A similar process goes on in the bar library systems. Here there is often an informal cover system operating between groups of barristers at different levels who operate in a loosely associated team. A breakdown in this system, or the intervention of such factors as a pupil master bringing on a former pupil, or a relative or contact influencing a career, means that work becomes available at the very junior end of the profession.

A similar effect is caused by a barrister's career development. In the normal trajectory of a successful career, there is a fall-out of cases which will have an effect on what becomes available at the bottom rung of the ladder. As we will discuss shortly, this career development is to some extent a result of an active clerk who is prepared to scale up fees as an individual, or indeed a chambers, develops. As one clerk insisted to us: 'if I didn't bother to increase the level of fees, how would the young members of chambers ever get started?' In the library system, career enhancement is the responsibility of the individual barrister, but the effect of the upward rise in a healthy career is similar. It produces an availability of work that has now been outgrown and which can be passed to a whole network of satellites, contacts and hangers-on.

Of course, despite the impression that clerks seem to like to give of young barristers as legal fledglings dependent on the clerks to feed them morsels of work, there are more mundane reasons for work being given to novices. Small, relatively unlucrative cases involving road traffic offences, petty sessions work, landlord and tenant disputes or pleas are generally sent to chambers only the day before hearing or sometimes on the day itself. The clerk may then, it is true, use his or her discretion in a time of famine to distribute this work where he or she thinks fit. To this limited extent, as Zander (1968: 86) maintains, 'the clerk sits at the fountain and can control the direction of the spray'. However, in a busy practice, the main concern is often to ensure adequate 'cover' for a firm of solicitors who provide a high volume of work.

The permutations of the laws of supply and demand relating to this low-grade work are thus rather odd. At a certain stage in a barrister's career, he or she will no longer want such low-grade work, as it will inhibit taking on more rewarding work. However, at the same time, as more senior barristers try to dispose of such work from their case loads, there will always be novices who desperately need a start to their professional careers. There are, of course, other competitors for this work. It was suggested to us that solicitors are increasingly undertaking work that was previously the preserve of the very junior bar. As one barrister who had just survived the first three years of practice pointed out:

> . . . it was very hard when I came out to get started . . . people coming out now are finding it so much harder, partly because the bar is over-subscribed, but, more importantly, because there are so many young solicitors and solicitors' firms have to find something for them to do . . . nine times out of ten what they're getting them to do is the petty sessions work.

A famine of work hits first and hardest at the junior bar. This is where any friction surrounding the interface between the two sides of the profession appears first. That is not to say that the current reforms in the legal profession are making much impact among the ordinary soldiers at the bar. We were unable to find anyone well-established who was particularly worried about new rights of audience displacing barristers. It was thought that solicitors

would find it uneconomic to come to court unless they did enough court-
work so that they became for all practical purposes advocates. However, the
petty sessions, where solicitors have always had rights of audience, provide
an excellent place to deploy the current surplus in that branch of the profession. Nowadays, it is commonplace for a large firm to have one or more
solicitors covering the busier petty sessions courts in a particular area.

There is much discussion by clerks and in barristers' memoirs of giving
young barristers a chance. Of course, in reality, and sometimes in contrast to
the memoirs, this is not a single, one-off chance that leads inexorably to
glittering prizes. It is rather a period of trial where mistakes can and are made
but where impressions are also formed by others in the system. The clerk
knows this:

> Once he has done a case in his own right and he's gone to court for that
> particular firm there is nothing more a barrister's clerk can do for that
> barrister and that firm ... he has got him the brief and it's up to that
> barrister to do the case well. I'm not talking about winning or losing: I
> mean winning or losing, rightly or wrongly in this country, doesn't
> seem to make much impression. If you win the case the client is only
> going to say 'Well, of course I won, I never expected to lose.' But if you
> lose, and you lose it well, pull out all the stops, put every point you've
> got to the court ... then the client knows there is nothing more that
> barrister could have done. Someone else sees that barrister in court and
> that is how his practice starts. You get more and more cases and more
> and more work.

Of course, the solicitor involved in a particular case that is covered by a
new barrister does not usually see these early forays. Especially on the sort of
minor matter on which a new barrister is likely to be engaged, it is rare that a
solicitor could be spared from more rewarding work in the office to hang
around at the courts. It will tend to be other solicitors in court awaiting their
(more important) cases, the clerk of the court and the judge who are the
audience for new hopefuls. We were assured in several provincial centres that
the legal world is very small indeed and that it is easy to get noticed. This may
be a mixed blessing, of course, as some of the cases that junior barristers end
up with are of such an order that it is often difficult not to create a bad
impression. As one young advocate put it:

> ... usually you end up with such dreadful cases ... you have no
> instructions ... the solicitor just arrives with the name and you go to
> court and you just cannot do your job well enough. . . . This does not
> look good to the other solicitors around.

It is more difficult to create a good impression in some of the busier London
courts, but even here there is generally room for new faces as solicitors
struggle to get someone who is available at the right time and at the correct
rate.

The clerk's role in shaping a career recedes as the barrister's career progresses. Hazell (1978: 106) maintains that even QCs need the favour of the
clerks. Although our evidence did not bear this out, we are unable to
contradict it. Indeed, as far we could make out, the more senior the advocate,
the less notice he seems to take of the clerk and the more deferential the clerk
becomes towards the barrister. However, even after the magic barrier of the
first two years is passed, and the barrister seems no longer to be almost
entirely in the power of the clerk, there is a process of shaping one's practice
that is carried on by, as well as through, the clerk. The 'rubbish' mentioned
earlier is shed as more lucrative work starts coming in. One barrister who
was doing fairly well after about three years talked in terms of being 'at a stage
when I can begin to pick what I do. I'm thinking of ditching domestic
violence if I can, and criminal work.' The clerks, too, think in terms of stages,
and for them it is very clearly the market that dictates this. If a barrister is
doing well, he or she must be shielded from the very petty court appearances
which consume time that could be better and more profitably employed
elsewhere. One clerk told us:

> . . . it's not only court appearances that solicitors take notice of, it's how
> quickly you do your papers as well . . . if you're in court doing magis-
> trates' court work, you can't do the work you should be as your practice
> develops.

Each clerk and each barrister will work out the details of the individual's
career timetable in terms of the work available, the demands of the chambers
and the level of success of the individual barrister. The use of the term 'work
out' perhaps dignifies what is an informal, reactive process but there is,
however, at least an *ad hoc* process whereby upward movement is detected
and responded to. So, for example, after two years, a barrister may be taken
off magistrates' court work. After another two years, a barrister may stop
doing legal aid scale one county court work to concentrate on the more
lucrative scale two and three work. If other work is coming in, it is counter-
productive to continue to send a barrister into court to do work that is less
rewarding. As a practice develops, the paperwork (opinions, drafting, etc.)
increases in proportion to the time spent on one's feet and time must be made
for this. In any event, there may well be in a large chambers new, young
barristers coming in and they too must be 'fed'.

Whether processed by a clerk or through the library system, work seems to
find the level of barrister to which it is most appropriate. (It is, of course,
interesting to consider what it is about a case – the level of fee, possibility of
custodial sentence, high award of damages or whatever – that makes it
important or otherwise and so determines its level. That issue will be considered later.) For now we just want to reinforce the point that within the
hierarchy that exists in any bar, cases which have little money supporting
them will filter downwards to those without experience or contacts who
have little else to do and are therefore obliged to take on such work. This
process whereby poorer work percolates downwards is matched by a process

whereby better work rises to a more appropriate level. We were given one particularly good example relating to criminal practice. Work in the magistrates' court is poorly paid and is generally the preserve of the beginner. The legal aid system does not provide for both a solicitor and a barrister in this type of work, and the barrister must be paid from the solicitor's fees. However, if there is an appeal from the magistrates' court, which takes the form of a new trial by a county court judge sitting as a crown court judge, legal aid is made available for counsel. Almost invariably, it is a more experienced barrister who is briefed for an appeal from the magistrates' court. This may be satisfactory for most parties involved: the client sees that he or she is apparently getting a better barrister, the solicitor is happy that he or she can be seen as providing a better service and the more experienced barrister is happy to get another brief. The junior barrister, however, is less than happy. He or she may have done some hard work on the case in the petty sessions, perhaps pulling out all the stops and putting in a level of effort that exceeds that of the more busy senior barrister. Nevertheless, that brief will be lost to them. As one aggrieved junior practitioner complained to us:

> ...we do all the shit but once the cream is available it's given to somebody else and, ironically, the barrister who ends up getting it often doesn't need it ... he's got maybe two or three other appeals on that day.

Career progression is, of course, the same in a bar library system; only here clerks do not undertake the brokerage role between barristers and solicitors. Here barristers must plan their own careers without the feedback that may be obtained from solicitors' offices via a clerk. In any event, in both the library systems and the chambers one, the career guidance towards a particular field of work seems to moderate considerably as market forces and the barrister's own abilities and contacts take over. That is not to say, of course, that the clerk's role in constructing what Flood (1983: 57) terms a 'career timetable', disappears. As we shall see, there is still the very important matter of fixing fees and keeping the flow of work at a steady rate.

DEVELOPING A CAREER

Every local bar has at least one individual practitioner whose career has not developed as it should, but who nevertheless manages to hang on precariously to a bare living undertaking low-grade work that should have been left behind long before. These embryo Rumpoles never attained the necessary exit velocity to leave the petty sessions. By dint of the sheer volume of cases that they do, they somehow manage to cling on and cut their cloth to meet their needs. The existence of such barristers as exceptions confirms the rule that there is normally a natural progression through various stages. Indeed, although this progression takes different forms depending on the area of practice and the local conditions affecting the availability of work, it is fairly obvious that there is a steady upward movement. Indeed, it is often manifested geographically or at least architecturally. In common with many organizations, chambers distribute office accommodation in strict accordance with ideas of seniority. In one set we visited, based in an old Victorian town house in a provincial city, there was a clear progression through the building awaiting anyone with a successful career. Conferences, etc., took place in specially appointed rooms but space for study rooms was clearly at a premium. At the lowest rung, there were 'the boys in the basement', as the other barristers termed them (even though they included several women). They inhabited a large room below street level containing four or five desks, which doubled as a library for the chambers as a whole. Progression from here led generally to rooms in the attic shared with only one or two others. From there, the next move was to a pleasant first-floor study inhabited by three or four senior juniors with the final prize – a study to oneself – available only to the very senior members of chambers. We did not stay long enough to discover whether, as in many universities, the presence of carpet and its size and quality had any significance.[2]

Another provincial set of chambers which had recently moved into very prestigious office accommodation had kept the same hierarchical form of allocation, albeit on a grander scale than other chambers and with much more room for the junior members. It was interesting that the move into these new chambers had required that one barrister take some months away from his practice to effect the move. His time had been paid for from his colleagues' earnings, but he felt that he had lost out financially due to work lost during his absence and the need to regain contacts. This suggests that the chambers system is not an ideal mechanism for coping with change: its goals are too immediate, and its members usually too committed to a short-term outlook to manage adequately non-urgent demands.

We found barristers on the whole to be very conscious of the idea of progression through a career structure and anxious to display that they were at least where they should be on the ladder. There is perhaps a feeling that work gravitates towards the successful and that it is important to give signs that one is doing well. This is so perhaps especially in the bar library system, where without the brokerage services of a clerk, it is necessary to advertise oneself and one's success as widely as possible. At the more junior end of the profession, barristers greeting one another generally declare themselves to be 'very busy' or 'snowed under with work'. While we invariably found members of the bar to be generous, it was noticeable that on our forays into pubs where barristers drink after work we found it almost impossible to buy a round of drinks. The competition among barristers to treat an ever-increasing circle was intense. At the more senior levels, the displays of success take a more subtle form. Indeed, those who are most successful – perhaps even being one of the 'six-figure men' (those who often earn in excess of £100 000 per annum) – paradoxically adopt a more nonchalant and relaxed demeanour.

Nan Wilson's study of Scottish Advocates echoes our findings. She notes how:

... prestige is assessed within the legal community not according to earnings directly but in terms of how 'busy' a particular advocate may be. Thus, for example, advocates' wives loyally complain to each other of how busy their husbands are; and not a few young advocates exhaust themselves each day in the Parliament House in their efforts to appear employed (Wilson, 1965: 178).

And her story of the advocates travelling up the Mound in Edinburgh captures the spirit of seniority: 'on an omnibus in which a number of advocates are travelling from New Town to Parliament House, the senior will pay the fares of the juniors on every occasion' (Wilson, 1965: 174).

The stages in a career timetable are less distinct as that career develops: different tracks are taken as relative specialisms are taken up and various ambitions are played out. However, whether the barrister has a clerk or whether he or she operates alone, there are still one or two milestones that can be fairly readily observed. For example, in the civil field, as a junior counsel becomes more active and successful, the proportion of county court work declines. Perhaps after a few years a decision will be taken not to do any more legal aid matrimonial work and so on. At a certain stage, it simply becomes uneconomic for the successful practitioner to spend time waiting around the county court when difficult and lucrative papers are waiting to be done and his or her practice will reflect this.

Many, if not most, of the career stages for a rising barrister will be encountered by happenstance and negotiated without any immediate aware-ness of their significance and certainly without recourse to anything like a developed game plan. One fairly typical story we were told illustrates not only how sometimes there are opportunities available for those who are able to take them, but also how the method whereby work arrives may well often impinge upon how such work is conducted:

Take for example a case I did the other day. . . . I do very little industrial tribunal work because I hate it and somebody rang me on Sunday afternoon and said 'Would I do this case?'. . . . I said 'Look Monday's my only day off and I need to catch up'. He said it was an industrial tribunal and I told him . . . 'Look I have no legislation, no books home with me'. . . . He said 'I think it's really straightforward but it's X's case'. As soon as I heard X's name I knew . . . I know what he's like. . . . It's always a simple case and usually the wheels fall off. . . . I rang the original person who had the case and they said 'Look, it will take you five minutes'. You know straightaway it will take at least half an hour. . . . He said 'it really is straightforward, net point, won't take long etc., etc., . . .'. I take it and find out it's a very serious, very important case; that there is a QC acting for the respondent; that I am the only one there, with photocopies of some legislation that I managed to get on the way down. . . . I didn't get finished till a quarter to three . . . luckily it turned out well . . . there was a lot of arguing and I'm going to get a good fee out of it. . . . But you just can't trust anybody: that's just the way it goes.

At most, it will be realized that, as in the very early days, a good performance in one area may lead to higher things. For example, at the junior end, if a barrister does well with a defence for careless driving in the magistrates' court, there is the possibility that an insurance company will capitalize on the expertise already gained on the case and retain the same barrister for a subsequent civil action. On a lesser scale, relatively small-time criminals will have a network of information about who's a good 'brief'. Alternatively, there may be wider factors relating to the policy of a private or public concern which have a knock-on effect on the legal profession. We were given an excellent example of this relating to one particular barrister in Northern Ireland who managed to get on to the panel, or shortlist, of barristers who are regularly briefed by a government department:

I have done a lot of tripping cases[3] for the Department of the Environment . . . that has been the mainstay of my practice for the last two years or so. . . . When I started doing them I was doing them . . . exclusively for plaintiffs, and at that stage the vast majority of them settled. . . . Unless there was some major problem with the plaintiff's evidence they are very difficult to disprove . . . the whole thing became out of hand, I mean the DoE [Department of the Environment] was swamped with claims . . . the Public Accounts Committee was just cracking up at the amount of money that was being diverted to meet these claims, so at that particular time . . . [the Crown Solicitors' Office] recruited a lot more staff. . . . Because they had more solicitors they also needed more barristers, so a few people who were at the right level of seniority got their chance, myself included.

Even more than in most occupations, luck is an important determinant in the career of a barrister.

One of the main divergences in a career relates to whether a practice is mainly criminal or mainly civil in nature.[4] It is, of course, possible to do a little of both and many barristers maintain a fairly mixed practice. What they do may vary from year to year and in relation to such factors as involvement in lengthy cases. Personal interest has relatively little to do with determining which type of practice a barrister ends up with. One young barrister, now building up a fairly vigorous personal injury practice, told us:

I'm thirty now: when I studied tort I was eighteen and I wasn't interested in it. I did it for one year, passed the exam and went on to do other things I was more interested in . . . then around the age of twenty-five I discovered there was such a thing as a tripping claim and suddenly I found myself doing tort again. . . . Really that is an accident.

It is only a few practitioners who can really pick and choose their cases. One successful senior junior operating in the provinces pointed out that even for someone at that stage:

the balance is dictated by the flow of work that comes in . . . it's really impossible to dictate the workload that you have unless you are so very busy and so much in control of your work that you can decide just not to do any criminal work or any civil work . . . basically I do whatever anyone asks me to.

This will include work that someone finds personally distasteful. Work is seen as just that for the most part. For most barristers whom we talked to, any reference to the idea of 'their professional role' was sufficient to enable them to overcome most personal feelings. As one counsel put it, 'barristers are supposed to be hired guns and I suppose that is what we are'. A senior barrister put it this way:

> I obviously don't enjoy doing, as I did ten days ago, a paedophile buggery case. I'd prefer to prosecute people charged with serious criminal offences as you do not have the pressure of a defendant's long sentence of imprisonment looming over you . . . with prosecution the pressures are different . . . probably less . . . you probably lose less sleep.

Another advocate commented that 'if you do criminal work you come across all sorts of nasty people and if you started drawing lines it would be hard to do any kind of criminal work'.

There seem to be few difficulties in obtaining personnel to handle terrorist cases in Northern Ireland. Although we picked up a few murmurings in another direction, it was generally held to be a great strength of the bar in Belfast that it was able to operate the Diplock court system on both sides without personal animosity. Indeed, some rather odd patterns have emerged whereby, for example, one of the leading solicitors' practices for loyalist paramilitaries is a Catholic firm and one of the premier defence counsels for republican paramilitaries was formerly active in Unionist politics.

Perhaps, however, this is not a particularly good indicator of barristers' attitudes on this matter: the level of terrorist work in Northern Ireland, not to mention its importance as a source of income, means that such matters can be handled in a much more routine way. Before we started our interviews, we had heard some stories that in England, terrorists – primarily Irish terrorists – found it hard to get good defence counsel. One leading criminal lawyer who we put this to said:

> I have never been involved in an Irish terrorist case. . . . I have acted for a member of the so-called 'Free Wales Army' . . . who had done a ten-year sentence for causing explosions, burglary and theft of gelignite . . . I then prosecuted him for importuning . . . (he happened to be unfortunate enough to proposition an off-duty police officer) . . . and I then defended him . . . for harbouring an active terrorist . . . it was a guilty plea but it didn't make any difference to me whether . . . it had been a trial. I wouldn't have associated myself with that for which he was campaigning. I would have done my job as a lawyer . . . in the end I

mitigated on the basis of the instructions that I had, making those points I thought proper to make. . . . It was no problem – any of it.

Leaving aside the idea of distasteful work, this perceived willingness or need to do whatever comes along, even when at a fairly advanced stage in one's career, may well of course have practical effects on a day-to-day basis. It may, for example, cause problems about timing different lists in different courts which may even be in different parts of a city. This may lead to difficulties with clients, solicitors and judges. It is no wonder that we constantly observed the urgency of barristers knowing that they should be somewhere else in just a few minutes – this may come as much from actually being busy as wanting to appear so.

However, for some practitioners there is, in the broadest sense, a fork in the career path that must be negotiated. The direction taken depends, to a large extent, less on the conscious decision of the barrister than on such factors as ability, aptitude and contacts. Some barristers we talked to made a distinction between a practice that involves law and one that is in the criminal courts. As one commercial practitioner put it: 'criminal barristers carry their law in a volume, two volumes now [Archbold, *Criminal Pleading, Practice and Evidence*], and we leave our library in chambers . . .'. That is probably slightly unfair, but undoubtedly matters of fact and issues of evidence and procedure predominate over matters of law in criminal trials. From the other side of the fence, the criminal practitioners are often dismissive of 'the cattle trading' that goes on as civil cases are settled. Undoubtedly, different techniques are important in each type of work. If the strengths of a barrister lie elsewhere than in a particular sort of work, it is unlikely that he or she will be asked to do very much of that sort of work. Market demand levels out many advocates' aspirations.

Of course merit, or a lack of it, is not the sole determining feature of the sort of work that a particular advocate undertakes. It may not even be the most important factor. As we have already said, contacts may be important. Clearly, once barristers move beyond the immediate fiefdom of the clerk, the number and level of contacts that they maintain with solicitors' firms is vital (this is considered more fully in the next chapter).

There are also other contacts that are significant. The pattern whereby a chambers that specializes in a particular branch of law tends to divert its members to that field, is also reproduced in the other organizations. While it is not true to say that under the bar library system barristers hunt in packs, informal groupings do evolve. While it is perfectly possible to operate alone, it is, as mentioned earlier, clearly easier to have a coterie of colleagues at various stages of experience to whom work can be passed as the need arises. In those bar libraries that we were able to observe for any length of time, it was perfectly easy to identify small groups working together in informal partnerships. For example, Belfast's Criminal Court in the Crumlin Road has a fairly small group of practitioners who work there regularly. One practitioner described it in this way:

There is a core of criminal barristers who would number no more than about a dozen at the outside – probably half a dozen would be more accurate. You could name the half dozen at the junior bar who would be up there every day . . . and then two or three who would be up there every day at the senior bar. . . . Then there is an outer circle of people . . . who would be up there fairly frequently but by no means necessarily every day or every week.

Another barrister, from outside the charmed circle, complained:

. . . in the early or mid-seventies there was a glut of work, there was more work than there were lawyers and a lot of people got into it . . . and made a very good living out of it, who perhaps in a more competitive climate mightn't have done so. Take the present situation, you have an ever-contracting amount of criminal work. Those people who have, in a sense, made their reputation on it are obviously going to guard their patch more jealously . . . it's not all institutionalized, it would be wrong to say that, but . . . it's very hard to break into the 'Crumlin Road Mafia' – at least enough to make a living at it.

This situation is not unique to Belfast or the criminal side. An advocate with a large civil practice elsewhere told us:

. . . you're in constant competition . . . there's a finite amount of work around and everybody's competing within a certain range for the same type of work. . . . If you become known as a civil practitioner on the defence side, and once you have overcome the initial resistance of getting into that band, you are inclined to look round and say 'We have a happy little cartel here and we don't want it upset by somebody sort of coming into it . . . and therefore we won't be overly enthusiastic about any newcomers'.

Clearly, there are such patterns in existence everywhere. Often they do not amount to much more than a tendency whereby, for example, particular junior and senior council work together. Such informal groupings are not always to be seen as sinister gangs operating to squeeze out others and bring on favourites. Friendships and contacts are not alone sufficient, but they may be the way in which a group that already exists fills the vacancies and provides the cover needed in the ordinary exigencies of practice. Without apologizing for nepotism, it can be said that barristers often need help and will turn to those that they know. They will know those who they see on an everyday basis and who are around when they are needed. This reinforces what was said earlier about young advocates needing to be seen to be active and busy in the right places. One barrister we talked to had for various reasons been sent down the road of mainly civil practice but still nursed ambitions to do more criminal work. He outlined a theory that because the civil and criminal courts were in different parts of the city, he was very rarely seen by solicitors or other barristers working in the criminal law field. As a result, he was not considered to be a barrister with a criminal law interest and was overlooked in the allocation of such work.

While this sort of thing may be a factor, we think it is simply one among many others to be considered. One barrister who we questioned on how these patterns built up commented:

> ... there's a lot of things ... many clients do not really relish the prospect of their counsel learning on the job ... they want somebody who knows what they're doing ... inevitably if you have done a lot of a particular type of work you have a greater expertise in it ... you know the form of the judges, how they will react to different points and consequently you can bring more to a case ... you find those people know the ropes, they know the solicitors and you find this extends into the solicitors' profession ... a certain number of solicitors tend to dominate ... they do a higher percentage of [a particular sort of work] ... relationships build up.

We will develop this idea of common understandings and practices in a later chapter. For now, we simply wish to make the point that there is no doubt that shared understandings between colleagues on both sides, and between solicitors and judges, make life easier for the barrister (and arguably the parties to an action). Points can be accepted without the need for full argument, working practices can evolve and accommodations can be made. These all develop in such a way as to produce patterns in the allocation of work as well as in the way it is done. The legal profession is not unique in this respect. It would be naive to believe that the patterns here produce themselves randomly: the social organization of the profession and the politics of being a player in a fairly small game have their effects. This is not always detrimental to the client as the quotation above suggests.

After a certain point in the development of a barrister's career, the sort of work that that individual undertakes does not change inasmuch that he or she does not appear in higher courts or in front of more important judges. Appearances in the Court of Appeal or the House of Lords are not necessarily a sign of success, at least in financial terms. However, what does change is the scale of fees charged. In those systems which have them, clerks have a significant role here. They are in charge of scaling up fees and so developing both the practice of the individual barrister and of the chambers as a whole. If a clerk maintains a fairly aggressive charging policy, always attempting to raise the fees of those in his or her charge as their experience increases, the careers of those barristers will develop. The chambers as a whole will also develop as work becomes available for more junior members. Inevitably, there are solicitors who say that on a particular case there simply isn't enough money either on legal aid or from the client to pay for a particular counsel at the new rate. In such a case, the clerk will have someone else next in line to recommend and in this way keep the chambers (and, of course, the clerk's own earnings) developing.

The process of raising fees to match the increasing success of a barrister's career must be done gradually. Often the clerk will prepare a solicitor in advance for a rise in the costs of employing a particular barrister. If the market research is done properly, there will be few problems – for the barrister, his collegues, the solicitor and, of course, the clerk. As one clerk put it:

> I've never had any real complaints from solicitors that I've priced anybody out of the market. . . . But does it do any harm? Because if I've priced somebody out of the market, his career has gone so high already that he can always get work anytime because there's always people who are going to pay . . . anyway doing it that way, it also gives a chance for the youngsters in chambers to come in and get the work.

In certain instances, high fees seem to be in everybody's interest. A clerk in the provinces told us:

> When I came here [from London] I realised that the fees weren't high enough. . . . I started gradually to increase the fees. . . . The feedback to me from solicitors is we are delighted that [the clerk] is putting up the fees because the more fees the barrister commands the bigger fees we can get from the insurance companies for preparing the cases and instructing them in the first place.

Where there aren't clerks in the system, barristers have to attempt to gauge these market forces themselves. Some younger advocates talked of the difficulty of knowing when and by how much to raise their rates in cases that were not publicly funded and therefore on fixed levels. Like building contractors, young barristers have to be careful not to overprice or underprice their services. A usual practice, apparently, is to ask a slightly more senior barrister what he or she would charge and make whatever adjustment the individual's modesty, ambition and conscience suggest.

We would not wish to over-emphasize the role of money *per se* in the life of barristers. Many do not plot a path remorselessly onwards or upwards but find themselves at a point of equilibrium where good and bad years come and go and their fees do not march very far in advance of the increases taken by the bar in general. However, getting on at the bar is, up to a certain stage at least, indicated by charging higher fees. This is simply how the market manifests itself through the supply and demand dynamics to which the bar is constantly subject. However, to identify the process of getting on at the bar solely with earning more money is to gloss over the many factors leading to the development of earning power which we are trying to at least hint at here. Money is simply a medium in which career patterns, produced by many other factors, can be traced. 'Busy-ness', it might be said, is almost as important.

Of course, where barristers talk in terms of no longer undertaking a particular type of work, what is meant is that they no longer undertake that work for the usual fee. So, for example, a very senior junior (i.e. someone not far below QC level) would not go into the county court at all for legal aid work, although he or she would do so for a minimum fee. If a solicitor wants a particular barrister to go into the county court, the solicitor would have to be prepared to pay, say, £350–400. We even had stories confirmed to us of eminent QCs being available – for a price – to appear in the magistrates' court for a road traffic offence. (Whether the deployment of such a heavy-weight in these circumstances is a useful exercise is a point we will consider later.)

This might seem to have some effect on the so-called 'cab rank rule' – the idea that everyone is entitled to the barrister of their choice and that every barrister is available for hire for a reasonable fee. Clearly, however, some cabs cost more than others and this rule seems to be something that the public (and the Bar Council defending the market position of the bar) are more interested in than practising barristers. One clerk did attempt a vigorous defence of his charging practice, claiming that:

> . . . it may seem unfair to the public that they can't get someone of their choice for under a certain amount of money, but it is the public who have put this person in that spot in the first place. If he still went into the county court after eight years call, how on earth is he going to get his paperwork done . . . and by now the paperwork he gets is complicated and they sometimes need two or three days to read the papers before he can give the answer . . . he doesn't have time to spend two days in the county court wasting time waiting for a case that only takes half a day to hear.

It seems that the fee charged for an appearance in a lower court must take into account the time lost that could have been otherwise spent doing something else.

There is, of course, a problem if all or most of the work done by a particular barrister is publicly funded. Charges cannot be raised in the same way. Indeed, the unified charging system, whereby a particular level of work attracts a particular fee regardless of who takes on the task, means that many more senior barristers find it difficult to raise their income if legal aid is their main source of remuneration.[5] This fact is not, of course, lost on the junior bar, and many of the more able younger barristers we talked to were aiming for a career in chancery work, whereas in the past a criminal practice might have had more appeal. One senior criminal practitioner took a very jaundiced view of the situation:

> . . . the amount that we get paid for basic knock-about stuff is in my view almost insulting. . . . I earn a good living, I'll not deny it, but I have to do high-volume work, defending or prosecuting, in order to tread water. . . . My earnings aren't going up at all in the last three or four years: I'm simply increasing my actual work load in order to tread water financially.

The consequences of this high-volume work do, of course, manifest themselves in the system: crowded diaries, double bookings, court hopping, pass-ons and poorly prepared cases are the obvious dangers of attempting to increase one's turnover. There are also unsavoury consequences for the quality of justice in some instances. A criminal advocate complained:

> ... the public purse is very carefully monitored these days ... most of the cases I do are standard fee cases where you get the same fee for prosecuting whether it's a plea or a trial. .... That is why so many cases go short, because certain members of my profession like to earn as much money for as little effort.

This instance, where pressure is put upon a defendant to plead guilty to the original charge or a lesser one in order to avoid the lengthy process of a full trial, is perhaps the most extreme example of the consequences of an individual barrister's struggle to get on. There are other pressures also and these effect the barrister's relations with judges, lay clients, peers and, perhaps most significantly as we shall see in the following chapter, solicitors. Overall, all such factors must encourage us to look to the complexity of the barrister's world and how not only the day-to-day struggle but also the process of getting on in that world impinge on what it is that the barrister does.

THE SENIOR BAR

The market orientation, with all the complexity of what exactly it is that makes up a demand for a barrister to supply, can be seen very clearly in the decision to move to senior counsel (or as it is termed in the UK, Queen's Counsel). This rank was first created in England in the sixteenth century and was originally designed to single out a group of counsel retained by the Crown to act as assistants to the Attorney General. Originally, they could not appear against the Crown without a special licence from the monarch, although there has long since been a general dispensation from this. The title is now an honorary one conferred on established barristers by the monarch on recommendation from the Lord Chancellor by letters patent appointing them to be 'one of Her Majesty's Counsel learned in Law'. Their privileges amount to wearing silk gowns as opposed to gowns made of stuff, and in England when they appear in the Supreme Court they may sit within the Bar of the Supreme Court (the now notional line dividing the personnel who constitute the court from those who merely attend).

Expressed in these terms, this may seem to differ little from the sobriquet 'By appointment to Her Majesty' on a jar of marmalade. However, it carries with it significant financial consequences. It is, in effect, a formal mechanism for raising fees. Senior counsel do not draft pleadings or write opinions on evidence. The result is that, except in a fairly restricted area of work, it is also necessary to employ a junior in order to make use of senior counsel. The two-counsel rule, which made it mandatory to hire a junior along with a senior and pay two fees, was formally abolished in 1977.[6] However, a

Queen's Counsel would today be unlikely to be involved on a regular basis in cases that did not support two or more counsel.[7]

What is in it for the Queen's Counsel? There is certainly prestige. If the bar resembles the set-up of a public school, then the QC appears as a prefect or a member of the First XV. Solicitors may well be more respectful and if briefs are imperfectly prepared it is, apparently, possible for a QC to send them back where most juniors would not risk offending the solicitor. We even heard that late payment is not quite such a common occurrence with senior counsel. However, the most significant feature about taking silk is the opportunity of raising one's fees. Although a busy junior may earn as much or even more than a senior counsel, especially in the period immediately after the transition, most QCs are able to command higher fees.

This raising of fees must be balanced against the danger of pricing oneself out of the market, not only by asking for more money for oneself but by requiring two sets of fees to be paid before one can work. In effect, in the period immediately after promotion, the senior counsel has to say to solicitors, 'although I am effectively the same person as I was last month with no more ability or special contacts, and I could have been employed then for £X, now I need to be paid £X+'. In many ways, this is very like the usual upward movement on the fee scale except that here it is impossible to revert back to former rates if the market does not seem able or willing to accept the new rates. There will always be some solicitors who will be unwilling or unable for the majority of their cases to brief a perhaps previously regular barrister. As one barrister is reported to have said becoming a QC is: 'a very simple process. You give up the practice you have got and begin again, and you run a very fair chance of incurring the risk of starvation' (quoted in Du Cann, 1980: 23).

It is a new market that is being tapped here. The decision to move into that market is clearly a complex one, depending on variables that are beyond the control of the barrister. A clerk may be able to advise on the state of the market and the possibility of a particular barrister finding a niche there, but there is inevitably an element of gamble in such a move. Many do not accept the odds as they apply to them. Although there may seem to be proportionately more senior counsel now, it is by no means an automatic career progression. One relic from a past age is reported to have complained that: 'When I was made a silk there were about 15 to 20 of us. It is no longer a distinction to be a silk when you get 40 to 50 made every year.'[8]

Notwithstanding such a view, it is clear that most barristers do not apply. Some of those who do are refused. What does making the transition involve? Do senior counsel undertake different work or is it simply a question of higher fees? One senior counsel we spoke to insisted:

> The fee's not the most important thing ... we don't charge astronomical fees so that people have to sell their motor cars and their houses in order to pay us, contrary to what the public might say.

In our initial researches, it seemed to us that QCs were more academically inclined than the other barristers we spoke to: they seemed to have more interest in points of substantive law than non-QCs. Certainly, there are QCs who are involved in specialist practice where points of law are the everyday stuff of their work. However, we now believe that it was because many of our initial contacts came from friends and colleagues who supplied us with people who they thought would be interesting to us, that we formed in the early days the false impression that senior counsel were the patrician element of the bar, aristocrats with a presence and command that singled them out from the ordinary cab for hire. Such a view is inaccurate. There are many work-a-day QCs whose bearing is much less than impressive and who undertake cases that are very similar to those undertaken by junior counsel. We then made a point of talking to senior counsel who were, as one informant put it, 'honest journeymen, craftsmen rather than artists'. From them we very much took the impression that the specialist QC is only slightly less rare than the specialist junior. The work they do is the same in kind with matters of fact and settled law predominating. One senior counsel put it this way:

> . . . to make a generalization, in the real world a lot of cases . . . almost certainly most cases, are really argued about the facts because everybody knows the law, the law is fairly obvious . . . a running down case, a factory case there is not much law about. . . . It is in a minority of cases therefore where the law counts in the sense that there are two views of the law. . . . There are three situations I suppose: one – there is no argument about the law, it's only about the facts: two – there is law but it is fairly clear, where do these facts fit into that legal framework? The third, and much less frequent one is what is the law? Cases where the law is generally uncertain are more interesting, intellectually more satisfying. . . . Broadly speaking, a QC is used where there is a point of law or where a lot of money is involved. . . . For example, I spent 7 or 8 hours this weekend on one particular aspect of a case I'm doing next week.

Another saw the difference between junior and senior counsel as one of degree rather than of kind:

> Having taken silk relatively recently, the difference is subtle in some ways between a senior and a junior. A junior tends to do more cases, and more simple cases and the earlier stages of most cases. The junior, maybe, tends to have more envelopes crossing his desk, more sets of papers crossing his desk. A senior has to spend more time on preparation. At the end of the day, he's the person who has to take the overview of the case – the law and the facts.

We will discuss in more detail later exactly what it is that a barrister, senior or junior, in fact does. The point that we want to make here is that progress through the career timetable at the bar depends on all sorts of things other than how good one is at law in the sense of law in books.

JUDICIAL APPOINTMENT

It is well-known that an appointment to the bench represents for many barristers an appealing prospect towards the end of a career of fighting it out in court. The highest prize, appointment to the High Court bench, carries with it enormous prestige (at least in legal circles), a knighthood and a pension from the state, something which barristers as self-employed persons cannot otherwise look forward to. Lesser appointments also have their advantages to barristers who may no longer be able to sustain the same level of interest in, and enthusiasm for, the struggle to prosper at the bar. There are a whole range of full- and part-time appointments, ranging from master-ships, registrarships through to magistrates and commissioners, which are open to barristers of some standing but not necessarily of senior counsel status. Indeed, the pressure on the courts that has resulted in recent reforms to the levels of work that can be handled in various courts, has made this a more viable prospect for more advocates.

Such matters are beyond the remit of this work, but for one particular aspect. There is, apparently, a judicial appointment track on which some careers are run. This may have some effect on the type of work a barrister does and the way that he or she does it.

We were not immediately aware that a judicial appointment formed part of so many barristers' career expectations. Perhaps this was because we began our research in Northern Ireland, which is probably unique among the jurisdictions we examined inasmuch as a judicial appointment there is now something that is taken on only through a strong sense of duty rather than because of its attractions. A permanent police guard and a place on a list of terrorist 'legitimate targets' outweighs any question of pensions or regular hours for most practitioners. However, in other jurisdictions, judicial appointment is a target that is within people's sights very frequently and at a remarkably early stage. It is not that there are two tracks – one concentrating on building up relationships with solicitors and establishing a solid practice and the other focusing more narrowly on the bench – but that, as one informant put it:

> You get more interested in judicial appointment as a career progression once you get established with solicitors and build yourself up ... but you are conscious of that from the start anyway ... it has always been a natural way up.

Local factors make a considerable difference of course. As one aspirant from the provinces pointed out:

> ... here the circuit bench has greater prestige than it has in some places. For example, in London the circuit bench is regarded as something of a joke ... the circuit bench salary isn't sufficient in London and people wouldn't want to get an appointment. ... Down here a circuit judge is fairly well thought of and quite respected and their earnings are

probably reasonably comfortable even though most people who get appointed probably take a cut in income.

On the question of whether career aspirations would affect the type of work taken on, we heard much about the need to maintain a balance in the sort of work that is undertaken. As one barrister put it:

> ... the traditional way to get advancement ... is to have a general practice, including crime, and then it is easier to take silk because most of the silks do lots of crime, and it's easier to get to the circuit bench.

The need to do criminal work seems significant in every jurisdiction. In England and Wales, a recordership is the most likely initial appointment and experience in criminal advocacy is clearly an advantage to a judge trying criminal matters. It was notable that several barristers in Northern Ireland took it as a considerable virtue that the current Lord Chief Justice there had at least once in his career defended an IRA suspect, even though his practice was in a different field.

It is not possible to be sure if a desire for elevation would affect the way a case is handled. One fairly young practitioner we talked to about sharp or sharpish practices in court declared that he would not wish to get involved in anything too different or imaginative as it would mean that he would be remembered for it by the judge who is, after all, someone to impress because he is involved in judicial appointments. This aspiration can seemingly act as a disciplining factor. As another informant put it,

> ... the judges do talk about individuals at the bar who are not reputable. They meet regularly ... a reputation will get around ... the back corridor of the High Court – they all live in the back corridor – is so small that if there is a problem everybody gets to hear of it.

Overly 'clever' dealings will be disciplined by one's colleagues (as we discuss later), but also by the feeling that judicial disapproval may have career implications. We are not impunging the independence of the bar as such, but say simply that, as in any other occupation, there are snakes and ladders that people need to keep on the right side of. Perhaps barristers are correctly represented by the Bar Council as self-employed, independent guardians of justice. But, as this section and this chapter generally has tried to indicate, they are also inevitably caught up in many of the games and struggles that in different forms beset anyone else in a work environment.

NOTES

1 We heard rumours that in Northern Ireland, masonic contacts or those from the Knights of St Columbanus (the Catholic version of the masons) were utilized but, of course, we could not confirm or deny this.
2 There does not seem to be any similar process in the library systems, where the (fairly basic) facilities remain at least formally standard throughout the various levels of the profession.

3 Cases where a member of the public has taken legal action against a public authority for failing to maintain pavements or roadways, with the result that the plaintiff has fallen and been injured.

4 There are important choices to be made within these too, most notably on the criminal side where prosecution or defence work often appear as mutually exclusive alternatives. This issue and related matters are discussed fully in Chapter 3, which deals with the relationships between barristers, solicitors and clients.

5 A guide published in 1990 by Chambers and Partners, a legal recruitment agency, suggested that a barrister of ten years' standing in the field of criminal law might expect to earn £40 000 to £50 000 gross per annum if in criminal practice, but £70 000 to £200 000 if working in commercial law. At the very top of the profession, a barrister with a criminal law practice might recieve £100 000 gross per annum, but the practitioner in the commercial field could expect to earn between £300 000 and £600 000 per annum. Overheads vary but rarely exceed 30 percent for any barrister. There is, of course, great variation within these figures. Many successful barristers outside London do not earn anything like as much.

6 Until very recently in the Republic of Ireland, a rule existed that stated that two senior counsel were required.

7 There have been moves in recent years in England and Wales to increase voluntarily the number of cases where senior counsel can act without the assistance of juniors. Under changes that came into force in November 1988, it was agreed that QCs could act without juniors in a whole range of cases and even without solicitors in some classes of action. However, figures published by the Lord Chancellor's Department relating to how the scheme worked in its first 15 months show that QCs have managed without juniors in only 8 out of more than 1700 cases identified as suitable for the new level of manning (*The Times*, 15 and 16 August 1990).

8 F. Ashe Lincoln, described as the oldest member of the bar in daily practice, with 60 years' service, quoted in an interview published in the *New Law Journal*, 20 April 1990, pp. 556–7.

3

THE SOLICITOR–
BARRISTER
RELATIONSHIP

INTRODUCTION

In this chapter, we look at the interactions between barristers and solicitors: how the need to attract the interest of solicitors and then provide them with a service affects both the type and level of work that a barrister does, as well as the way in which this work is done. Once again, it is useful to look briefly at the orthodox view which prevails and which infiltrates most of the thinking in legal education. This view of the barrister–solicitor relationship is of a general practitioner working in concert with a specialist in the interests of a non-professional client. The most common model is that of the family doctor and hospital consultant: the solicitor is seen analogously as a channel of reference to someone expert in a difficult or unusual area.

The view that we take and develop here is somewhat different. If, as we said earlier and will develop later, the judge is the centre of the advocate's world in court, then out of court it is the solicitor who fills that role. We shall argue that the real client of the barrister is not the lay client, whose case is being presented, but the solicitor. Understanding the solicitor thus helps make sense of the barrister's world.

Importantly, there has been some limited research on the solicitor's profession in the UK. This has tended to suggest that solicitors are not the powerhouse of legal inquiry for which some might wish (Napley, 1983), but rather that they are best viewed as small businessmen running an operation the main concern of which is negotiation and the resolution of various types of cases. These cases are, in the widest sense, legal; but they do not normally require any particularly full understanding of substantive law in order to be carried out. Most legal knowledge held by solicitors is fairly general or is of a procedural nature, i.e. knowing the correct forms and precedents to use in various types of cases. This knowledge and business acumen is directed towards the sole goal of keeping the client happy:

Scottish solicitors explained that on average they would deal with law, in the sense of technical knowledge, for something around one hour a week. The rest of the time – taken up with handling personal relationships and business negotiations, and with consultations and meetings – involved little legal skills; either they used totally routinised legal knowledge or else moved out of, or beyond, specifically legal work. Solicitors confirmed that in their practice, the most important factor in terms of client satisfaction was *not* careful research, technical skills, or even (when a dispute was involved) winning the case, but rather maintaining relationships with clients on proper grounds. As my earlier reference to client satisfaction suggests, the lawyers do achieve remarkable success in managing their relationships with their clients. . . . To maintain the relationship the lawyer may 'involve' other individuals and use institutional excuses. Thus a lawyer, to put it crudely, may blame the law, blame other lawyers, blame the judicial process; should things go wrong – or go too slowly – it is never the lawyer's fault but always that of other people. Clients thus emerge satisfied with their own lawyers but less than happy with the legal system as a whole (Campbell, 1976: 209–210).

As we shall see, the role of the barrister in supporting this client/solicitor relationship on proper grounds means that the barrister is obliged to see his client as the solicitor, rather than the lay person involved in the case in hand.

In this chapter, we will also provide a background for a discussion in Chapter 4 of the solicitor's role in directly shaping the individual case through the supply and structuring of information. In Chapter 4, we will consider the brief – the written set of instructions plus relevant documents and statements – which provide the formal nexus between the solicitor and barrister. The way in which the brief is presented and processed, the manner in which the real world of the client's problem is sliced up and presented for the legal process, clearly structures the content of the case and has a determining role in the way in which a case is dealt with by a barrister. In this chapter, we will begin to look at the brief chiefly in order to bring out some further points about the relationship between barristers and solicitors and how this in general affects what barristers do. In a later chapter, we will look at how the barrister carries the case through.

The need from both sides of the profession to perform the barrister–solicitor relationship adequately is built into the way the legal system in the UK is organized: in order to be successful, to do the job of advocacy properly, the correct handling of this relationship is almost certainly more significant than a spectacular performance in court.

WHO IS THE CLIENT?

Relatively early on in our researches, we found that our more orthodox view of the barrister–client relationship was errant. The first two intimations of this came from reports of errors made by solicitors. A very junior barrister had, she told us, put a substantial amount of effort into preparing her first case to be heard before the Appeal Court in Belfast, but had discovered that the solicitor had not forwarded the prepared documents within the necessary time limits. The case thus had to be dropped. We asked the barrister if she had told the client who was to blame, but she informed us that she had not because she did not want to antagonize the solicitor. On another occasion, when speaking to a very senior civil barrister, we asked him whether he would feel obliged to inform his client if a solicitor made a mistake. The senior barrister informed us that he would not, because solicitors would not like it.

This sense of detachment from the client was found among most of our interviewees and, as we see below, is seen to be advantageous in several respects. However, our reporting of this fact to fellow legal academics did cause some surprise, since the orthodox view – analogous to that of doctor/consultant – would have the barrister responsible to the client as the consultant is responsible to the patient, rather than the doctor.

Barristers in ordinary practice may find themselves representing a whole variety of people and agencies, including citizens as defendants in criminal proceedings or as litigants arguing over an accident, a will or action of government. They may be businesses suing over a contract, applying for planning permission or licensing, or contesting a negligence action. Alternatively, barristers may find themselves representing the Crown, either in prosecuting criminal actions or by acting on behalf of government departments in a whole range of civil matters. In all these instances, a barrister is not strictly acting for the party who is directly involved in the legal action but for a solicitor. The solicitor is thus more than simply an intermediary between the bar and the public. This is why we see the solicitor as one pivot of the barrister's world.

In legal practice, this view is commonplace. Several barristers have told us of judges who, if a novice barrister unwittingly refers to 'my client' when they clearly mean the person for whom their instructing solicitor is acting, will inquire if they are referring to the solicitor or the person sitting next to them. Notwithstanding the current impetus to transform the legal profession into a consumer-led service, barristers remain at all times independent consultants who advise solicitors rather than acting directly on behalf of a solicitor's client.[1]

In the archaic traditions of the bar, the barrister's fee was an *honorarium* and the fee pocket that is still sewn into the back of the barrister's gown allowed payment to be discreetly made during the course of a trial. These traditions do, however, have their modern-day consequences. Even today, most barristers leave negotiation over the level of fees to their clerks. Indeed, payment must take the form of a fee for each piece of work done and not a salary or lump sum paid over a period of time. Counsel cannot sue for their fees, and long delays in their payment are commonplace. Furthermore, a party to a legal action cannot sue a barrister for incompetence in the conduct of a case.

This is not merely a technical point about the exact nature of the legal relationship between the client, his or her solicitor and the barrister. We maintain that the lay client, the solicitor's client, is in practice very much of secondary importance compared to the solicitor. As one barrister put it: 'the lay client, as such, does one case and goes away . . . but you give a service to the solicitor, hopefully, time and time again'. Another advocate saw his relationship in this way:

I suppose I think of the client as being the person that is hurt, the person making the claim – although I appreciate in strict parlance you have a solicitor client. I suppose you are working on two levels . . . from week to week I am hoping to keep satisfied, give a good service to, a number of solicitor clients and part of the way I can do that is by treating their lay clients well . . . hopefully there will be a coincidence of interest between both [lay client and solicitor], but ultimately I suppose you do right by them [solicitors].

This idea of giving a service to repeat players (as opposed to one-shotters)[2] is, we believe, central to understanding the dynamics of the client–solicitor–barrister relationship: it has an effect on much of what barristers actually do in the conduct of individual cases in particular and their work in general. Solicitors who regularly brief a particular barrister clearly have much more influence over that barrister than a one-off client. Of course, it is not only solicitors who are repeat players in the justice game: there are large private and state bodies who use the courts on a day-to-day basis. Insurance companies, local authorities and government departments are involved in litigation over accidents, benefit entitlement and employment disputes, debt and child-care wrangles. Their interests will also be looked after, but this is done through the solicitor. As one barrister put it:

I have some lay clients who come back time and time again . . . corporations . . . and therefore they are a client and clearly I would look after them. But in so doing I would look after the solicitor of course – it's all part and parcel of the same service. . . . With insurance companies . . . you have to service them, so they are the client as well as the solicitor and you, in servicing the insurance companies, are servicing the solicitor's interests in terms of insurance companies. . . . In looking after one, you are hopefully looking after the other at the same time.

We will return to this point shortly and deal in more detail with exactly the sort of influence a solicitor as opposed to a client routinely exerts on the way a barrister perceives both individual cases and his or her work in general. We will also consider the influence of the prosecution authorities – The Director of Public Prosecutions (DPP), Crown Prosecution Service (CPS) and Procurator Fiscal – who are also, of course, major repeat players but who exert a slightly different influence.

THE SOLICITOR'S CHOICE

We have already discussed some of the factors which determine which particular barrister will end up with a given case, e.g. cost, availability, level of work and the role of the barrister's clerk. However, the general process by which solicitors choose barristers to work for them is less well-known. There are a variety of guides and directories available in the various jurisdictions which are intended to assist the solicitor – presumably when the usual channels of personal contacts, recommendations and salesmanship from the barrister's clerk have failed. These are, apparently at least, purchased by solicitors' firms. *Waterlow's Directory* is the market leader in England and Wales and is bought by 80 percent of solicitors. Several of the chambers that we visited had recently reacted to the relaxation in the rules about advertising in particular and the market orientation of the Lord Chancellor's reforms in general, by publishing brochures listing the members of chambers, their experience and their expertise. More controversially, several of the independent guides are now attempting to move beyond providing a simple list of practising barristers; they are moving towards a consumer guide detailing the merits of particular barristers. As we write, *Haver's Directory* is aiming to include not just information about the specialisms of individual barristers but also their charges. Another guide, *The Legal 500*, contains a section on how different chambers rate and there are plans to expand this to include evaluations of the merits of individual barristers. In responding to the controversy that these initiatives have generated, the producers of the various guides have pointed to how the Lord Chancellor's reforms have opened up the bar to other professions (accountants, surveyors, etc.), who are now able to brief counsel directly. Information about which barrister to employ may be important to such people, and indeed there are all those potential clients in Europe who in theory need not now approach a barrister only through a solicitor.

Much of the controversy over these guides is centred around objections from the bar and misses out on the fact that these guides are potentially more threatening to the solicitor's profession. They purport to take on one of the central roles of the solicitor. Indeed, the knowledge as to individual barrister's abilities that is acquired by acting as a go-between for client and barrister is an essential part of the solicitor's expertise. In some ways, for the solicitor, who you know is as important as what you know. After all, solicitors do not conduct cases themselves and part of what clients are paying for is knowledge about who is the best barrister for the job given its nature, the funds available, local conditions, etc.

This information is generally beyond the understanding of barristers. A common theme among those we interviewed was the apparent irrationality of solicitors. As one pointed out:

> Where we get our work from is sometimes a bit of a mystery to us in
> that some people are briefed by certain solicitors and certain insurance

companies and nobody knows why or what the connections are or how they get it.

This sometimes causes resentment:

> ... to actually get to a professional standard ... to put in all that work from school onwards ... and to have to rely on somebody else getting you work, getting you quality work, and somebody else paying you for that work and you being at the beck and call of somebody ... I mean there are solicitors you can work for, do lots of work for, and you do nothing wrong and everything's right and then maybe for three months, four months, you don't hear a word from them and then the next thing they arrive with something totally shitty and expect you to sort it out.

One barrister we talked to put the successful cultivation of solicitors down simply to 'regularity of contact. They get to know your form and you get to know their's ... you get a feel for them.'

The idea of personal relationships was a recurrent theme among barristers' evaluations of how they attract solicitors. One provincial barrister declared:

> ... the extraordinary thing is, if you do a piece of work really well for a solicitor (I mean what you do in court, what you do for the client rather than how you make the solicitor feel), you quite often don't see them again. But if you cock a case up, they seem to remember you and send you more work.... I know it sounds strange but I think that probably I get more work from getting on well with the solicitor than necessarily doing well – as long as I reach a certain standard in the quality of my work.

The importance of this is not lost on senior barristers and has an influence on many wider decisions affecting a chambers as a whole. We were told:

> We are toying with the idea of moving out to somewhere like a small industrial park outside town ... where you haven't got the problems with parking, you're in between the two major centres where you do most of your work ... a perfect location but, on the other hand, you haven't got the drop in ability – in other words, there's no solicitor who is going to come in to you after court for a cup of coffee, to say hello.... That, we feel, is going to lose us a lot of business.

Undoubtedly, the relationship between solicitors and barristers is far from being a purely legal one based solely on assisting the person in court. There is, of course, the well-known spectre of touting, the idea of treating solicitors in order to encourage them to channel work towards a particular barrister. When we raised this in our interviews, it elicited responses that varied markedly from area to area. As we noticed in other areas of the barrister's work (particularly the role of the judge in chambers), there were small local differences and traditions which produced variations in attitudes and behaviours. On this matter, as elsewhere, the conditions that prevailed locally were invariably defended as being the more honourable/workable/realistic/effective way. For example, in Northern Ireland, and as far as our limited experience in the Republic of Ireland indicated, it was, apparently, rather unseemly to even mention the matter of touting. The view that was taken of touting varied from one which acknowledged that it might go on, but not by they themselves or anyone known to them, to a more forthright denial that the practice exists at all. Perhaps the most commonly expressed view was: 'I don't want to get on that ladder: once you start it you have to keep at it.'

In most parts of England and Wales, the situation was somewhat different. One provincial barrister commented:

> . . . naturally, as in all business you find yourself having to take them [solicitors] out to lunch once in a while, keep them cheerful, invite them to the Christmas party. . . . It's a pretty cynical business really but I don't think it is any different from any other business. There are 5500 practising barristers in the UK and there is always someone who will do it cheaper than you . . . you have to give some reason for that solicitor to come to you.

Sometimes what may seem routine and unobjectionable to one practitioner was regarded in a different light by another:

> I suppose a good word for it is prostitution . . . there is so much of it about – you know, nicey-nicey to solicitors, 'Oh come out to lunch', 'How are you?', 'How's the family?' It's very ungenuine.

In Scotland, the situation was strikingly different. Transfer between the two branches of the profession is more commonplace there and work is very often channelled through old contacts who are kept at reasonably close quarters. In our interviews, Scottish advocates were genuinely surprised that close links between solicitors and barristers were forbidden in the rest of the UK. In Scotland, it was seen as highly advantageous to have these links, particularly given the high early costs of becoming an advocate. If a solicitor wished to change to the other side of the profession – for whatever reason – it was seen as beneficial to him that he knew and had worked for a firm of solicitors, since they would be prepared to support him in his early days as an advocate. It was also beneficial for the firm of solicitors who knew him, as they could trust him to act on their behalf.[3]

There are undoubtedly large lunches being given everywhere. However, as we hope to indicate in the rest of this chapter, touting in the sense of giving money or treats is in fact a rather unnecessary icing on the cherry. This is so because the nature of the service that barristers give to solicitors is such that the barristers are already controlled by the solicitors in all the important aspects of their work. As one barrister put it, perhaps a little self-righteously:

> . . . you can 'tout' by providing a service and if you are working for sensible solicitors they are perceptive enough to realize that the guy who's licking his backside is not perhaps as good as the man who is providing a quiet service and getting the work done.

A related but perhaps more interesting issue is that regarding contacts. We have already mentioned contacts at the bar, but there is also the matter of contacts within the solicitor's profession who are able to direct work towards a given barrister. We heard quite routinely of careers made by wives or husbands, uncles or fathers in solicitors' firms, who briefed particular barristers regardless of whether they were in fact the most suitable advocate for a particular case. Indeed, in several of the jurisdictions we visited, we were told a remarkably similar unkind story of a barrister who married a solicitor mainly in order to improve his flow of work. There are other sorts of contacts that may be important also. For example, we heard from a barrister based in Belfast that:

> ... the law like every other aspect of ... Northern Ireland society is influenced by the sort of divisions that characterize this society. . . . It's not really a sectarian division all along the line by any means . . . but . . . the sort of work you get is determined to some extent by your political connections and . . . by your religion. For example, if the majority of plaintiffs in actions against the police are Catholics, then they generally would have Catholic solicitors and Catholic barristers . . . there are no strict rules obviously but, realistically, you have to recognize that that happens. . . . The nature of the practice that you have is determined in the first year or two at the bar. . . . By chance? Yes, but also by design in the sense that if you have certain political connections . . . whether as a republican or a loyalist . . . then you will get work from republican solicitors or loyalist solicitors – as far as you can make those sort of divisions which are never universal because most solicitors will get some work from both sides.

This apparently extreme situation in Northern Ireland is no doubt reproduced elsewhere, if in less extreme ways. The badges of belonging to one establishment or another may be different but the process and the consequences are not.

While there is undoubtedly a certain amount of patronage in operation everywhere, we did hear another explanation for the number of stories and allegations that abound. We were told:

> There's a lot of personal and professional jealousy at the bar . . . particularly among your own peer group. You are watching. What is someone else doing? Are they doing better than I am? . . . The one reason which I think most people find hardest to swallow is that so and so might have more ability than I have. You tend to cloak it and say he knows X or his uncle is Y or something like that to overcome the unpalatable truth that somebody might just be very good.

Of course, as far as the barristers' clerk is concerned, there is no mystery about why a solicitor chooses a particular barrister: it is all the result of careful handling by the clerk's office. All the clerks that we talked to were convinced that solicitors were fairly comprehensively controlled by the clerk's recommendation. Certainly, as Flood (1983: 75) concludes, much of what the clerk does is salesmanship, persuading solicitors to take whoever is available within the chambers rather than letting the brief go elsewhere. As we discussed in Chapter 2, if solicitors are unable or unwilling to pay increased fees, the clerk must persuade them to take the next best alternative. One clerk who we spoke to had no doubts as to his importance in that role and the significance of his performing it inadequately:

> . . . the solicitor and clerk relationship is trust. I can't afford to lie . . . I mean bearing in mind that the solicitor will always believe what I tell him, if I tell him Mr X is good and I believe inwardly that he wasn't, I may keep a brief in chambers but in the long term I would be losing the respect of the solicitor and I may lose the firm entirely . . . they [solicitors] depend on me.

The relatively few solicitors we spoke to gave only a very rough indication of the process whereby they chose a particular barrister. Clearly, it is beyond the ambit of this study to pursue in detail what is undoubtedly a complex process. Several solicitors gave us checklists of the qualities that they would in general look for in any counsel who they regularly briefed. Qualities such as 'efficiency', 'robustness', 'style' and 'the human touch' generally came towards the top of such lists. Some solicitors talked of looking for 'someone to see the compromise'. Most referred to 'horses for courses', the idea that different cases require different qualities depending on the subject matter, the court or tribunal, the money available, etc.

A solicitor's client is generally not involved in choosing a barrister; after all, in many instances, this is part of the service that the client is paying for. In the case of large-scale, repeat players such as insurance companies and government departments, however, a panel or list of recognized and acceptable barristers will be used. In some ways, this may make it easier for the solicitor to make a choice of barrister, but more difficult in others. A barristers' clerk described the situation in this way:

> . . . solicitors come to us and insurance companies go to solicitors . . . We've got one . . . Eagle Star, they use a firm [of solicitors] . . . and they in turn use us. This is where it becomes very, very hard because [the solicitors] . . . would know exactly the calibre and expertise of every member of chambers as they put all their work here. . . . As far as Eagle Star are concerned, they perhaps have on their panel just three barristers . . . we have a problem here that when these three barristers are all engaged elsewhere . . . I ring up [the solicitors] and say I can't get any of these three tomorrow for you . . . but I can recommend Mr A. . . . Now although [the solicitors] know exactly what Mr A is like . . . they use him for other work . . . they have then to persuade Eagle Star 'OK he's not on your panel but . . .'. Eagle Star will say 'He's not on our panel – I don't want him then' . . . they don't know him . . . he [the solicitor] then has to persuade Eagle Star . . . to increase their panel.

With some clients, particularly prosecution authorities, the list is exclusive inasmuch as it cannot be extended without much formality.

Most solicitors who do any amount of work that ends in court will themselves keep a small stable of such barristers who they brief regularly. It is difficult for us to guess how, in practice, such a stable is chosen, but we would suspect it is a complex mixture of various factors including contacts and personal relationships, cheapness and availability, inertia and tradition, convenience and satisfaction. Overall, our conversations with solicitors tended to confirm what we had learned from barristers – for a barrister to become part of a solicitor's stable and for that relationship to continue, he or she must provide a good service.

PROVIDING A SERVICE FOR SOLICITORS

We have already referred to the sort of description of the relationship between barristers and solicitors that can be found in many texts on the legal system and which refers to the generalist passing on difficult problems to the specialist. Textbooks for trainee solicitors reproduce this idea of solicitors referring to barristers on difficult points of law and for specialist advice (see, e.g. Blake, 1989: 41).

This is undoubtedly part of the job that barristers do for solicitors but it is, for us, only one part of a much more complex service. We see barristers as primarily offering a service to solicitors that goes beyond simply giving specialist advice. In this section, we will describe in more detail the nature of this service and how in performing it the barrister's work is circumscribed, shaped and controlled.

In arguing for this view, we do not maintain that solicitors are all-important in the sense simply that they provide work to barristers. The fact that solicitors are the link between barristers and remuneration is significant but not completely determinant of the role of barristers. It is rather that solicitors provide the focus for what barristers do. Solicitors are, in a sense, a conduit: it is through solicitors that the pressures and demands of individual client's cases and the wider world are processed. This has its effects for the individual barrister in terms of what type of work he or she does, what volume and level that work is at and, most significantly, how it is done.

We have already talked about the necessity for, and the difficulties of, keeping a practice that is mixed in terms of the type of work that is carried out. On the whole, barristers aim to keep their employment base as wide as possible. They tend to avoid putting all their employment opportunity eggs in the basket of one solicitor. However, the requirements of the service that barristers must give to solicitors often means that this is difficult to sustain. In particular, it is often hard to manage a criminal and civil practice. The reasons for this, as we noted above, do not lie directly with solicitors, but it is through solicitors that they often come to bite. One barrister described it this way:

> There are those who try a mixed bag. The difficulty with it is . . . in civil
> cases you tend to get notice of the case being listed, say three weeks or

possibly four weeks ahead. You put that in your diary, tell your solicitor that you're doing it and you're committed to it . . . maybe even consult in it. Then if you're doing a criminal case the notice is somewhat less – it can be two weeks or maybe even days . . . you're going to get awful clashing in your diary and somebody has to give. . . . I don't like ringing up solicitors saying 'I've got a criminal case and your civil case has to go by the board'. . . . Eventually, solicitors get disgruntled and . . . there's plenty of other people to pick up if you leave off and you can lose out in that regard.

Even within a general civil practice, there are divisions and sub-divisions into which people sometimes fall but are sometimes pushed by solicitors. Most commonly, there is the categorization of women into family law. Many solicitors require, and maintain that their clients prefer, a female practitioner in divorce or child custody actions. We did hear from several women barristers that it can be extremely difficult to avoid that stereotyping. Unexpectedly, it was also argued that women found it easier to get work from male solicitors, rather than from female solicitors. One female solicitor suggested: 'women instructing women, that is not something I come across at all . . . women instruct men and men instruct women . . . I think it is the old biological feature'.

More generally, though, if a barrister is perceived by solicitors to be working in a particular area – be it personal injury, chancery or business contracts – the label sticks. As one barrister put it:

I find that if you exhibit a natural interest in a certain kind of work, you are sent that work and if you are perceived as someone who wouldn't favour [working in a particular area] . . . then you generally wouldn't get that kind of work.

This doesn't mean that advocates are forced into specialisms. It is rather that the initial career direction taken is reinforced as expertise, working knowledge and above all contacts with solicitors are built in the day-to-day working in a particular field. Another barrister told us:

. . . most lawyers are completely mercenary in the sense that they represent the interests of whatever client they have to represent . . . at least that's the theory of it and that actually does apply in practice . . . except that . . . it generally happens that certain kinds of people are identified or perceived by solicitors as suitable for certain kinds of work.

If an advocate regularly operates in a particular area, he or she will develop the sorts of skills, personal relationships and inside knowledge that make it a difficult or even perverse choice for a solicitor to choose someone from outside. For example, we found that most of the licensing work that was done by barristers in Northern Ireland was conducted by only a handful of barristers. Solicitors acting on behalf of pubs, hotels and restaurants know that such work is often not difficult. However, because the outcome of a licence application has considerable financial consequences for their clients, they tend to be cautious and brief one of the perceived experts. The fact that the work could be done by someone else for a smaller fee is insignificant when set alongside even the remote possibility that the expert might be successful where an outsider might not. The general process in operation is one where being considered suitable for a particular kind of work is a consequence of doing that kind of work, and has the result that the barrister will largely continue within that work.

Again, although most barristers aim to litigate on both sides – to appear for the plaintiff as well as the respondent in civil matters and to prosecute as well as defend in the criminal courts – this sometimes becomes difficult in view of the type of service that solicitors require. As one well-established barrister commented: 'it is more difficult than it might appear to represent both sides on a regular basis – you tend to get branded'. We were told by another advocate that 'if the state bodies . . . or the insurance companies see that you're a plaintiff-type, they are probably less likely to let you into the secrets of how they deal with their side of things'. There are, of course, good reasons for this. As we were told:

> . . . plaintiff work is probably easier . . . it's certainly easier to get . . . it tends to be that the barristers doing civil defence work have a background of doing plaintiff work before. . . . I think the people briefing the defence barristers [i.e. acting for insurance companies, government bodies, etc.] appreciate that having had the experience of one side it's probably useful then to get them on the other side . . .

There is some movement, although it is largely in one direction only – from plaintiff to defendant as the barrister's experience develops sufficiently to satisfy a panel that he or she should be regularly briefed on the other side. It also seems that this movement comes mainly, although not exclusively, in a barrister's early days at the bar. It is, of course, difficult to estimate when exactly a barrister is no longer a beginner and becomes a 'plaintiff-type'. However, it is certainly true that, generally speaking, if an advocate hasn't heard the call from the defence side by a certain stage in his or her career, it is unlikely to present itself.

Another barrister explained the plaintiff–defendant split in this way:

> . . . insurance companies do rely heavily on panels . . . there are some barristers who they would not regard as suitable for their work . . . you know they don't like the poacher turned gamekeeper as such. . . . If you take the [Northern Ireland Housing] Executive in particular . . . they have a system of operation in terms of litigation which has many little problems in it – not all of them evident to plaintiffs' practitioners. . . . So if I, defending Executive cases, turned into the poacher . . . I'd know the warts in the Executive system. . . . For instance, one of the things that quite often arises is the recording of complaints before an accident happens . . . a tenant injures himself and the case will only really get off

the ground if the tenant can establish that the defect over which he tripped was reported to the Executive well beforehand and they failed to repair it within a reasonable time . . . then he can show a good cause of action. The system of recording complaints is absolutely vital . . . the Executive have what they regard as a good system of reporting complaints, but in point of fact it is full of pitfalls and those pitfalls will be known to those of us who do Executive work but not necessarily to plaintiffs' [counsel].

The situation is similar, if not identical, on the criminal side. A successful criminal barrister maintained:

. . . most people will either be prosecution counsel or defence counsel. . . . I would be identified as someone who would do lots of actions for plaintiffs against the police, certain kinds of judicial review work, criminal defence work and therefore I wouldn't be sent or asked to do criminal prosecution work . . . it just doesn't arise.

Some of this career-typing is the result of deliberate choice, but most comes from what solicitors choose to perceive about a particular individual. Another criminal advocate told us:

I do draw lines to some extent, not hard and fast lines by any means . . . I started off . . . drawing the sort of lines that were drawn by the chambers where I did my pupillage in Wellington Street [the former location of a 'radical' set organised by Tony Gifford] . . . like never doing . . . any prosecution work. . . . A lot of the lines, I should say are still there, not necessarily because I still feel it's appropriate but because, having established those lines in the first place, it has just carried on . . . having been identified now as somebody who wouldn't do that kind of work it just doesn't come my way.

There is also the process whereby barristers are adopted by the prosecution authorities and put on their panel. This will then become their regular and major source of work. In several of the jurisdictions we looked at, there was a recognized career path which began when advocates were taken up by the prosecution authority at a point in their career, usually in their late twenties or early thirties, when they had acquired a degree of experience in minor defendant work. Regular work and close supervision from the central authority may have the result that, in the eyes of some solicitors, they become prosecution-minded and even adopt a particular house style. In some jurisdictions, this can lead to a permanent arrangement whereby a barrister does exclusively prosecution work, although of course he or she is still paid on a case-by-case basis. For example, in Belfast's Crumlin Road criminal courts, there are three seniors and two juniors who perform this role and if they are unable to cover the five or so courts that run each day, other younger barristers further down this career ladder are brought in. In Scotland advocates generally accept the Lord Advocate's invitation to be one of 12

Advocate Deputies (prosecutors in the High Court) for a three year period. Most successful juniors will do a stint.

In criminal work there is not, however, always the same exclusivity about moving back and forth from prosecution to defence work as we noticed on the civil side. A senior barrister informed us that about five years previously, his practice was about 90 percent prosecution, but that now it was about 60 percent prosecution and 40 percent defence. The exact reasons for this were uncertain, although chance factors seemed to be important:

> . . . these days they [the Crown Prosecution Service] seem to be slower off the mark than certain defence firms that use me . . . and in the last six months I have had probably twelve occasions when I had been briefed or booked by the defence two or three months before the prosecution brief comes in for me . . . in certain of the cases I would have preferred to prosecute rather than defend.

Of course, the solicitor's perception of a barrister's expertise and experience is not always accurate. Sometimes a label is outdated, mistaken or otherwise misapplied. But even if this is the case, the nature of the service that the barrister gives to the solicitor is such that the interests of the barrister will very often be stretched to accommodate the label. Work is, after all, work, and the solicitor as customer is always right. One very senior barrister whose practice was now almost exclusively in the area of planning law told us:

> I only do personal injury work for one client . . . I have done it through the years . . . [but] I have deliberately abandoned the general range of civil work . . . keeping that element of civil work [i.e. personal injury] really to give a service to a particular solicitor.

The nature of the relationship with the solicitor is such that the requirements of a solicitor may well override the normal stages in the development of a career. In this way, the level as well as the type of work is determined ultimately by the solicitor–barrister relationship. For example, one practitioner told us:

> I was called in '81 . . . I'm doing an Order 24 possession action this morning which really – well, I've got a pupil against me on the other side, that gives you an indication. It's relatively simple work and something that really I shouldn't always be doing, but if a solicitor wants you to do it you have to offer that service because that encourages them to send . . . more important, more interesting and, let's face it, work that will pay more money.

The requirements of a solicitor also influence the volume of work that a barrister takes on. As one advocate pointed out: 'There are those who cram their diaries as full as they can but basically they're taking a chance as regards servicing the solicitor.' At its most extreme, this may mean that solicitors run the risk of being severely embarrassed. There are barristers who we heard termed 'court hoppers', who schedule numerous cases simultaneously in various courts, and 'travellers', who work in two or maybe three provincial centres. Obviously, the tactics of such practitioners carry a high risk, and very often their late attendance or non-appearance infuriates judges, opposition counsel and clients alike. It is often the solicitor attending the case who fields this trouble. In extreme cases, it has been known for the judge to dismiss the case, award costs against the solicitor or even sometimes in the county court require the solicitor to run the case. Given this, these species of barristers are fairly rare and their practices are not frequently emulated.

However, the whole system is built on the idea of settlement, and courts as well as barristers list many more cases than they can possibly handle. They do this because they know that in civil cases there are always settlements, and on the criminal side many contests will be turned into guilty pleas. There is always the temptation to take on too much work or at least more than is safe. There remains, of course, the option of passing the brief, but again the demands of the solicitor determine how this is done. One experienced barrister explained it this way:

> . . . what happens is, for one reason or another, barristers hold on to papers for too long when they know that the chances are that they are not going to be able to do it . . . you have something in your diary for three weeks ahead and you get papers for the same day and hold on to them waiting to see if anything develops in relation to the case already in there. . . . It is a feature of the individual nature of the employment that you tend to hold on to the papers longer than perhaps you should do. . . . You say to yourself, 'Well, if something happens to the other case I'll be able to do this one, whereas if I pass it now and something happens to the other case next week I'll be unemployed!' . . . Solicitors know when you're being greedy. . . . Solicitors rightly feel a bit displeased if you wait until the very last moment to pass the work where it isn't because you're in a running case . . . but because you knew there was a conflict [in timing], thought it might resolve and held on to the papers accordingly.

The situation becomes more complex when one takes into account how the remuneration system of the bar operates. Basically, the barrister who conducts the case is the one who gets paid, although payment may be made if an opinion is written or a consultation held or for any drafting done. A barrister with conflicting duties must take into account how much money each case will lose as well as the difficulty that a late pass may have for replacement counsel making up the case. This was explained to us in the following manner:

> I suppose, as quite often happens, you might have quite a complicated case where there was very little involved on the paperwork side [and therefore very little to charge for before the hearing] and where you have spent quite a long time looking into the law . . . then it is of course rather frustrating to have to pass it on to someone else. . . . I suppose as a

result, a lot of barristers, if they are in a complicated case, will give it preference simply because they have done the work on it. And it's harder to ask the solicitor to put up with a new counsel at the last moment when the case is complicated. . . . I suppose where you are put to your mettle is if the competing case is a lucrative one . . . maybe simple but lucrative, but the one that you're in is complicated but not lucrative . . . that's where the crunch comes . . . are you loyal to the solicitor?

For many barristers, the answer to such quandaries is clear. One practitioner we interviewed clearly spoke for many when he laid down the rule that: 'If you are really stuck you select the case for passing from the solicitor you do least work for.' When a barrister needs to pass a case, he or she must again take into account the solicitor and whatever panel system or stable he, she or the client operates. The same barrister set out a second rule: 'if you have to displease a solicitor, displease him least by passing to someone he knows'.

The relationship that a barrister has with a solicitor – the need to provide him or her with a service – clearly shapes that barrister's practice, in terms of its nature, level and volume. It also affects the way in which that barrister will in general approach cases.

THE INFLUENCE OF SOLICITORS ON THE CONDUCT OF CASES

As well as looking at the general way in which barristers and solicitors meet in the dispensation and acceptance of work, we must consider further how the general demands of the barrister–solicitor relationship, i.e. the need for barristers to give a service to solicitors, introduces pressures and demands that affect the way in which barristers perform their role. Here relationships from the outside world as mediated by solicitors, and the social arrangement of the profession, operate to influence how cases are dealt with. We see how the idea that barristers should supply a service to solicitors operates to ensure that barristers perform in a way whereby the solicitors are satisfied. This will involve solicitors being:

- facilitated,
- unburdened, and
- enhanced in the eyes of their clients.

Facilitating the solicitor's practice

There are, of course, large variations within the demography of the solicitor's profession, which are attested to by Abel (1988). A one-man, or one-woman, practice in a country town operates in a very different way from a multi-partner, specialist firm. Different again are those solicitors who act from within a government department or an insurance company. However, there are some key elements which are common to most solicitors' practices and these effect what it is that a solicitor will expect of a barrister.

A solicitor in private practice is, as we have argued above, a business person. In a sense, a solicitor makes his or her money like a shopkeeper turning over goods. The solicitor's objective is to open a file, get through the file, bring it to an end result, close the file and get the bill of costs out and charge the fee. A high volume and quick turnover make the business successful. In order to achieve high volume, it may be necessary to employ staff – secretaries, outdoor clerks, assistants, etc. The overheads are great and, especially if there are partners who are going to take the cream off the top of the profits cake, it is important to have a quick turnover. Barristers are very aware of the business reality of the solicitor's world. As one advocate told us:

> If I'm sent out papers to draft proceedings or . . . replies to notice for
> further and better particulars . . . or whatever . . . if I sit on that for three
> months and don't do it because I'm not organized or I'm lazy, that's
> three months passing by where that solicitor might have got that case
> listed, the file closed and another one open . . . getting the paperwork
> back quickly is one of the main, probably the most important, reason a
> solicitor will brief a barrister. I think a lot of them would trade that
> virtue for a lot of others . . . to make his business more efficient and
> more lucrative.

Another barrister, asked what was the secret of success, took the view that:

> The successful people at the end of the day don't mess about with their
> paperwork . . . they're not successful just because they are aggressive
> and can bluster or . . . [because they are] . . . intelligent . . . or whatever
> . . . they are of course hardworking, but the fundamental thing is that
> they get their paperwork done on time.

Although the general public as consumers of legal services might find it difficult to believe, speed and efficiency are valued in the legal world. They are valued for healthy commercial reasons. Of course, solicitors in government departments do not have direct commercial pressures, but no doubt the drives towards greater efficiency that have come in all aspects of public life have a similar effect in terms of increasing the speed of turnover.

We were told of solicitors expecting barristers to facilitate their practices in ways that go far beyond the textbook relationship. One experienced barrister told us:

> There are a number of solicitors in this area, and they are a growing
> proportion, who will make a case fight . . . they make it difficult during
> the pre-litigous stages . . . when you're writing the first few letters you
> sense that they are being awkward just to make it fight . . . sometimes
> the client's interests are undoubtedly coming second . . . there is un-
> questionably a move among some solicitors just to make a buck and to
> hell with the client.

Problems like these, and as we shall see shortly, solicitors who interfere or use barristers as scapegoats, provide some interesting challenges to the scruples of barristers.

Unburdening the solicitor

A considerable part of the barrister's role seems to involve relieving the solicitor of problems. This may in part be an aspect of the referral role which the solicitor plays in opposition to the barrister's role as specialist. However, much of the relief solicitors seek is not from merely difficult or technical points of law. Some barristers we spoke to were contemptuous of solicitors' legal abilities, declaring them to be business people rather than lawyers. In many cases, a referral to a barrister is an almost automatic reflex by a solicitor. Details of difficult points of law are not necessarily what is sought. One solicitor working for a government department told us: 'Basically what I want to know is what to do next . . . I need clear and concise directions for proof or whatever . . . nothing wishy-washy. . .'.

Despite the dismissive attitude taken by some barristers, there are reasons for this other than a solicitor's inability to deal with law. Barristers are very often in a position where, as someone from outside the case, they can move in, resolve issues and make things happen. As one barrister expressed it:

> If you provide a practical service, and quite often a lot of the time you are taking a burden off a solicitor's shoulders . . . they have got so deeply into a case that they can't see the wood for the trees and that's why they employ you . . . so if you come back with a robust opinion on something, even if it may be slightly wrong, they rather enjoy that, they like that weight being lifted off their shoulders . . . you're making their life a bit easier, maybe allowing them to make money doing things that are more profitable to them.

The very act of sending a brief to counsel may encourage cases to clear up. Poor cases will be highlighted and settlements may become possible. As one practitioner put it:

> . . . very often . . . because you are slightly removed from the case, and so is the barrister on the other side, it will be possible to reach some sort of compromise that will be workable.

Even if a pre-court resolution is not achieved, at least the issues become crystallized. Objectives can be identified, strategies can be decided upon and pleas changed. As one criminal practitioner told us:

> We're independent . . . we get papers – defending or prosecuting – we take a totally objective view and if the client is totally up a gum tree or being stupid I can advise him so. . . . By the same token, the prosecution service may be obsessed with the guilt of an individual even though there's bugger all evidence against him and I, by looking at it afresh from an objective standpoint, can advise them to the contrary.

Barristers are also useful for disciplining clients. One counsel described it in this way:

> Because we come from outside we can tell them things that their solicitors, who . . . don't want to upset them and so forth . . . and are perhaps more involved, can't tell them.

Another barrister said:

> . . . some [solicitors] are very practical and expect you to read the riot act to the client, let's say in a domestic injunction situation. . . . Then [there is] the solicitor who says 'I know he's telling me lies, I've brought you in to be able to talk some sense into him'.

Again the solicitor may not be able, for various reasons, to do what is necessary. One country solicitor we spoke to maintained that: 'it's easier for the barrister to be more cut and dried than the solicitor . . . we have all sorts of factors . . . local feelings . . . to take into account that he doesn't'.

Overall, we were given the very strong impression by both barristers and solicitors, that the role of the barrister is to side-step many of the personal relationships that surround the client–solicitor relationship and act as a problem solver. A fairly commonly expressed view was, as one practitioner put it:

> If they could sort themselves out they wouldn't come to us, that's why we're there . . . to sort them out. It's different if you have a very legal case . . . a complicated building dispute . . . but even then the way out is usually fairly clear. . . . You can say 'Look, the probabilities are this . . . if you go ahead you're going to lose in costs, you might as well agree to this' – (a lesser sum without costs or whatever). . . . If any of them could work it out themselves they wouldn't need us.

Part of the reason for this focus on problem solving seems to lie with the fact that, generally, when a barrister is brought in on a case, there is something happening. The legal process is moving things along: if the party to a case does not do this, then that consequence will follow. There is an action or order or whatever to be initiated or defended. Even where general advice is being sought, it is because a lay client wants to do something or stop doing something: advice in the abstract, for its own sake, is not commonly sought. Against such a background, barristers take on the role of problem solver or at least problem resolver. This is what the client wishes for and the solicitor requires.

One practitioner we spoke to, who worked mainly in the criminal and family courts, saw his role as being very different from those solicitors who were, in his opinion, like social workers concerned with how their clients felt about the situation and what their clients wanted:

> At the bar you realize in objectivity what is going to happen. You tell your boy 'Well listen, you can do this and this but at the end of the day

this is going to happen and if this happens I want you to do this . . .'. If certain things have happened you must decide on balance what the consequences are and act accordingly.

He supplied us with an example:

> Today I had a case . . . I'm for the mother who has refused access to a child; father wants access; I'm under instructions to make a cross application to deny access. . . . Now I know he's beaten her up but that doesn't make any difference in relation to access because . . . you have to be really bad not to get access. So on balance he's going to get access to the child. . . . I don't say 'What do you want?' – I say to her, 'Look I understand your feelings, I know he's been a silly bugger, he's messed you around, he's attacked you but at the end of the day he's going to get access. Now it's up to you, we can either adjourn it today for another date, and you can give evidence . . . but at the end of the day he is going to get access. You might as well agree now.' (The court's going to do it whether she wants it or not, it's up to you to make her agree rather than put her through cross-examination . . . she's going to feel worse . . . she's going to cry, she's going to go home unhappy . . . whereas if you persuade her . . . she's going to be much happier.) She agreed with me. I've only had two clients ever who have refused my advice . . . my experience in these certain areas allows me to predict the outcome . . . it's then a matter of persuading the client. . . . That's my job.

Enhancing the solicitor

Many of the barristers we talked to declared that they were not in the slightest interested in pleasing solicitors. When pressed on this, it generally turned out that they were not prepared to allow solicitors to interfere with their running of the case. They would not make 'solicitor's points' in court simply to impress the client of their solicitor's keenness. Control is an important value for the barrister. Generally, barristers appeared unwilling to allow solicitors to intrude into what they saw as their role. Of course, as we have just discussed, this coincides with what many solicitors require from those they instruct. However, within the limits of the roles that barristers and solicitors in general play, and taking into account the variations within individual relationships, there is clearly a process whereby barristers act to make solicitors look good in the eyes of lay clients.

In saying this, we are not claiming that the vanity of solicitors, combined with the financial power they hold over barristers, operates to the effect that the personal enhancement of solicitors becomes a primary goal for the advocate. It is rather that solicitors stand at the junction between the consumer and the services consumed. Solicitors provide the important nexus between the paying public (or in the case of publicly funded action, the choosing public). If a solicitor is well regarded, then the client will on the whole be satisfied irrespective of the outcome of the action and will likely return to that solicitor. In a sense, what we are arguing for here is similar to the point made by Campbell (briefly extracted above, p. 50), who explored why participants in the legal process are generally dissatisfied with the justice system but happy with their own solicitor. Campbell suggests that this is because solicitors will attribute any shortcomings to other players in the system, while simultaneously performing a vigorous public relations act for their own benefit. Although Campbell did not discuss advocacy, the role of the advocate is a supporting one to the solicitor's. Advocates must convince clients that they are getting a good service from their solicitors. As one barrister expressed it: 'What they [solicitors] want you to do is turn up and impress the client.' Another, with a different level of practice, said:

> It's very difficult to know sometimes what the client thinks the barrister is. . . . Eighty percent of the clients I work for are on social security, they're unemployed, they are getting legal aid, they are probably not very familiar with the workings of the legal system. For all they know, I might be a sort of appendage to that solicitor's office.

At whatever level the barrister is operating at, he or she must take part in the public relations aspect, whereby the solicitor's service is viewed in a satisfactory light. One senior barrister recalled:

> I made a comment to a client that was critical of the solicitor . . . that solicitor took me to one side and said 'Don't ever, ever do that again.' It taught me a lesson. I certainly don't make a point of doing that now . . . you have to use discretion and make the best of what you've got.

A considerable part of the public relations role involves 'cooling the mark out' as Goffman (1952) termed it, the process whereby someone is persuaded to accept as satisfactory a situation which falls short of their expectations. Aspirations and outcomes must be matched upwards as well as downwards. One barrister said:

> I always like to see the client before the case if it's of any import at all because I can then put the client in the right frame of mind to save his time in court . . . so that he won't have any greater expectations or they're not cowering, thinking they're going to get nothing when they might get something.

Generally, solicitors expect counsel to explain the proceedings to a client. We were told:

> As a matter of plain PR, the solicitor will quite often say, win or lose would you mind speaking to [the client] which is usually a fairly cursory little chat: 'Well done, you were very good in the witness box and the judge believed you, don't spend the money all at once.' Or it might be 'Well, as we warned you before, this case might succeed and it might not and it didn't. Too bad. Do you want to appeal it? Maybe you should think about it overnight, sleep on it and come in and see [the solicitor] in a few days.'

Another recalled how unpleasant this role could be:

> You have to tell certain plaintiffs that, sympathetic as you might be, they just have no remedy, the law doesn't accommodate it . . . the most tragic thing I had to do was go and explain to a mother that the value of her child who had been killed . . . was three and a half thousand [pounds]. . . . It stuck in my throat but you have to do it . . . it's up to you to sit down and explain it – that's your job.

Solicitors clearly value this function, perhaps even more than some barristers realize. One of the solicitors we spoke to told us of how she had dropped one barrister from her firm's stable in favour of another who was less technically able but prepared to talk to clients in a way that they were able to relate to.

This public relations function sometimes infringes on how the case is conducted. Although, as we have already seen, the solicitor often wants someone else to take on the burden of the case, and the barrister sees his or her role as persuading a client to accept a certain option, there are cases where the solicitor wants a 'hands-on' role. Seemingly, such solicitors are not always popular:

> . . . [different] solicitors expect a different approach . . . some . . . want you to believe everything the client says . . . even where it clearly won't be accepted by the judge . . . it's a pointless exercise but they want you to fight it all the way. . . . Solicitors like that make it difficult for us.

Sometimes it may be expedient to accept this. As one barrister told us:

> . . . if the solicitor thinks on occasion they can push you around a bit, if they want a certain thing, and you can see that coming, then you can be a bit more pliant in certain circumstances . . . it's something you have to do.

On occasion, this need to please the solicitor can be taken a bit too far. The solicitor may see the barrister's role in terms of taking the blame. This tends to happen mainly at the junior end of the bar. One young practitioner complained:

> Solicitors are not very loyal . . . some stand over you, back you up to the hilt, but there's others who try to blame you for everything . . . you have to know in advance and make sure you're well covered.

Of course, the attitude of a solicitor may result from pressures from the client. (This is considered by some to be a very significant variable in accounting for the success of certain types of actions: see, for example, Rosenthal, 1974.) In the ordinary course of things and with the ordinary client, these pressures will be resisted. The backing of the solicitor is important here, but generally most barristers insist on doing the case their way and resist demands that the court be told of certain facts that the client wants aired. Sometimes, however, the pressures from clients are not direct. One barrister told us:

It makes the working day very easy when you get a client with a big case who says 'Well look, there are more important things in life than money. Do your best and I'm not too worried if nothing comes of it'. . . . Clients like these don't come along too often unfortunately. . . . You tend to be infected by the client who is uptight about everything, and wants this done and wants that done and is very upset about his case, maybe financially or emotionally. That has an effect on you. You tend to make more effort.

A criminal practitioner said:

The most worrying cases that I have, strangely enough, are not those of great public importance . . . they are of great importance to the individual. For example, the person with a clean character who is charged with something as relatively trifling as shoplifting. Only once or twice have I defended someone, women in each case, who I actually believed in my heart of hearts was innocent. . . . If you reach that stage you're making great problems for yourself . . . you are literally living their acquittal or conviction with them . . . it gets too much.

Institutional clients as repeat players provide other sorts of pressures. There are general commercial and financial pressures which may require that a particular case or, more usually, a category of cases, be dealt with in a certain way. Several barristers recalled fondly the days when county court personal injuries cases were settled before they reached the courtroom to a much greater extent than they are now. The general economic climate of the 1980s was held to be largely responsible for a change of attitude. As one barrister with a large insurance company practice said:

. . . the days when you could say the majority of my cases are going to settle . . . particularly in the lower courts . . . are gone. . . . Insurance companies want you to justify your existence. They are saying why should these cases ever get to counsel. . . . Counsel are going to go . . . [to court] . . . walk up and down outside the hall and settle the case when that could be done by a solicitor six weeks before . . . saving quite a lot of money. . . . There is a lot more vetting going on and insurance companies are insisting that when counsel is briefed, in the main, unless there is a very good reason for it, those cases are fought. . . . [This vetting] means that there isn't as much work going around; the work that is available is . . . more likely to be contentious work . . . [and] that in turn means that you have to spend more time in court. And you have to pass more work . . . [because, without settlements,] . . . you can't arrange to be in two places at one time.

Similar pressures on the public purse have caused a similar situation on the criminal side of the law. Legal aid shortfalls and economies on the prosecution side have produced a bureaucratization of the barrister's role in pursuit of savings. One criminal practitioner complained:

There is a greater tendency these days to look at what people are doing and what they are being paid. . . . [It's almost arrived at the situation where] there is a clerk to tick you in in the morning and tick you out in the afternoon and if you leave the fact is noted.

Inevitably, this is linked to money:

Somebody in London decided that that was a lot of money for not doing very much . . . and do we really need counsel at all? The bar went on the defensive . . . tried to justify itself . . . and part of the result of it is that they had to concede ground on fees. . . . What you might have got two years ago you will get slightly less now. . . . The net result is that there is less work, the pay is not as good and . . . money is not so easily available.

Changes in the way the financial relationship is organized have brought not just changes in the barrister's role but alterations in his or her working practices. For example, there is beginning to be a change from the days when payment was on a brief basis and a global sum was marked for the barrister. This has meant that although sometimes absences from court are quite justifiable professionally (if, for example, that part of the trial had no bearing on the client), the barrister is no longer as in the past paid irrespective of whether he or she actually attended every day of the hearing.

A solicitor may require of a barrister that, because of the demands of large institutional clients, he or she conform to a particular way of handling an individual case. In some instances, the client may be pursuing a general policy through a series of cases and the instructions that the solicitor gives will contain very detailed orders to be followed. This happens at the criminal bar. In at least one of the regions that we looked at, there was slight resentment that even very senior advocates working for the prosecution authorities were compelled to refer back to the central office for instructions on the most routine developments in cases. In civil cases, the pressures are often even more intense.

We heard of the 'Goliath chasing David' situation that sometimes occurs when a large business organization may, for commercial or competitive reasons, wish to pursue a smaller rival through all stages of the courts regardless of the objective merits of the particular case. With insurance companies, there may be pressures of various sorts depending on the institutional goals and policies of the moment. One barrister we spoke to consoled himself for not ever having got on the panel of a particular insurance company who brought a lot of work in his set by saying: '[insurance companies] want a particular style: you have to do things their way . . . and the pressures to give in are enormous'. An insurance company may decide to come down hard on a particular sort of claim. One barrister whose practice came mainly from insurance companies told us:

If you get a particular insurer who insures one firm, some of the meat plants [for example], and you start off with a succession of cases, someone may decide, 'Look there's a bit of substance in these claims, let's get rid of them cheaply.' The next year they may look and see double the number of claims. At that point they may say 'Forget about the niceties. We are going to start fighting these to let people know that we are not just going to pay out money.' There is the tactical contest, I think that's becoming very evident.

This may be to deter doubtful or fraudulent claims or, more rarely, to try to work on a particular aspect of the law in order to alter it. We did come across an example of this latter phenomenon, although it was difficult for us to determine if the change achieved was the result of deliberate pressure or not. In Northern Ireland, claims against the Department of the Environment and other bodies, for injuries caused by tripping over paving stones that have been inadequately maintained at one time, reached epidemic proportions. There were newspaper reports of multiple claims originating from particular localities and even from individual families. Among all the barristers involved in this lucrative work, there was agreement that, at its height, there were a large number of false claims and an even greater number of dubious ones. We were told that barristers working for the DoE were encouraged not only to resist forcefully suspicious claims, but also to look out for any individual cases that could be used to develop the law in a way that restricted liability. A case was finally brought that restricted liability in a significant way (see *Brady* v *Northern Ireland Housing Executive*, 1990, unreported). This may have been regarded as a great victory for government lawyers, but it must also surely have been seen as a somewhat pyrrhic one.

More common is the first type of institutional goal, where limited budgets or policy decisions impinge upon the barrister's handling of a case. We came across a good example of this from someone who had just got on the panel of a local authority to defend it against accident claims. The message given from the client was clearly heard:

> The word basically came down the line that we were to take any possible lines of defence that were open to us ... [and] because we hadn't been in it when it was, if you like, 'a settlement culture', we were keen ... we were trying to establish ourselves. We would tend to take a robust view of a case and if that meant cross-examining a seventy-year-old granny with one leg we would have been doing that as we reckoned that this was our leg up to what was a very lucrative source of work.

CONCLUSION

In this chapter, we have tried to suggest some of the various ways in which the barrister's relationship with solicitors controls what it is the barrister does. This relationship determines the volume and level of a barrister's caseload and also what is required as the barrister deals with cases. This construction of the barrister's world in turn impinges on the 'real world' of the lay client and his or her case by dictating the terms on which a case is admitted into the system and how it is perceived and processed there. In Chapter 4, we will look closely at the brief, which is the formal connection between barrister and solicitor, and examine the sort of influences and controls that might be present there.

In Chapter 4, where we begin to discuss our notion of legal information and what it is that goes to make up a case, we will look at this issue of the brief as a limited, selective and necessarily distorted slice of information about the client's problem and the particular world in which it exists. In this chapter, our intention was mainly to reinforce the general point about how the exigencies of the barrister's world, including their relations with solicitors, affects how information is selected, perceived and handled. Before moving away from this, it is perhaps worthwhile to conclude by highlighting how the dynamics of the barrister–solicitor relationship affect everything the barrister does, including his or her first moves on receiving a brief.

Relationships with solicitors do, of course, differ among individuals and in relation to factors such as regularity of contact, seniority, etc. However, the idea which we developed above of servicing a solicitor, means that a barrister approaches a brief with particular objectives in mind. A question that we asked many of our interviewees was what did they actually do on receiving a brief. The answers we received highlighted the roles of barristers and solicitors. Nearly all barristers indicated that, in various ways, they usually tried to at least give the impression that they were looking after business for the solicitor. For example, one practitioner told us:

> The first thing I do when I get a brief is draft out a letter. I just have a pad which I use . . . I get a brief in, open it up, pull it out, write down the name and address of the solicitor, 'Dear Sirs, Re (write the name of the case), Thank you for your letter and enclosures' and just have a quick glance at . . . once I know I've written it down it is not going to go into a corner or be put at the bottom of a briefcase and forgotten about . . . therefore it will get dealt with . . . in its turn.

Clearly, turning the matter round and responding quickly is important. Another advocate told us:

> A lot of the time, if there is a fairly simple matter to be dealt with, I can do a draft answer to whatever the query is, fold it up and give it to my typist. . . . Alternatively, if they want draft proceedings or draft replies to particulars or an opinion or advice, I would tend to have a look, see what is required and either write it out or put it on tape as soon as possible . . . the idea largely being to get back to it as quickly as possible.

The type of advice that is required again highlights our earlier points about facilitating the solicitor's business and making him or her look impressive to the client. We were told:

> . . . my impression is that most solicitors want to open and close a case as quickly as possible. They are not interested in opinions that give lengthy academic arguments about the pros and cons of this or that –

unless it's very relevant. What they want is an answer to the query and what to do next, how do we get this case on and dealt with and the client happy.

All these answers to the same basic question about the preliminary steps on receiving a brief clearly indicate that the barrister is very aware of wider issues and relationships as he or she commences work on a particular case. In Chapter 4, we will look in more detail at how exactly the brief is constructed and handled and try to develop how the relationships discussed here, and other factors, impinge on how exactly the barrister proceeds on the path towards court.

NOTES

1 The bar can now be approached directly by members of certain professions (e.g. accountants, surveyors, etc.) without the intermediary presence of a solicitor. Though we did not find evidence of this, it may affect the workload of a number of barristers over the next few years.
2 The terminology used here comes from Galanter's (1974) seminal article on how the legal system is arranged so as to privilege those who use it most frequently.
3 Our findings directly contradict those of Wilson's (1965) study.

4

THE BRIEF: THE CONSTRUCTION OF LEGAL INFORMATION

INTRODUCTION

In the next two chapters, we will move from the relationship between the solicitor and the barrister to that between the barrister and the court. There we will find that the pre- and courtroom circumstances are just as hostile to the barrister as is the work-seeking environment. Here it is useful to discuss the formal means whereby a case is documented, discussed and processed. Although the solicitor is – once again – of prime importance in the drawing up of this, the brief is the result of a whole variety of complex interactions. There is the relationship between the various parts of the legal process (prosecuting authorities, opposing party, etc.) and the process of negotiation that goes on there. Other aspects of the legal system, e.g. documents such as leases, wills, contracts, etc., as well as determinations from other courts, also assert their influence. The process of obtaining information and processing it into witness statements, expert reports, etc., also has its effects. All this comes to the barrister in a form that is mediated through the solicitor and constrained into a 'brief'.

Our interest in the brief and its construction is to demonstrate that legal information arises from a whole host of disparate sources, and that the collecting and structuring of this information is as much a social process as is that of finding work as a barrister. In looking to this, we are building our theory of the complexity of legal information which we mentioned earlier. We will in particular note the timetabling mechanism which cuts, slices and moulds the preparation of the brief. We also note the roles that are played by substantive law and by facts in the construction of this brief. We suggest, contrary to the view of barristers as academically inclined lawyers, that much of the law which barristers deal with on a day-to-day basis is routine, standardized or anecdotal in character rather than formally researched, specific or specialized. Meanwhile, the basic factual information with which barristers must work is more akin to 'hearsay' or stories rather than formal evidence.

Indeed, one of our arguments is that the traditional separation of 'fact' and 'law', which posits these as two sides of the coin of legal argument, is not really appropriate. We shall see that in the construction of 'facts', there are a variety of elements at work: the nature of the information that is available to the barrister (from solicitor or expert or other data-gathering means); the need to make a closure and agree to agree or disagree on the 'facts' of a case (i.e. to decide where to make one's stand in negotiation or trial); one's view of how the argument will be seen in the light of the courtroom (which we look to more fully in the next chapters); and, importantly, one's view of the legal rules and policy decisions of the court which might be brought to bear upon the raw information. That is, one does not just begin with the 'facts' and then see how these relate to the 'law'; rather, the facts are moulded at the same time – and as part of the same process – as the legal rules. It can only be a *post hoc* rationalization which separates the two, and allows us to discuss them as though they were relatively independent of each other.

Generally, our view is that it is better and more informative to consider the entire gamut of materials which the barrister works with to be 'legal information', rather than to break this down into the two traditionally suggested component parts of 'fact' and 'rule' and ignore the rest.

THE BRIEF AS INFORMATION EXCHANGE

Blake's (1989) *A Practical Approach to Legal Advice and Drafting* (3rd edn) tells its readers, who are in the main trainee solicitors and barristers, that 'The brief is very important as, with very few exceptions, the barrister can only act in a case if he has a brief, and should only act on the documents and instructions contained in it' (Blake, 1989: 41). This short description contains what are, for our purposes, the important aspects of a brief. It reminds us that a barrister can usually only come into a case via a solicitor. This means that the case exists and is 'a case' before the barrister is allowed to mediate or advise. The definition also helps us to begin to understand how a case is handled, i.e. through written documents.

Importantly, it also indicates that the information the barrister has is created by, or at least processed by, someone else. It is made up of written materials selected and ordered by someone else as best they can, given the general role that they must play and the various exigencies that affect a particular case. It is not in any sense a complete picture made up in any comprehensive or 'scientific' way. Yet it structures the activity in court.

A basic definition of a brief is a set of documents that a solicitor sends to counsel when asking him or her to advise in a case. There may be slight differences between jurisdictions in the details of presentation and in the traditions surrounding this formal link between barrister and/or advocate and solicitor, but the job it does is much the same everywhere. The contents of the brief will vary depending on the nature of the matter involved. Generally, the instructing solicitor will have met with a client, interviewed that client to determine the nature of the problem and then perhaps collected some evidence surrounding the matter, taking notes and organizing what needs to be clarified. The brief will contain documents detailing this process. There will usually be a statement of facts from the client or a summary from the solicitor. There may be statements from witnesses or medical experts. There may be copies of any existing correspondence with the other side. There may be photographs, maps, plans or diagrams to help the barrister understand the situation. There will also be any existing legal documents in the case, such as deeds, wills, contracts or copies of pleadings or proofs which contain allegations of facts or the evidence of witnesses prepared by the instructing solicitor. There may be a summary of all this from the solicitor.

There might be a note which sets out the instructions to counsel from the solicitor asking for advice generally, advice on a particular point or how to conduct the case in court, or there may simply be a handwritten note saying simply 'Please advise'. There will also be a backsheet which is folded around the rest of the brief or placed on top of it. This has written on it the basic details of the case – the names of the parties, the counsel, the solicitors, the instructions to counsel, the court in which the case is to be heard, and the fee or the fact that the brief is a legal aid brief. By tradition, the whole bundle is tied together with pink tape (white if a prosecution brief), although it is becoming more common for solicitors to use a thermal binder to produce a 'book' containing all the papers between plastic covers.

It is this that the barrister receives. Additional documents or information may be required of the solicitor or it may be necessary to meet the solicitor and possibly the client in conference, particularly if the matter is complicated. The barrister is then expected to refine and re-order the points at issue as presented by the solicitor and form a general view as to what is involved and what might be done about it. What will generally be required here is sound practical advice as to whether the client has a legal case or not, whether the case merits legal aid, what are the evidential issues in the case, the measure of damages (quantum) that might be expected (and then the level of court in which to issue proceedings), or whatever else is required. In criminal cases, issues like bail for the client and obtaining legal aid impinge on the advice sought. Generally, this centres around advice on the plea that the defendant will make to the charge, any possible election as to the level of court in which the case is to be heard and the general conduct of the case. In civil cases, the barrister will generally be asked to draft the pleadings, which involves setting out the precise allegations of fact which are to be presented before the court and draft the other formal documents, applications (for injunctions or special orders) and affidavits (sworn statements from witnesses) which are necessary for court proceedings.

When the work requested by the solicitor is completed, or the case finished, the barrister will endorse the brief to this effect by making a mark through the title, writing the date when the work was completed and signing his or her name. The backsheet is used to record the brief fee. In some jurisdictions, this must be agreed and written on the back of the brief before the barrister goes into court. In others, e.g. Northern Ireland, fees are usually agreed and marked on completion of the case – only before in exceptional circumstances. In a legal aid case, the words 'Legal Aid' should appear on the backsheet and the barrister is paid from costs which are met in civil cases by the unsuccessful defendant or, if necessary, from the sum allowed on taxation (a process whereby the taxing master, or auditor of court in Scotland, assesses the costs involved).

The above is perhaps best regarded as a formal description of what goes on as a brief is prepared by a solicitor and received by a barrister. In reality, of course, all sorts of practical exigencies, personal factors and relationships enter into the process to make it much less straightforward. The version of the client's problem that the barrister receives is very far from a complete, objective or accurate one. What the barrister gets from the solicitor is both determined by the practical limitations of representing the world of the client's problem through papers and complicated by the relationships between the client, solicitor and barrister.

While most barristers that we spoke to were ready to blame solicitors for the inadequacy of information contained in briefs, this was not always the case. In the first place, there are obvious difficulties about representing accurately what are often complex events. Documentary evidence, including witness statements, etc., is the only thing that a barrister can deal with. A court, although it may call witnesses and assess their reliability, does not go too far beyond what the barrister sees written down. Indeed, that which constitutes evidence for a court may be narrower than what the barrister can take on board, since rules of evidence may preclude much of what is contained in the brief. Often, events and problems cannot be fully or accurately represented in written documents or reports. The reality of a client's problem cannot be mirrored in a brief to counsel. Evidence, even in the more relaxed form that counsel – as opposed to a court – can deal with, is incapable of containing all the meaning that might be required.[1]

Leaving aside these epistemological, linguistic and textual issues, there are often practical limitations to what the solicitor can obtain for a barrister. The solicitor may have difficulties understanding, collecting and assembling the material. The solicitor must interview his or her client, but there are all sorts of problems involved in this, including incomprehension, distortion and a breakdown in communications (see, e.g., Sherr, 1986). Even if the client's problem is understood fully, the solicitor may face difficulties collecting information to substantiate it. Other parties may have relevant documents, and although it is often possible to obtain them, it may be difficult and their value may remain uncertain. It might also be difficult locating witnesses or finding that they are unwilling to cooperate.

One solicitor we spoke to complained of difficulties experienced in personal injuries cases of getting surgeons' reports and reports from hospital staff who had treated a patient. Although medical reports for legal actions are paid for, many medical practitioners are overstretched as it is, without undertaking work that may result in time-consuming court appearances. The problem is often worst when a specialist report is required, for example from a neurosurgeon, and solicitors often have to settle for information that is far from complete and less than the best available.

The process of collating the material necessary to enable a barrister to do his or her job should, in theory, be an interactive process between the solicitor and counsel. However, solicitors are sometimes unwilling or unable to do what is required by way of organizing the material and identifying issues. One barrister we spoke to complained:

> ... solicitors simply hand things over to you because they don't quite know what they are doing or because they panic. They want an outside opinion. Because of that, I find quite often that they haven't identified the issues, they don't know what they want you to advise on or what they want for their client in their instructions to you. . . . I think that's wrong: instructions are instructions. They should be saying to you 'We want X Y and Z'. . . . I accept that I get asked to advise generally (I probably get asked to do that more often than I do anything else). I can handle that, but I don't like it because it means that I have to spend more time on a case working out what our goals are.

Another stated:

> It is definitely easier for them to give their secretary a pile and say 'Copy this and send it to counsel' and for it to come here. That is the easiest way for them to brief counsel. And effectively for it to come here and us to do the donkey work.

As we argued in Chapter 3, solicitors see barristers as being there to offer them a service. Undoubtedly, some expect more from their barrister than others. Poor instructions were a very common complaint. One barrister even told us that with a certain solicitor it was invariably necessary to arrange a conference with the client to get even the most basic information about the nature of the problem and the advice sought. However inconvenient that might be for that particular barrister, he still accepted it as part of what he had to do within the context of his working relationship with a particular solicitor. Another told us that one particular solicitor simply made a verbatim report (omitting punctuation) of what the client said from entering to leaving his office, and sent this to the barrister as 'the brief'. However, poor instructions do seem to affect junior practitioners to a greater extent than more experienced counsel. One young barrister told us:

> You can't complain about poorly prepared briefs. However much you would like to . . . you can't just say 'I return the papers. Take some statements from the witnesses and send them back and then I will direct your proofs.' Some of the seniors can, it's one of their advantages, but I certainly couldn't.

Another seemed to insist that it was the bar at large who were prepared to put up with poor-quality instructions:

> The bar puts up with laziness . . . they put up with it . . . we are getting a bit more bullish about it these days . . . I don't want long briefs with great powers of analysis. I would quite like a brief that says these are the issues, we would like your advice on these four points. The words 'Advise generally' are a solicitor trying to get as much out of you as he can, because he hasn't done his job.

Problems with inefficient solicitors do not stop at poor instructions. We heard several horror stories of solicitors failing to produce the information required to make a case. Generally, this affected younger barristers most, and the cases in which it happened were clearly regarded by the solicitors as unimportant. For example, as one junior barrister complained to us:

> You send a direction for proofs and you get to court and you find nothing's been done. . . . It's usually a plaintiff's case, where you're trying to get the poor sod some money . . . and you're going to win but nothing's been prepared properly. . . . You've done everything but they haven't checked with you before . . . you can't afford to make too much fuss about it [with the solicitor].

The constant cry we heard from barristers was of the poor briefs they were sent:

> The [brief] varies. Some do it very well . . . but not many. I have one [solicitor] and he is the only solicitor I know that I can put my dictation machine on, and – in a few minutes – I can do it because he will have put everything in I need and won't have put anything else in. Others . . . [pointing to a large pile of papers] . . . at least half of that will be rubbish . . . there will be stuff in there which is there three times . . . I said one man, but there is another who is not a solicitor . . . he is a legal executive.

Legal executives are non-qualified members of a solicitor's staff who are often left in charge of an area of work, e.g. personal injury or conveyancing. Rules governing solicitors' offices dictate that legal executives will never attain the status of solicitor, nor become a partner in a firm of solicitors. Neither do they usually cover the whole gamut of cases which a typical solicitor has to deal with, and are thus able to specialize in the preparation of documents in one or two particular areas. This specialization was welcomed by barristers:

> . . . on personal injury and licensing, my instructing solicitors are never solicitors, they are always legal execs employed by the various authorities. To a man, they are all better than the solicitors who instruct me on matrimonial matters . . . they know the work, they are on top of everything. . . . Legal execs are goldmines . . . an insurance company has radio adverts out for legal execs – they don't want solicitors . . . to

do personal injury work. They are making £25 000 to £30 000 and a good car.

Another barrister noted how legal executives were being brought more into the structure of the legal profession, and then talked wryly of the lack of foresight of his own side of the profession in not making use of employees in a similar way:

> ... they are making them [the legal execs] litigation managers and putting them on the notepaper. The bar never realizes the reason that solicitors make more money is that they employ people.

Some of the barristers that we spoke to maintained that, in general, large firms of solicitors produced better briefs than solo practitioners. This may be a consequence of greater resources, allowing larger firms of solicitors to employ more staff, including legal executives, and to undertake a greater volume of work. This in turn encourages the build up of expertise and the formation of personal relationships with the police, accident investigators, medical experts, etc., who provide the regular cast in the early stages of a legal production. Information is not automatically attracted to a brief: facts have to be hewn out of the world and anything that assists in this process produces a better brief. Of course, another factor that improves the flow of information is the resources a client is able to bring to bear to back up the process. One of the ways in which cases appear difficult or important is if a lot of money turns on their outcome. An important case, in the sense of a well-funded case, may well produce a brief that is correspondingly well-informed and structured. There are clearly a whole variety of factors which affect the quality of the brief, although the solicitor's input is of most importance.

Sometimes, however, the problem may not be a poorly prepared brief or a solicitor asking too much of a barrister. It can be the other way around: solicitors know only too well what they want from counsel. The textbooks state that solicitors should avoid infringing on the barrister's role by offering too much by way of suggestion or observation (see, e.g. Blake, 1989: 43–4). However, the temptation must be great for an experienced solicitor to influence a young barrister. Even our limited sample of solicitors yielded one example of a solicitor who claimed that he regularly disagreed with counsel and, despite the supposed professional embarrassment of doing so, he made a point of telling them. Of course, more experienced and established barristers are in a better position to resist such pressures from solicitors. However, the influence may be indirect. The type and level of information that is sent to a barrister may carry with it the implication that a case is of a certain sort or at a particular level of seriousness. For example, detailed statements about what a vendor of a defective motor car actually said when selling it might indicate that the case involved misrepresentation, while the inclusion of specialist medical reports in a personal injury case might suggest that the case was of a certain gravity. Several of the solicitors we spoke to acknowledged this, although they maintained that if it went on it would generally be an unconscious action in the more general process of sifting information.

Lay clients also have expectations and these impinge on the way that a case reaches the barrister and the form that it takes when it gets there. One advocate with experience of large commercial clients made the point that:

> ... the case has gone through a lot of different hands before it reaches counsel. This is particularly true on the defence side, less true on the plaintiffs' side. . . . My experience on the plaintiffs' end of the business is that solicitors are less inclined to take it upon themselves to do a lot of the work by way of drafting pleadings . . . and generally advising. (In the most extreme examples . . . solicitors have become just administrators and have ceased to use any legal training that they had.) On the defence side, insurance companies are, I think, much more conscious of basically justifying their outlay to their shareholders . . . they will investigate [a claim] and refer it to their solicitors. At that stage, a preliminary view of the case will be formed. . . . If it is a difficult one, on the law, counsel might come in at that stage. . . . If it's a typical, ordinary case the solicitor would normally advise. . . . They would more or less make the decision at that stage how they want to approach it. Do they want to approach the plaintiff's side . . . to see if settlement can be reached or do they think this is one that they want to set up for trial?

In many civil cases, having gone through the legal department of a commercial concern, and having been fitted into line with general corporate objectives and budgets, the case comes to the barrister with fairly rigid instructions to attain a given objective.

The position is more extreme in criminal practice where clearly what the client wants the barrister to do is paramount. The brief is structured around the plea to be made. In criminal cases, the defendant's account – be it of his or her *mens rea* or of some factual situation – is very often central to the way the case will be handled, especially on the defence side. The brief is therefore often composed primarily of what the client says, with witness statements, etc., acting only in support of that. In other words, the brief, the raw material with which the barrister is to fashion the case, is to a large extent dictated by the client. Information is slanted by the client towards his or her account. We were given a good example of the determining role of the client in criminal practice:

> ... instructions dominate, especially in defence. You've got to stick to what your case is. . . . You cannot run what is called in this country the 'Irish Defence': that is the client is saying one thing but you think it is the better course for him to be arguing another. . . . For instance, I defended a youngster, fourteen or fifteen years old, on a rape charge about two years ago. His defence was alibi, 'I wasn't there'. It was as plain as plain to me that that wasn't true . . . his defence should have been 'I did have intercourse with her but she consented'. But that was

never my instructions and I couldn't run it on that basis.... I initially
cross-examined [the woman] as if his defence was 'He was there but
with your consent' and then put it to her, much to everybody's surprise
no doubt, that he wasn't there at all ... the judge had [another] reason to
call us into his chambers halfway through the case ... and the words he
used to me were 'You're running the Irish Defence. You can't do it ...'.
He was quite right.

On the prosecution side, it is equally difficult to go outside the scenario
contained in the papers. We were told:

> ... you have the prosecution papers ... and you cannot start running an
> account contrary to your case or your witnesses even if it seems the
> better one to run ... you've got to stick to what your case is, as you get
> it.

We will return to this issue of the brief as a limited, selective and necessarily
distorted slice of information about the client's problem and the particular
world in which it exists. However, in the next section, we will look at the
various ways in which the written materials that comprise a criminal brief are
collected together, in order that we are able to see more clearly how the
barrister is, in effect, tied and constrained by decisions, negotiations and
timetables that arise elsewhere.

THE CONSTRUCTION OF A CRIMINAL BRIEF

The criminal process provides an excellent illustration of the way in which
the information that is presented in the brief to the barrister – prosecution or
defence – has been subject to a process of creation which structures it in
fundamental ways. The original incident, i.e. the alleged crime, is interpreted
and encoded by various actors and agencies in the criminal process in a whole
variety of ways, each of which bears the stamp of complex social and
professional patterns surrounding the role of each agent. Furthermore, there
are institutional features in the criminal process – chiefly centred around the
need to work to timetables and the time-saving value of a guilty plea – which
structure what the barrister gets and constrain what he or she must do with
that material.

The most obvious determinant of what will eventually end up as the stuff
of the case is, of course, the criminal incident itself. It has been calculated that
over 95 percent of the cases that are cleared up by the police are not solved by
detection but rather are proceeded with on the basis of information received.
Criminals are very rarely caught red-handed by a police officer in unequivo-
cal circumstances. Cases against defendants need to be made from the ground
up. Generally, all cases begin with the defendant being interviewed by the
police. The information that the police obtain is very clearly influenced by
what they know from witnesses and informants, the procedures under which
they work and the level of cooperation and truthfulness of the person(s)
interviewed. On the basis of what is obtained at this stage, the police may

release a suspect or prefer holding charges. If a suspect is charged, a solicitor may be brought in, although research on the operation of the Police and Criminal Evidence Act suggests that recourse to a solicitor is by no means automatic even in remand hearings (see, e.g. Sanders *et al.*, 1989). The information that is available at this stage is in a fairly crude form, at least in legal terms. It will contain allegations and intimations that may not necessarily be supportable and make connections and assertions that are perhaps not capable of being upheld within the laws of evidence. However, all that is required here is that there are reasonable grounds to connect the suspect with the offence.

While the suspect is detained on this holding charge, the police are able to continue to investigate the case – obtaining further evidence, statements, etc. When their investigations are complete, the file is sent to the prosecution authorities. They will assess it and, if proceedings are to be taken, will arrange for 'new' changes to be drafted and statements to be put into legal form. There are, of course, variations between jurisdictions and between offences at different levels of seriousness. However, to follow the example with an indictable offence, someone – maybe from the Crown Prosecution Service, the Office of the Director of Public Prosecutions, the Procurator Fiscal or the police – will begin to construct a case and perhaps draw up new charges that can be brought against the defendant at the next stage. Although the timetabling effect in the criminal process has started, inasmuch as the suspect must be brought before a magistrate on a regular basis (especially if remanded in custody), there is not as yet any real pressure from the court system itself. The pressures and constraints come instead from the internal dynamics of the government agency involved. The difficulties that were experienced in setting up a new Crown Prosecution Service in England and Wales, and the effect on the success rate of prosecutions that factors such as inadequate funding, organization and personnel had in the early days, indicate that what goes on at this stage is very much captive of social and logistical forces. The processing of 'raw' information into legal information is far from straightforward or unproblematic in any set-up. It will be very much constrained by the nature of the agency as well as factors in the real world which make information difficult to obtain and uncertain in its effect.

Of course, what needs to be obtained at this stage is not at a very refined level. It is not necessary to provide a hard and fast case in legal terms that would justify acquittal or conviction. Generally, if the action against the suspect is proceeded with, he or she will only be committed for trial in a hearing presided over by a magistrate or equivalent. All that is required to return a suspect for trial is that there is sufficient evidence for a reasonable jury, properly directed, to convict. Generally, the evidence will be in the form of written documents, depositions containing statements of facts made by witnesses under oath. Although these may in certain circumstances be challenged by the defence, they are generally accepted at this stage and matters such as legal aid certificates are dealt with.

The effect of this procedure, i.e. committing a person for trial, is that the defendant is thus propelled into the court process proper. Once it has been decided that there is a case to answer, a date for arraignment is fixed. It is at this time that charges in a bill of indictment are put to the prisoner and he or she must plead guilty or not guilty. Generally, there is a time limit running from the committal hearing to the arraignment. The prosecution must fashion its case from the information it has. It must process what it has into legal form. It is a barrister, generally a junior Crown counsel, who performs this role. Meanwhile, the defendant will begin to fashion a defence. Counsel will generally be appointed and the material from the committal hearing will be combined into a brief with other information that the solicitor is able to produce. The quality of this brief will, of course, vary enormously depending on the diligence and ability of the solicitor, the availability and quality of witnesses and experts, the nature of the relationship between the barrister and the solicitor, and the position that the defendant takes up. In no way could it be said that the flow of information into the brief is automatic or not subject to a host of practical, personal and professional exigencies.

While this information is being gathered, there is also the possibility that the case is being redefined through a process of negotiation between the prosecution and defence counsel. It is commonplace, although it does not invariably happen, that discussion may occur over the exact charge in the indictment. For example, the defence may be prepared to take a different attitude if the charge is one of grievous bodily harm alone rather than grievous bodily harm with intent to endanger life. Also, it is well-known that mitigation is more effective if the Crown or police can be persuaded to help by reinforcing what is claimed. The information that counsel will deal with is thus potentially subject to constant change and negotiation. However, this is not the material of simple 'fact'.

When the prisoner is arraigned, he or she must make a plea. There are advantages in making this plea known early. Generally, if the plea is 'guilty', the case will be dealt with there and then. If the plea is 'not guilty', then the whole operation of producing a jury and calling witnesses must be begun. A date must be fixed between the listing officer and the solicitor and questions of judge availability must be resolved. The problems and costs that are necessarily incurred by a contest lead to a situation where there may be a clear discount for a guilty plea. However, as time runs, the discount for a guilty plea may diminish. The further down the road towards a trial that a defendant goes, the more costs that will be incurred and the less will be the credit given by the judge during sentencing for a guilty plea. However, much depends on the circumstances of the individual case. Thus, for example, in a potentially lengthy and complex fraud trial, a guilty plea may well carry more weight. Also, if there is a very strong Crown case where, for example, the defendant was caught in the act, the guilty plea will carry less discount than where the Crown case is weak. Factors such as these may negate any adverse effects that a delay in pleadings may have. This basic fact of life in the courts is only an extra-legal one if we take a narrow view of what the law is. The factors that determine how a case will be run in the criminal courts come from myriad sources. Moreover, they are constantly changing as the process runs its course and the pressures of timetabling reduce discounts, decrease options and require an adjustment of tactics.

Much more will be said in the next chapters about how cases in both the civil and criminal fields are actually conducted. Here we simply wish to make the point that the information with which barristers deal is not straightforward law alone, or even merely the application of uncontroversial facts to a framework of law. The example of the criminal brief indicates that there are a wide number of social and institutional factors that control the material with which barristers have to work and the framework within which they must act. This framework and the information within it changes constantly. There may well be abstract law, such as one would find in a textbook or law report, as part of the raw material with which barristers work, but an understanding of the law element alone is not sufficient to perform the role of barrister. The information which barristers receive in order to do their job is already heavily ordered and sorted in a whole variety of contexts. The editing provided by barristers in further sorting the information is just another stage in the process of a case heading towards court.

LEGAL RESEARCH

Much of what we have said so far has suggested that substantive law is not the main concern of barristers. We have thus argued against the orthodox view in legal education which suggests that, if solicitors do not carry out a legal interpretation of books, cases and legislation, then it must be being done by barristers. Contrary to this, we have suggested that just as solicitors work in a hostile environment which is not conducive to carrying out detailed research, so too do barristers: time is short, cases are many, and the brief in large part acts as a constraint upon how the case can be interpreted anyway.

Even that part of the barrister's role which is most usually seen to be oriented to substantive law – *counsel's opinion* – is not simply a picture of abstract rules of law and how they fit in with the facts of a case. It is, we argue, only inexperienced barristers who take that path, pushed no doubt by their experiences in academic education. Counsel's opinion is best seen as a reply to the brief sent by a solicitor. It is not always used – in particular, not in minor matters – but it is an important element in the construction of legal information. A counsel's opinion is also an important piece of information in deciding whether a case can actually be taken forward or not: it can be passed, by the solicitor, to the Legal Aid Committee for its view as to whether, for example, there are sufficient non-factual reasons for taking a legal aid case onto appeal. Blake (1989: 56), in her text for trainee barristers, writes:

> Once he has been sent an initial brief in a case a barrister will normally have to send back a written opinion setting out his advice to the solicitor and the client. Once he has read the brief properly the barrister should have a basic idea what his advice is, though he may need to get extra

documents or information, talk to the solicitor and client in conference, or *research legal points in detail before he writes the opinion* [our emphasis].

On the traditional view, then, it is the opinion which requires the poring over legal textbooks and legislation. It is here, more than anywhere, that we should see barristers working directly with law as in the popular image and the academic assumption. Our argument, below, is that legal points are less relevant in the opinion than is often thought. This does not mean that we believe that barristers do no legal research, only that there are pressures upon them which limit the research which they can, in most cases, do. These pressures, we will argue for example, tend to cause opposing barristers to reduce the potential for substantive law conflict by agreeing common interpretations of the law. Effectively, this means that, rather than arguing about law in court, there is a tendency to agree on the interpretation of law in order to get through the court workload.

The size of the Statute Book (i.e. all the legislation in effect, which is being extended by our move into Europe), the number of reported and unreported cases,[2] and the large number of different approaches to law taken in textbooks and academic articles, mean that barristers have, potentially, a huge number of sources where they can find/discover legal rules. Barristers who wish to run a case on legal issues would, surely, be able to find material on which to base a case.

The existence of this large corpus of legal materials has been seen as a problem since modern, written law began. Edward VI complained: 'I would wish that . . . the superfluous and tedious statutes were brought into one sum together, and made more plain and short, to the intent that men might better understand them.' The fact that the UK (like North America) is a common law country, too, has made the difficulty of keeping track of all legal materials more pronounced. In essence, common law countries are those where the legal system has a large customary element to it – where the previous decisions of courts in their written judgements are seen to act as constraints by being precedents which have to be followed. In countries with codified legal systems, the judge is directed only to the legislation, while in common law countries, the judge is directed to both legislation and case reports. The potential sources of law in the latter systems are thus enormous and confusing.

One of us has an interest in the provision of computer-based systems for research (Leith, 1991), and this interest led us to ask our interviewees about their perceptions of such systems. Basically, these are either large databases of legislative and case texts which are indexed by word and can be searched through (the prime system in the UK is called Lexis), or systems which use less text and which provide summaries of cases and various other sorts of information (such as Lawtel in the UK). Although such computer-based legal research tools have been available for some time, they have not been as successful as was first imagined. The reason for this lack of success – or lack of immediate success – is not easily identified. However, there are issues of cost, system flexibility and the difficulty of training barristers to research (rather than just 'use') the systems: thus, if the systems were cheaper, would more barristers make use of them?

We thus asked interviewees about these systems and whether they had used them. All of them were aware of the availability of the service (particularly Lexis) and many had seen a system in operation. They all thought that such systems were a 'good thing', but did not themselves use them. One QC even told us that he had been on a committee to oversee the introduction of such a system to Scotland, and welcomed the introduction of that system, but did not see any use for it himself. A junior civil barrister told us that he too thought they were a good thing and that he was on a committee to ease the introduction of such a system to Manchester, but did not think he would have a great deal of use for it himself. Generally, this reaction follows that reported across Europe (Lloyd, 1986) where most lawyers welcome the systems and consider them 'good', but fail to use them.

Another important factor is the social organization of the profession into chambers or libraries where generalists and specialists and those with pre-dominantly criminal and civil practices are mixed together. As one barrister explained it:

> It would have to be a chambers' decision to use Lexis. I don't know exactly how much it costs but it is quite expensive and I think that we probably feel that it wouldn't be worth the expense.

Part of the explanation given for this lay with the often-held view that there is usually enough law already available and, in any event, material on databases can generally be obtained in other ways. Significantly, however, it was also said in a mixed chambers that it would be very difficult to get Lexis even if the 'civil boys' thought it was worthwhile:

> I think there is a growing divide – this is my own view – between civil, especially non-legally aided civil practitioners, and general or criminal lawyers. Things like Lexis involve major capital expenditure which civil people can afford because they can stick it on their fees and criminal people can't. There are already quite a lot of disputes in chambers about the extent to which criminal boys are having to pay large rents and subsidise the library which they rarely use. This will probably in the end create pressures for specialist chambers on the circuit.

Obviously, it is not the case that no barrister makes use of systems such as Lexis. If that was the case, then it would be unlikely that the companies providing these services would still be in operation. However, it was illumi-nating that none of our interviewees saw their own day-to-day research being enhanced by such computer-based tools. This tends to imply that either barristers do little legal research, or that they have other ways of doing it.

Alternatively, and this is the position we take, barristers do undertake some limited formal legal research, but most of their knowledge of law is gained through routinized methods in the courtroom and from experience or, more infrequently, from asking fellow barristers. These latter, informal sources of law, tend to suggest that law is treated in a 'hearsay' fashion, i.e. that barristers accept the interpretation put on a case or on a piece of legislation by other barristers and do not go into great detail in the interpretation of the sources themselves (except in those cases – such as licensing – where their clients are prepared to pay for this research). In the hostile barristerial world, where time is short and pressures are constant, we can easily see why this approach is taken. There is no doubt that most barristers work very hard. A barrister whose career was beginning to flourish told us: 'I work every weekday without fail. . . . Last Christmas I said "No more Sunday nights". I tried really hard to keep to it but. . . . Generally, I find it all bloody hard work!'

It does not necessarily become easier as one moves on. Another barrister, commenting on the working habits of a senior counsel who often leads her, said:

> . . . all those guys . . . someone like . . . [a well-known QC] . . . wouldn't be going to bed until at least midnight if not later every night. And I know for a fact that he starts each day at 5.30 . . . it's just incredible. I don't think my health would stand it.

In a singular book written by John Parris in 1961, there is a description of the barrister's day that captures certain aspects that seem from the evidence of our conversations to be relatively unchanging. Having retired from the bar, Parris wonders what he would otherwise be doing:

> Early November. The fogs have started in the North of England. Already I would have left home; stiff collar, grey tie, black jacket . . . no umbrella; the car was my umbrella. I would be crawling through the atmospheric mire towards some distant courthouse, my mind full of the case I was to do, and in a panic lest I should be late.
>
> Arriving at the court nearly late but not quite (I was always, whatever the weather, nearly late but not quite) I would have flung off my collar and tie, thrust on a wing collar and tabs, slapped on my wig and gown, and rushed to relieve myself before dashing into court just as the judge entered.
>
> Then there would follow two and a half hours locked up . . . the windows are always shut. . . . At one o'clock another dash to the lavatory, and then to join the queue in the barristers' mess room. . . . Across the road there is a hotel which serves excellent meals, but by an unwritten rule of the profession no counsel dare venture in. At one-thirty – swept off by my clerk into conference; at five to two, swept out again and another dash for micturition before further incarceration.
>
> When I should be released from that session would depend on the whim of the judge . . . whatever time it be, there would not be an interval for tea before I would be pushed again by my clerk, like a piece of paper before a carpet sweeper, into another conference. Then, when I

had signed the papers I had dumped on him in the morning I would be free to crawl home through the fog, now black and dense to eat my dinner . . . and then afterwards to settle down to another five hours or so of paperwork; and crawl into bed about two o'clock so charged with black coffee and ideas that I could not sleep until the daylight was already creeping in the window (Parris, 1961: 209–210).

This seems to capture a flavour of the pressures that might keep a barrister from doing any more by way of legal research than was necessary or useful.

The fear of embarrassment was mentioned as a motive for doing general legal research. However, it would seem that most of the legal research that is undertaken is, almost invariably, connected to a particular case rather than in an effort to keep up generally. The various bar libraries and most sets of chambers have a library. Most barristers subscribe personally to a set of law reports – often the *All England Law Reports* – and to *Current Law*. Some read other journals, often relating to a speciality or interest on a regular basis also. Despite the opposite view that was expressed to us vehemently by a barrister who also writes practitioner texts, many barristers purchase personal copies of the leading books in their specialist field. However, these are rarely perused for their own sake. One barrister explained it this way:

> Time's short during the week – trying to get time off and time to work – and basically if you have a briefcase full of paperwork you try to turn it round as quickly as you can. You don't have a whole lot of opportunity to go to the library and study the journals as you want to or in a way that is not related to specific cases.

There are clearly pressures on barristers and these exert an influence so that in struggling to handle a practice a barrister will neglect all but the most important aspects of the job. Legal research, especially of a very general, keeping up-to-date sort, is here what economists call a soft variable – something that will get squeezed when the going gets tough.

When talking to barristers about the level of legal research that they undertake for a particular case, we did see large variations among different practitioners. There is the obvious demarcation between civil and criminal practice. In criminal practice, it is much more commonplace to hear boasts about how a particular practitioner (although, significantly, never our interviewees personally) had survived in practice without opening a book for decades. One experienced criminal advocate assessed the situation in this way:

> . . . you don't need much law knowledge to be a criminal barrister. You have to have a working knowledge of the laws of evidence and a basic understanding of the criminal statutes but . . . if you haven't got that up to scratch by the time you've been in pupillage six months then you never will and you shouldn't be practising anyway.

Another equally senior criminal barrister put it this way:

> ... about ninety nine percent, I would have thought, of criminal cases
> really depend upon the facts and the arguments put forward by the
> prosecution and the defence and the jury having to make up their minds
> about which they are sure and not sure about. . . . Subject to an inherent
> understanding of the law and an appreciation of the rules of evidence,
> really it's all about facts and the persuasion of advocacy . . . the impres-
> sion that a jury gets.

This does not mean, of course, that barristers with criminal practices do not
work on their cases; rather, their research is of a different kind. This was
explained in the following manner:

> ... it's very easy to do it badly. . . . The job in my view, to be done
> properly, entails thinking long and hard about it, as long as it takes,
> even in a simple case. . . . The art of being a competent barrister is the
> preparation. . . . Yes, oh yes, I think about the questions in advance,
> two or three days in advance . . . I write some of it down but I really
> never look at it usually . . . if you don't know the details of the case well
> enough to look the jury in the eye then you shouldn't be doing it.

The situation is generally somewhat different in the civil area and especially in
a commercial specialism. For example, one barrister working largely in the
commercial field told us:

> ... lots of them say you never have to use the law you learned at
> university but that's not my experience. . . . I use quite a lot of law,
> largely the kind of basic law that one learned at university . . . you have
> to make quite a bit of reference to contract, equity and that sort of thing.

Conversely, another declared:

> ... when you come to running a case, the law about it doesn't really
> matter a lot. . . . I mean you're not going to get *Wagon Mound* out every
> time . . . the sort of argument that one was used to at university is not
> always of great value – even on the chancery side.

Much of what barristers do in civil practice relate to their making evaluations
of the value of claims. The legal background of those assessments changes
little and is easily absorbed and retained. One personal injuries barrister
explained it this way:

> ... often there is no law in it, it is just facts. What injury has he got?
> What is it worth in your experience? End of story. . . . They're mostly
> straightforward . . . you have to refer to the books now and again . . .
> *Charlesworth on Negligence, Munkman*, stuff like that. With employers'
> liability cases there are big issues as to whether they are employed or
> self-employed . . . there are a lot of cases on that but once you have done
> a few you retain it and it is just a question of checking up if necessary.
> Much of it is run-of-the-mill – until a really horrendous one comes off
> the conveyer belt.

Clearly, much will depend on the type and level of practice that a barrister has. However, in a healthy career there will generally be a balance between the familiar and the new. As one middle-aged civil practitioner told us:

> The sorts of cases that I'm involved in – say 75 or 80 percent – there is a certain amount of law involved but I know it well enough by now that I wouldn't really trouble to look it up. But the other 25 percent of cases – which are probably cases for the same solicitor – I would spend a lot of time looking things up.

Contrary to our initial expectations, we found that the specialist bar did not inevitably deal more with legal arguments. One practitioner, one of the 'six-figure men' whose earnings are rumoured to be in excess of £100 000 per annum, told us:

> You don't necessarily have to go into it in that much detail. The sort of opinions I'm delivering, they're adequate, they're a fairly generalized view of matters . . . enough to allow the clients to make decisions. . . . Cases where you have to read all the authorities and go into all the arguments are fairly few and far between.

Another very senior barrister was dismissive of the amount of detailed law involved even in the appellate system. He declared:

> There are only a few principles – that's all you need to know . . . when you're waiting for your case you see [the Court of Appeal] dealing with a planning matter . . . then maybe a taxation point. . . . All they're using is a few principles.

Of course, here as so often elsewhere, the way the solicitor (and maybe the client) wants the job done is all important. The barrister will give the service that is required and, generally, what is required is problem solving rather than legal scholarship. As one barrister told us:

> . . . the solicitor doesn't give a toss if you have read an article in the LQR and incorporate it in your opinion. He is interested to know what you believe basically: what you think the chances are.

It is practical advice that is being sought – as in a doctor's surgery, there is nobody there who has not got a problem. Purely legal research is not always thought to be the way to get results. One senior counsel we spoke to quoted with approval the distinction made by Lord Denning between what the law is and what the law does. He saw himself as concerned exclusively with the latter. Another practitioner made the point:

> . . . there is a completely different sort of barrister to the one I hope I am . . . the one who enjoys playing with the law. . . . Funnily enough we've got one in chambers . . . he loves taking technical points, and all the judges know it . . . he's a very bright guy . . . he knows ten times as much law, a hundred times as much law, as I will ever know but I don't believe he's as practical in his approach and that I believe causes

problems. . . . Who are you serving? . . . At the end of the day, technical problems can usually be overcome. You're only delaying the evil day in most cases.

Another barrister with a large family practice with whom we discussed the difference between academic and practical approaches to law said:

I think when you're faced with real people . . . that's the thing. As an academic you are more often faced with problems rather than people. People bring you down to earth. . . . People come to me, particularly in ancillary relief proceedings, and they're worried sick. They think they're going to be turned out on to the street with their children . . . you can see what they want, what is going to settle their mind. . . . That makes you think of the practical solution.

This barrister subscribed very strongly to the view that there is something about the practice of law that makes an overly academic approach inappropriate. He told us:

There is a judge up at Luton . . . he was an academic from Cambridge . . . after a remarkably short career as an advocate he became a county court judge. . . . We all think he's very good; absolutely practical, I don't know where he's got all his experience from. He's superb. Doesn't bother with the law too much – even though he's written a number of books on family law!

The attention that is paid to the practicalities of cases as opposed to their strictly legal niceties was demonstrated to us by a barrister from the south of England who told us:

I had a set of papers the other day . . . the liquidator of some company was suing a chap for the price of goods he had bought some years ago. . . . He had no very good defence but we simply raised in the defence that the contract was made in Scotland and the proper law was Scottish. . . . It may be a very spurious point but the liquidator discontinued (as we hoped he would) because he couldn't afford the fag of going up to Scotland or arguing the point.

As we have said before, and will reiterate, a 'good legal point' is one that works – its merit in strictly doctrinal terms is secondary.

This focus on the practicalities of the situation is reflected in the legal research that counsel do undertake. There was much mention in our interviews of 'time-honoured precedents' and even 'time-honoured articles' which are wheeled out regularly to cover the academic side of things. In certain types of practice, particular works become adopted by judges and practitioners alike and assume a status akin to the law itself. This is most marked in relation to the role of *Archbold*, a work on pleading and evidence in criminal cases. One barrister told us:

. . . in the leading case on murder – *Maloney* – does foresight of probable consequences equal intention? House of Lords said that it was only

> evidence of intention not proof of intention . . . but the reason why the
> case reached the House of Lords was because the judge directed the jury
> at first instance that it did equal intention and the reason why he did this
> was because *Archbold* said so.

In an environment where a particular work is universally relied upon, it is
little wonder that many barristers seldom feel the need to look far afield.

We will discuss further the role of law arguments in running cases later. For
now we would simply like to reinforce the point that what law that is used is
either drawn from memory or researched as needed and that it is practically
oriented rather than technical or legalistic. This is reflected in the sort of
sources that barristers use. One barrister we spoke to pointed out:

> Textbook writers' views about what the principles and propositions of
> law are are much more useful than ideas about what the possibilities or
> expanding these principles and propositions are. There are very few
> judges who are prepared to break new ground. Academic law is less
> relevant than a good working knowledge.

We were also told:

> You get to know your own favourite books . . . and you tend to go to
> them . . . you have to find your area in the index . . . there are a couple of
> sets of *Halsbury* that are always a good starting point . . . something like
> Atkins, *Courts Forms* are useful for giving precedents of draft proceed-
> ings and also there is a text attached which may refer you to what is
> relevant.

It was widely accepted that the key to good practice was knowing where to
find specimens and drafts that could be adopted. An ability to draft from
nothing, a Rolls-Royce agreement, was held to be much less important than
knowledge about where to find one ready-made. As one commercial practitioner put it:

> If you're a novelist or an academic, plagiarism is a dirty word, but if
> you're a practitioner it isn't . . . whether you're copying your own
> precedent, a textbook precedent or somebody else's precedent or if you
> get six precedents that are roughly in the area but not quite and you
> chop and change between them . . . so long as you've got a draft that is
> the right answer and is going to progress that case the step required and
> you get that back quickly . . . that's what you're being paid for – getting
> the right information down on paper and back to the client as quickly as
> you can . . . yes, the solicitor client. . . . That's a better service than
> locking yourself up and attempting to do it all out of your own head.

Many barristers we spoke to – especially young barristers – emphasized the
help that they got from other barristers, either in their chambers or in the
library. For many of those operating in jurisdictions where there was a library
system, this help was seen as a feature which gave their system a certain
superiority:

. . . a lot of assistance comes from each other . . . day to day I have people coming up to me and saying 'What would you do in this situation?' or 'What do you know about this?' and equally I'm going to them, especially one's contemporaries, saying 'Have you been involved in a business tenancy situation recently? Have you dealt with this point?' . . . It's a starting point to find out more.

This information exchange works most busily at the more junior end of the profession. Here points that are unfamiliar to the barrister appear with more frequency. Not only will the junior have less experience to draw upon but the informal network of friends, colleagues and working groups that a more senior barrister might use to collect information is not as clearly in place. Also, there are logistical and personal reasons which come into play. As one informant told us:

I would be one of those people who spend most days either out in court or in the bar library . . . the reason I do that is because I use the books and generally it's a fund of information . . . there are other people who don't use the library much and don't talk about their cases but I think the library is a very helpful exchange of information.

The information exchange works in the chambers system too. Here again the junior end of the profession make more use of the time-honoured custom of seeking help. Their opportunities as well as their needs are often greater. For example, the pressure on space in chambers may mean that junior barristers are accommodated in rooms occupied by several colleagues. In these circumstances, help from one's contemporaries is easier to obtain and we often heard of brainstorming sessions taking place with ideas being thrown in from a whole variety of sources.

Obviously, there was a tendency not to over-ask, nor to ask those who one did not know too well. But, generally, this process was supported by more senior barristers who intimated that they would not feel able to decline to provide advice to younger barristers. One senior barrister we spoke to took a very strong line on the custom about helping colleagues:

. . . if you get a medical report in, there is practically nobody who, no matter how busy they are and no matter how senior or junior they are . . . [who will not help]. If you hand a medical report to someone they will have a look at it and confirm or disagree with what your evaluation of it might be. . . . I usually stop whatever I'm doing (unless I'm really pushed), and read a letter that somebody has received if I feel that I can help . . . that sort of general reciprocation helps me even now.

But it was particularly on questions of procedure, rather more than on legal interpretation, though, that most of our informants felt that they were able to ask advice. One barrister suggested that this was because matters of procedure were seen to be matters of professional pride. It is easy to see why procedural questions are so important to barristers. Procedure provides the way in which to make things actually happen. In contrast to the more analytical and reflective exercise that is carried on in law schools, barristers in professional practice must act on the world to bring results. It is only through mastery of procedure that a barrister can bring out his or her case in the way desired and direct the proceedings towards a preferred conclusion that is recognized by the judge as possible and valid.

A barrister with just a few years experience noted that procedure is the most difficult aspect in the early years:

> I think that probably procedure is the most difficult to learn because it is much more difficult to work out than substantive law . . . if I ask people about anything, I'll ask about procedure . . . you really have got to, and ask someone who has done it. . . . The problem with these procedural points is that you don't realize that they can be sprung on you . . . people don't feel generally embarrassed asking other barristers . . . it's a lot less embarrassing than . . . not knowing what's going on in court.

Procedure is (quite properly, we believe) not something which is taught in an undergraduate law school, being left to postgraduate professional courses, though many implied that this training was not really satisfactory. However, on the matter of technical legal research, we began to feel after some time that this – in the manner of law school training – really did not impinge too much upon the thoughts of barristers. Few claimed to do any really extensive research before taking a case, although most would not go to court without a copy of the necessary legislation. One barrister even suggested to us that Industrial Tribunals (where legal aid is not available to pay for representation by a barrister) are more legally inclined than the typical courts and thus require more technical legal knowledge.

In some areas of family law, particularly that relating to children in danger, it was suggested to us that the system relied upon a small number of expert judges and barristers who, effectively, know the ropes and difficulties are found only when new judges are brought in as replacements:

> All the family division judges that sit, until recently, were family practitioners at the bar. They were in the [well-known cases] as leading counsel and they know it backwards and forwards. Hence they don't want an outline of the legal authorities. . . . I would remind the judge of the principles when I state the case at the beginning and any issues of policy which I think are relevant – the unwritten policy of the division which comes from the senior judges in the High Court. . . . In front of a deputy, they need more reminding and they may need more law as well, because they are not as conversant. . . . The only time I would lead a High Court judge is if I am transferred to a [non-family division] judge. Then you have your work cut out, because they expect you to be as on top of the law as if you were doing a commercial case. . . . He then says, 'What are you talking about?' when you are talking about a precedent which has been there for . . . twenty years or more . . . then you really have to go through it in classic form.

... if a High Court judge is against you [on a point of law], unless you've got some terrifically compelling point [of law], then you just sit down, because you have to appear in front of him again.

Pressures not only come from judges, but from one's colleagues at the bar. One barrister noted that a particular QC in his chambers might well increase his earnings if he was to become less inclined towards legal research:

The one person [an ex-academic] we have here who does any lecturing is a brilliant lawyer and is also a very good advocate ... he is sometimes not as practical as he ought to be in the way that he runs his practice – I won't say that about his cases – but certainly ... if he was trying to make money at this game. ... When I go in to ask him a question, I come out with more words than I went in with.

There are areas of advocacy, however, where barristers are expected to argue legally and to use as much law as is required. These, by and large, are those where commercial interests are involved and where a large amount of money is at stake. Only a few of the barristers we interviewed were involved in this kind of work themselves, but we would expect that those doing cases in the central London commercial field would exhibit this 'rule bending'.[4] One barrister we spoke to reinforced this view when he commented:

The Lloyds Reports [of commercial litigation] have the most interesting cases ... that is because there is more money and more research in those cases ... [the parties] are better able to afford it ... [but] normally you only get a day or a half a day to do the research.

One example of 'rule bending' which we did come across fairly frequently was in the area of licensing law. Frequently, these clients are large brewery chains and every legal avenue is sought in order to get a satisfactory result:

... the one area where I do refer to cases is in licensing and I do that a lot ... I never ever go to court without *Patterson* never ever ... because there are a hell of a lot of authorities ... it's all statute law anyway and every single word of the statute has been defined in various authorities ... it is the ultimate cut-throat world, licensing ... because it is all commercial, there is no emotion involved in it, it is all to do with people making money somehow and therefore they are going to take every tiny little point they can ... they will pay the silks an awful lot of money to argue a point ... and things nearly always go to appeal if it goes against a brewery, so you have got to get it right at the beginning.

Generally, though, it is striking how rarely is recourse made to technical areas of law in the day-to-day work of barristers. Most seem to get by largely through routinized knowledge, sometimes referring to a textbook, but never wishing to be seen to be too legalistic either to their colleagues or to the judge.

And, even in the research for counsel's opinion, experience makes the barrister limit the substantive law research which is carried out in its preparation:

I think [having experience in court] makes you a lot more realistic in considering cases . . . in the first few years I would go straight to the textbook and produce a model essay on what the law is and how it applies to those facts. I wouldn't take into account the fact that it was going to be heard before a judge who might quite often be prepared to waive aside certain inconvenient decisions or principles in favour of what he saw as a meritorious case. So, it has become a lot more practical because you are always considering 'How would I put this in court' and 'Could I really put forward this legal principal in court if it was quite clearly technical rather than meritorious'. That's where you gain your experience as well, because it is very difficult to assess the prospects of success in isolation from envisaging it in court.

CONCLUSION

The world is a noisy place. There are few elements of the world which are agreed upon through consensus – the voice of debate, argument and shifting ground are always to be heard. Perhaps more so than in most other areas, is this true of the world of law. Clients fight for their freedom, for money, for revenge. The court system fights to handle all the cases which come before it. And the actors in the system fight for their livelihood. Law is not a system which can be accurately modelled by a division into fact and rule, as though these were clear and distinct categories which were of central importance.

Our argument is that law is richer than this. Law is a social process where information is constructed, passed on and mediated through a myriad of ways. Each element of this legal information is as important to the barrister in his work as any other – no one or two aspects can take precedence and be all-important. Indeed, the art of the advocate might be said to be the deciding of the relative importance of each of the various elements for each particular case. But by describing the product of the process as 'information', we do not want to suggest that it is something concrete which can be taken out of the context of the legal process. It is not 'information' as in 'information' processed by computer. It cannot be looked at beyond the way it is constructed and used by actors in the system. Legal information is only legal information by being a part of that context: it cannot be formalized, coded and processed by a computer to arrive at a 'just decision', for taking it out of its context makes us unable to appreciate it properly.

Yet to the academic lawyer, this acontextuality is indeed how the legal world is presumed to be best understood – facts which can accurately be extracted from reality, rules which can be extracted from legislation and case reports. The textbooks of law, the teaching of law and the discussion of law omit so much of the other aspects of the moulding of legal information which we are describing. They ignore the pressures on the barrister to find work, the time limits and peer-group pressures which preclude academic legal research and such like. And they ignore the pressures we look at in the next chapter which come from the court.

And on the other side of the coin – that of barristerial writings such as Du Cann (1980) – we find the same ignoring of the complexity of legal information. While barristers rarely write with the same perspective as the legal academic, they too bring a simplistic view and present a simplistic picture. They downplay how they are fixed into the role and career structure dictated by their occupation. They ignore their captivity in the solicitor–barrister relationship. They underestimate how the legal information with which they are presented captures them within its framework. As we shall see in the next chapter, the captivity of barristers within a set of limits constrains them all the way to the courtroom.

Our general picture is that barristers help to construct a form of legal information which then holds them captive.

NOTES

1 This is not a novel insight as far as academics are concerned, many of whom have been affected by the studies in the literature (see, e.g. Jackson's, 1988, semiotic approach).
2 Despite the difference in terminology, the difference in actual fact is less than might be expected between these two types of cases. The former are 'officially' reported, whereas the latter are 'unofficially' reported.
3 In Colin Campbell's (1976) research into solicitors' research practices (see p. 50), he did not ask solicitors how much research they undertook, but which texts they had looked at and for how long during the previous few days. This gave evidence both of the nature and extent of the 'research'. Though we did not undertake this approach, it is perhaps one that would pay dividends in the analysis of barristers' research practices.
4 By rule-bending we mean that the lawyers attempt to mould the interpretation of the rule to suit their clients' interests.

5

GOING TO COURT

INTRODUCTION

The proceedings in the courtroom are a possible final stage in a very much longer and more complex process. We have already considered some factors relating to the barrister's role and career which affect the job that he or she performs. We have also considered the relationship between barristers and solicitors and the way in which information is passed to barristers. Now we must look at how a case is actually handled. We will look at the processes by which a case is evaluated, how it may be settled or negotiated and, finally, how it is run in court. Here, as elsewhere, the focus will be less on the determining influence of law or even arguments of law and fact (although they are present at all stages), than on the social factors which influence the way in which a case gets to court. In particular, we will focus on the influence of personalities – the opposition counsel, defendants and plaintiffs, witnesses and, above all, the judge. Here we will see how factors and relationships at this level are significant. We will consider in the context of both civil and criminal practice how each of these actors in the legal process, in combination with other factors, exert an influence on how a case is handled at each of these stages.

EVALUATING A CIVIL CASE

As we begin to consider how barristers evaluate cases and make the strategy decisions that will be so influential in determining their outcome, it can be seen immediately that there is an important difference between those barristers in criminal practice and those advising on civil matters. Usually, barristers in criminal law practices are involved with people who are already in trouble. General advice is not often sought and, in the main, criminal barristers are called in for a matter that will end up in a courtroom. As we saw earlier, where we looked at how the criminal brief is produced (see pp. 84–7), by the time a barrister is involved, the lower reaches of the justice system have begun to process a suspect. Barristers are generally required to react to what has already happened either by drafting charges or advising on a plea.

In contrast, barristers advising on civil matters are not often restricted to a reactive role. Quite a proportion of the barristers we spoke to, especially those working in the commercial field, emphasized how their work was largely advisory and non-contentious with court work restricted to the occasional appearance to argue interlocutory matters (those issues that arise during the course of an action and before any final determination). Opinions are provided on a whole range of matters which will never be argued inside a courtroom. Indeed, generally, a high proportion of matters in respect of which solicitors are consulted never require the institution of proceedings. Even in an adversarial situation, actually going to court involves using the big stick when everything else – threats, negotiations, etc. – has failed. So when a barrister is brought in, it is not invariably because the case is going to end up in court. Court proceedings are the final resort and because of their expense and uncertainty they are a weapon which must be used carefully. The role of the barrister involves more than just running a case in court. Indeed, several of the barristers we spoke to emphasized that handling a case in court was much less difficult than making decisions about their client's aims and how best to achieve them within the limits set by the case, the personalities in it and the resources supporting it. The sorts of skills that are used here are far from purely legal ones.

One of the major problems can be in deciding what to aim for. As one barrister put it: 'What do you want? That is the hardest question of all to get an answer to. Once you know that you can get started.' As we discussed in Chapter 3, it is often part of what a solicitor expects from a barrister that issues relating to a client's problem be clarified. Another barrister with a large commercial practice told us:

> You have to know what they are after. Sometimes it's quite surprising. They [the client] have to stop short and think about it because they haven't worked out what exactly it is that they're actually after.

As we have stressed before, generally what the lay client is after is a solution to his or her problem – be it a dispute with a neighbour, failure to pay up on a contract or the existence of rules seemingly preventing the client from doing what he or she wishes. These problems are rarely simply legal problems only. The context in which they exist will impinge to a great extent. The barrister must be able to appreciate the large number of various factors relating to the nature of the client and his or her problem and, perhaps above all, to the financial resources supporting the case.

The matters that need to be taken into account will, of course, vary with individual clients and with different problems. One barrister we spoke to who worked almost exclusively with small business people commented:

Very often the nature of their business is at the heart of the matter – for example, whether a franchising agreement would work for them or whether they need to amend their articles of association . . . you need to know something about business to be any good to them.

In contrast, a barrister acting in a family law matter might be required to take into account factors that were not strictly legal in deciding on custody applications or whatever. Even in commercial matters, the objective value of the case is not inevitably determining. For example, we were told of a case where a businessman pursued his former partner against all the odds out of a sense of betrayed trust.

It is often the issue of costs that is of central importance. Generally, as a barrister looks through the papers in a brief, he or she will be looking out for the client's best interests in terms of the costs of going to law. The famous view of the US judge Learned Hand, that a law suit was to be dreaded 'beyond almost anything else short of sickness and death', found an echo with many of the barristers we spoke to. One remarked: 'It's a misfortune for the client to go to court – it's expensive, it's time-consuming, it's stressful and nearly always unnecessary.' In view of this, most barristers assess the case in terms of its overall value to the client. As one very senior barrister put it: 'a healthy appreciation of the economics of litigation is essential'. This often involves knowing when to drop out of an action. As one advocate told us: 'I always put myself in the client's shoes; at the end of the day would I want to spend £10 000 chasing £5000 or would I rather be told that it's not worth it?'

The availability of legal aid may well be of crucial importance in decisions such as these:

> There's no point in advising a privately financed client to spend money unless it's worth it. It's all too easy to say 'Yes you've got a good case. Yes we'll issue proceedings', but you have to be able to look right down the line. Where is this going to end up? . . . What could possibly happen that would involve further legal costs? . . . It's very often a commercial decision . . . money is usually the prime determinant of all cases.

Almost all the lawyers we spoke to took the view that a very high-quality of justice is available but all of them then qualified this by saying that money is essential to get access to it. The so-called 'middle-income trap', which has the effect that those with moderate means are denied legal aid but are also unable to afford taking the risk of losing a legal action for fear of costs, was frequently cited as being of central significance to the advice offered. We noticed a very great awareness among barristers of questions relating to money and the relative value to a particular individual of proceeding at law. As one civil practitioner pointed out:

> Quite often a solicitor will write me a letter saying 'By the way this client isn't going to be legally aided: should we proceed with this case?' Then it's a different story. . . . I suppose in a legal aid case you would say there are risks but I suppose there is a prima facie case to be argued, you

should go ahead. . . . If you don't have the cushion of legal aid you'll be saying seriously to the client that there are risks and there are costs involved . . . unless you're getting legal aid it's too risky.

Where the financial factor is not such that it scares off the potential litigant completely, it may well determine strategy in important ways. Another barrister told us:

The decision to put out feelers for settlement or to run it is often the most important one because it greatly affects costs . . . . If you're going to set it up for trial you might have to get expert witnesses, your own medical evidence, [senior] counsel, etc., etc. Even in the county court it's all very expensive.

Conversely, if resources are unlimited and objectives are clear, then it seems a case can almost always be made. We found it initially surprising that law arguments, as much as factual ones, were used here. As one advocate put it: 'every problem has a legal element to it if you want to find it – if you're being paid to find it you can generally come up with something'. The same barrister went on to illustrate the point with an example from his own experience:

I was involved in a case where a multinational [company] sued someone who I acted for, for breach of copyright and passing off. He had a video shop. . . . He hadn't done that . . . but they kept it going and going and going . . . on all sorts of spurious grounds . . . until he ran out of money . . . so they achieved their aim: they closed him down.

This capacity for a case to stretch in proportion with the resources available to it appears to hold true even at the higher levels in the court hierarchy. There, indeed, law in a pure sense (rather than in the sense of the process of the law and the delay and cost involved there) seems to be the variable factor. One senior counsel, unencumbered by modesty, told us: 'In a really important case . . . you can always find law, make it up if necessary . . . I know as much law as they [the Law Lords] do.'

When a barrister has worked out what it is that the client wants, and what the client can afford, there is still the problem of deciding what you have got and of making the bricks of a case out of the straw of a brief.

Barristers found it difficult to describe exactly what it is they do when they first read the brief to evaluate the case. Several talked of reading the whole thing through quickly once or twice and marking out a skeleton on to which they could hang various arguments – or at least try them out for size. Others referred to a process of continually summarizing and refining the issues. None talked in terms simply of slotting facts neatly into categories provided by clear rules. When asked if he looked for controlling issues of law, or law and fact, in a brief on which a case would turn, one senior junior represented a fairly commonly held view when he replied:

I suppose I do but I don't think it's quite as mechanical as that . . . there's an element of instinct and experience . . . you just read the papers and

the issues . . . scream at you . . . it's usually crystal clear . . . it is very rare
that they are hidden in any way.

It seems that most issues in a brief, although undecided, are not unclear: the
problem is assessing their value or anticipating what a court might do.

Sometimes, undeniably, these uncertainties are points of law. One barrister with a large practice at the High Court level insisted: 'The law is crucial in
High Court practice . . . at the end of the day [if you get to court] . . . if you
don't see it the judge probably will.' Another reported:

Some barristers are very good at picking up points of law in briefs . . .
there are some very good lawyers – in the academic sense. . . . They will
see points of law and then research them and have something in their
hand.

As if to redress an impression that we did indeed form from various sources,
another barrister who was just beginning to graduate to more High Court
work maintained:

If you have a point of law in your favour in the High Court, but even in
the county court, it is very important . . . it will be listened to. . . . You
can win cases on legal points in the county court . . . despite the view
that you sometimes hear.

If law points can be important in this evaluation, so can matters of fact.
Indeed, one barrister summarized his role by saying:

The main activity of barristers in the county court [level of practice]
would be consulting with the client and mastering the factual side of the
brief. If there is any applicable law you have to look it up, but otherwise
you are simply negotiating and generally running the case.

Matters of fact will very often determine outcomes both in the sense of win
or lose and in the level of damages or type of remedy awarded. Barristers
spend a lot of time studying the details in the brief with what one lawyer
called 'a minuteness and precision which passes far beyond the bounds of
what is interesting or permanent' (quoted in Du Cann, 1980: 16). Their task
is, in theory, to thoroughly understand all the relevant factual information
that could possibly have a bearing on the case. The wealth of information in a
brief might mean that in a personal injury case, for example, a barrister may
have to evaluate medical reports, perhaps working out how much a person
has suffered or what the likelihood of arthritis developing in an ankle joint is
worth, and balancing this up against the strength of medical reports or
accident reports on the other side. Intellectually, these factors are all totally
different things, but from the point of view of the plaintiff they must be
brought together in a recommendation to seek an offer or risk a contest or
whatever.

We enquired how barristers went about mastering the factual information
needed to evaluate a case. One senior advocate said: 'Yes sometimes I see
what I'm reading in the brief as a picture . . . and your job is to be able to show

your picture to the judge and convince him to see things your way.' One barrister, with experience in a wide range of civil practice, talked in terms of forming a picture from the brief but said that he edited his view of the case in accordance with the quality of evidence and what could be proved:

> You have to present a case strongly but the only way you can do that is from the papers before you ... you form an image of what has happened ... but you may overdo it, you have to make sure that you can back it up ... if you put it too strongly it will go against you if the evidence doesn't come up to your standards. ... If you've got strong, good evidence you pitch the story right up, if your evidence is weak you pitch it down.

Another agreed with the idea of forming a picture (at least in certain cases) but added: 'Say if it's an accident, perhaps you fill in with detail from somewhere you know, that helps, but it can be misleading.'

Facts as they appear in the brief are uncertain: it is only after they have been through the process leading to the courtroom whereby they are negotiated by the parties, sifted through the rules of evidence and orientated by the judge that they become sufficiently settled for the areas of dispute to become clear. One very experienced barrister warned about drawing too firm a conclusion from the papers in a brief:

> I'm a great believer in keeping an open mind. You must listen to the other side and take on board what they are saying and, if necessary, change your opinion. Sometimes I have taken a view about a case and been wildly wrong. ... There are two sides to every story and no matter how much investigation you do, how many witnesses you interview and how many people you get into one of these [conference] rooms ... you will never know what the other fellow's evidence is going to be.

The element of instinct was referred to on numerous occasions to describe what seems to be a fairly complex process as factual matters are evaluated. One barrister who acted for government departments defending personal injury claims maintained that in the sort of cases he was involved in it was often very difficult at face value to evaluate cases. If the plaintiff gets the story moderately right and can provide a witness, there is often no evidence to directly contradict what is claimed. In these circumstances, our informant maintained:

> ... you get a nose for it ... knowing what cases to run ... there are certain indications like the injuries are not consistent with the story, multiple claims – maybe from the same address, improbable circumstances ...

Factors like the demeanour of the plaintiff can be important here, even at this very early stage. Another practitioner told us:

The other thing you have to bear in mind about your client is what he might be like if he had to give evidence . . . some are disastrous . . . they get worked up, they get too involved, they lose their temper . . . exactly the kind of witness who won't be quiet when told to by the judge, who will shout out from the back of the court . . . that kind of thing doesn't go well and you have to bear it in mind when deciding how to proceed.

The witnesses who are important to a case must also be considered, as any obvious weakness or strength there can have a significant impact on the decision about how to proceed. One advocate explained how he weighed up potential witnesses for their effect on a case: 'Will he immediately answer questions? Does he answer them directly? Is he comfortable? Would you buy a second-hand car from this witness?' It seems that it has always been this way: Aristotle maintained that 'we believe good men more fully and readily than others' (quoted in Stryker, 1954: 140). Most barristers are aware of this and evaluate witnesses carefully. We were told:

You will gain an impression if they can tell a story that is important to the case coherently . . . you also judge if they seem honest and seem straightforward . . . or stupid or intelligent . . . or if he is someone who will just exaggerate no matter what you do. . . . Sometimes you get witnesses who you know are just beyond the pale . . . there's not much you can do, it's just one of those things.

An important factor is the witness's sense of balance and proportion concerning the matters in the case. One informant maintained that:

. . . a good witness will not exaggerate in their own favour . . . indeed, if they play down their own case it may assist them enormously . . . usually they are too keen to promote their own case and knock aside all contrary points.

Really good, well-organized witnesses are, it seems, rare. One barrister made this point:

Chronology is a very important aspect in producing order. There are very few people who think chronologically . . . when you meet them you want to hug them: they do your job for you, they are the very best witnesses.

Even professional witnesses who appear regularly – social workers, probation officers, police officers, etc. – were thought to be very variable in quality and usefulness. On the other hand, expert witnesses, such as doctors, engineers, etc., do not prove too much of a difficulty. As one very senior barrister explained it, 'The solicitor gets the evidence you need. If a specialist doesn't say what you want . . . you go to another.'

Before we move to consider matters largely unconnected with the brief, which can, nevertheless, determine how a case is evaluated, it is perhaps worth considering another description of this basic evaluation role as it applies to the information contained in the brief. This view seems basically to be an attempt to summarize the complex process of assessing a case in a way that goes somewhat beyond the general and bare reference to instinct that we frequently heard. It is a view that we came across often enough for it to seem significant. We were told:

> I think the merits are very important. When I pick up a set of papers I try and forget I know any law to start with. I will speed read through all the documents . . . I will just ask myself what is the general impression I have – because that is probably what a judge will do . . . he will have an impression one way or the other about who has behaved badly and who has not.

This idea of the merits of the position taken by a party to the case was considered to be of great importance – even for this particular barrister who described his practice as being at the 'law end of the profession'. The question of merits, and their relationship with any legal element, was for him ultimately determining of how a case was evaluated. He set out a whole classification based on this: '. . . if you know that the merits are on your side, and then you research the law and know you have legal arguments too, you have a good case'. However, he continued, '. . . if you find the merits are on your side but the law isn't . . . in my view you really only have to find one good legal argument and the court will find for you on that one legal point . . .'. There was also a third scenario: '. . . if you know the merits aren't with you but the law is, you should be wary . . . your opponent only needs the one good argument . . .'. Finally, there is the situation where '. . . the merits and the law are against you . . . [and] you have got a real no hoper'.

We pursued this idea of merits, and what exactly it might mean, with other counsel. The idea was one with which many barristers were comfortable. Again, though, reference was frequently made to instinct and intuition to describe the fairly involved process of evaluation that goes on. One barrister told us:

> . . . you know it when you see it – usually if somebody has lied or broken promises . . . restitution (an area that I am very interested in) is basically about asking people to keep their promises . . . the idea is that it's wrong that somebody should go back on a promise be it a trust situation or in a contract.

Another barrister with a large personal injury practice told us that for him the main question in any case is: 'Is this a decent citizen who deserves compensation?' It seems to us that this reference to the merits of a case is significant. It puts in some sort of summary form the processes through which a barrister goes as he or she evaluates a case. Also, it introduces an element relating to the 'fairness' of a case indicating the way that the law would go. This may perhaps suggest that the operation of the law is basically pragmatic with the formal doctrine of law being subservient to notions of what is a 'good' result.

Factors outside the brief itself will be of importance too. Not only is there the personality of the plaintiff and witnesses, but there is the question of the opposition. The importance of who is acting for the other side as a factor determining outcome is probably highest at the stage where a settlement may be arranged, but even here it may have some effect. One counsel saw it like this:

> Is the person on the other side going to be reasonable? Are they going to make a very good job of presenting the case? You might see that there is somebody on the other side who maybe wouldn't make a good job of this and it's your chance to put the boot in . . .

The barrister's specialized knowledge will include such matters as this and his or her research will often involve keeping up with the triumphs and (especially) failures in colleagues' careers. Another barrister told us:

> . . . if the case looks on paper that it hasn't been set up terribly well you know that you can put the person under incredible pressure . . . in open court you will be able to say 'This isn't right', 'He hasn't pleaded that', 'This hasn't been done'. All these things enter into a judgement [about the case].

This view is reinforced by a writer of a textbook about legal drafting. In a section urging the importance of authoritative, well-designed pleadings (the document in which a claim is framed as a basis for a court hearing) he makes this point:

> After many years in the profession, I confess still to a tightening of the stomach when I am confronted with a pleading drafted by someone who clearly knows what he or she is doing. I know that I am not going to be able to get away with anything, that the weakness in my case will almost certainly be ruthlessly exploited and that if I have any reservations about the wisdom of proceeding with the action, now is the time to see if a 'deal' can be done (Rose 1990: 11).

The judge, too, can be of importance at this stage although, of course, his or her significance in a case reaches its highest point at the later stages. Indeed, at the very early stages, exactly which judge will preside is not certain. However, those who regularly practise in certain courts will know the composition of the bench in general and may be able to make evaluations about how certain arguments will be received. One barrister working mainly in the area of personal injuries, and in particular claims against public bodies arising from falls, commented that she assessed cases with this factor very much to the front of her mind:

> This is one you might pay on a compromise basis, this is one you might fight. In making that decision [to settle or to fight] I would apply my mind to who is going to be the judge. Is he basically going to be sympathetic to the plaintiff? Is he a judge who is quite cynical about these tripping cases?

Another barrister said:

> Obviously there are some cases that are so clear-cut that it doesn't make
> any difference, you are going to lose the case or win the case no matter
> who the judge is. But there are very, very few cases like this. . . . The
> success of almost every case is dependent on the judge . . . there are
> certain judges who if you knew in advance were going to hear your case
> you could virtually determine what is going to happen to it.

It is not often very easy to predict far in advance who the judge will be and so
this factor while significant cannot yet be said to be determining.

Beyond matters such as these, there are the sort of factors relating to the
barrister's role and career and the barrister's relationship with the solicitor
(see Chapters 2 and 3). These may affect the way individual cases are seen.
One or two examples might serve to remind us of the sort of thing we mean.
A barrister's progression on the career ladder and the relationship that he or
she has with a solicitor may well introduce factors that are important and
determining although well outside any information contained in the brief.
One barrister told us:

> Sometimes you say 'this is a case I can win, the probabilities are in
> favour of me . . . the people who instruct me need to be reminded that
> I'm not a soft touch, that I can do the business for them . . . this is a good
> vehicle for me to justify my existence: I could look good doing this
> case'.

Also, for example, it must be remembered that the barristers perform for
solicitors who in turn transmit the clients' wishes. Ultimately, barristers
must do what is required rather than what an uninvolved reading of a case
might indicate. The client, especially if a repeat player (see p. 52), may be
pursuing strategic objectives beyond the particular case in hand. This will
effect the evaluation that is made of the brief. As one barrister put it:

> . . . insurance companies work on percentages. . . . They can afford to
> go in and get duffed every now and again where there is a chance that in
> the long run they might save money in these cases.

Also, there are institutional and organizational factors of various sorts which
may impact on how a brief is assessed. For example, it is fairly well known
when certain insurance companies have money left over in their pay-out
funds towards the end of the financial year. A factor such as this may breathe
life into what might otherwise be a fairly moribund case.

Considerations such as these are not legal ones in the orthodox sense, but
they are of central importance in evaluating a case. As we move on to look at
the next stage, that of negotiation and settlement, we can see how several of
these assume greater importance. In particular, we will see how the point is
reached where the factor of the opposition becomes at its most significant and
how the significance of the judge increases, although it does not reach its

zenith. We must now look to the same process of evaluating the brief as it applies in the slightly different context of criminal practice.

THE CRIMINAL CASE

Many aspects in the process of evaluating criminal cases are similar to those outlined in relation to civil practice. Both the defence and the prosecution must evaluate the brief in terms of the evidence provided by the police and prosecution services, as well as by the defence. For the Crown, charges must be drafted or re-drafted and both sides must assess the value of a case in any negotiation process or for its strength in court. However, there are significant differences from the civil brief.

Chief among these relates to the fact that in most instances where a barrister is involved, the defendant must make a plea of guilty or not guilty when arraigned (see p. 86). Unlike in civil practice where the aims of the parties may not yet be clear, in criminal work the existence of a brief generally means that a case will be heard in court and that, on the defence side, this basic choice of how to plead must be made. On the face of it, then, there would seem not to be the same difficulty about ascertaining what the client wants as there is in civil practice. However, this decision about how to plead may be problematic. It introduces an extra and very crucial stage in the process of evaluation. Although the vast majority of criminal cases go forward as guilty pleas, with the barrister's formal role in court restricted to making a plea in mitigation, there is, as we shall see in the next section, a great deal that goes on to bring the case to that position. It is vital that the case be thoroughly evaluated to make the most of that process. Charges can be reduced, police support can be enlisted and discount off the sentence can thus be won.

Accordingly, it is a very important aspect of the barrister's job to evaluate the case in order to advise on the plea. We were told:

> I think it is one of the most important things a barrister can do . . . tell his client that his chances are zippo of being acquitted – in the barrister's considered opinion – and if he fights it it will only get worse and maybe he should put his hands up.

As we discussed above in relation to the construction of the criminal brief (see p. 86), the guilty plea is the most potent mitigating factor in a sentence. Because of this, there is an important decision to be made and, although ultimately the barrister must do as instructed, he or she has a vital role at this stage in evaluating the case in order to decide whether to go for a plea of not guilty (and the chance of an acquittal) or whether to settle for damage limitation with a guilty plea (and a discount from the sentence in recognition for saving the court's time).

On the defence side, the most important determinant of this basic strategy is, at least ostensibly, the accused client. One experienced defence barrister told us: '. . . the first thing you want to know is is he going to plead guilty or contest it . . . the solicitor may indicate it in the papers but you never really know until you see the guy'. The situation may not always be clear from the information that the solicitor has passed on:

> Sometimes the papers ... don't give you an idea. ... There's a state-
> ment only and he says the police beat him or whatever. ... Also, the
> police want to clear things up so they say 'Well you're going to go down
> anyway, we'll get you bail or whatever if you admit to these ...'. You
> don't know.

It is the case as outlined by the lay client that the barrister must present. As one advocate put it: 'One of the unfortunate realities that people don't understand is that you have to act on the instructions of your client; if he instructs you to say something you ... [generally] ... have to say it.' Sometimes this may not always be the best course of action. A very experienced criminal advocate complained:

> In reality you're dealing with the stupidest people imaginable. ... You
> very rarely get a brief for a sophisticated criminal ... I mean they're
> [often] streetwise to an extent but they do the most appallingly stupid
> things. Ninety percent of them are pissed when they get caught and a
> big percentage of them would be caught red-handed ... staggering up
> the road with a TV under their arm. ... You get very few cases where
> you read the brief and say 'Well, this guy's got a good fight'.

A very important part of the job of evaluating the case is to provide practical advice on the plea not just for trial but for the negotiation that may go on prior to trial. The client's own wishes are, in theory, ultimately determining, but most of the criminal barristers we spoke to saw it as part of their role to evaluate the situation in order to persuade their clients, forcefully if necessary, to take the option that provides the optimum result with the least risk. This involves taking a broad view of the case. As one advocate told us:

> Let's put it this way, I'm not easily fooled and in many cases I get a clear
> impression that I'm being lied to but it's not for me to make the decision
> whether the ... lay client is telling the truth or not. That's up to the
> jury.

However, he continued, it is important to try and ensure that the client does not continue with a hopeless case. He or she must be persuaded that the barrister's view as to the best course of action represents the correct one: 'You don't say "I don't believe you". You say "I don't think that the jury would find that credible". ... You have to make value judgements like that in every case.'

Thus the barrister uses his or her professional judgement to evaluate the case in order to represent to the client what is the best course of action. The client's own wishes while determining in the last resort are not always paramount. Another criminal advocate told us: 'What colours your advice is the strength of the case ... you give him your professional advice; you say

"Your chance here of getting a result is about ten percent".' Sometimes, the judgements that are made are very fine. One barrister commented:

> The most difficult cases are where the guy's got a bit of a record and you know that inevitably if he is convicted he will go to gaol. . . . But on a plea he might just stay out with the discount given for a plea. But you're not sure. All you can say to him is 'On a plea you might just stay out of gaol, there's a chance that the sentence might just be suspended but if you fight it you'll definitely go to gaol [if you lose]'.

The factors that are involved in these assessments are varied. Thus it may be the case as the prosecution have it that is important. As one barrister said: 'You will have read the depositions, know the strength of the case against him and, hopefully you will have seen his criminal record. These are the two main things.' Another put it more widely:

> There's always pressure on you. While you can't force him to plead guilty, there is often good reason for him to plead guilty for his own benefit. . . . Like who the judge is, whether or not he is already pleading guilty to a lot of offences of the same nature . . . (if you're pleading guilty to nine shoplifting offences there is no point in fighting the tenth charge . . . you lose all the credit for pleading guilty to the other nine and the tenth is not going to make any difference in the sentence).

Very often, of course, the decision about the plea is not based on the case itself but on the tactics that are to be adopted with the prosecution side. As we shall see in the next section, there may be much negotiation and the plea is the most significant thing that the defence have. Also, the plea may be determined by a perceived need to use the system with a view to gaining as much as possible for the defendant. For example, we heard of defendants initially pleading not guilty in order to be released on bail over Christmas and subsequently changing their plea to guilty.

Leaving aside for the moment the possibility of negotiation, we must concentrate on how the criminal brief is assessed when it is first received. After all, no-one can be sure that negotiation in any given case will be possible or fruitful. As barristers evaluate the criminal brief, on both the prosecution side and for the defence, the sorts of matters that were mentioned in relation to the civil brief are also relevant here. There are matters of fact and law to be considered along with the same sort of factors relating to the defendant, the witnesses, the opposition and the judge that we reviewed earlier.

Matters of law were (again) not considered to be of particular importance. One senior counsel outlined the situation in this way, declaring there to be three possibilities:

> One, there is no argument about the law, it is only about the facts. Two, there is law but it is fairly clear – where do these facts fit into that legal framework? The third, and much less frequent one, is what is the law? . . . this is very, very much less common.

Another experienced practitioner declared:

> There's no law in them. Ninety percent turn on their facts. You have
> the charge and the depositions . . . the charge has almost always been
> drafted by Crown counsel . . . it's nearly always right . . . on your
> reading of the facts you will know it is right.

Part of the reason why this is so comes from the nature of the criminal
process. One fairly senior barrister, who managed to maintain both a civil
and criminal practice, told us:

> . . . people who practise in the civil courts are more likely to be involved
> in legal argument because more civil cases go on as contests than
> criminal cases . . . criminal cases obviously go on all the time but as
> pleas: they are based on the facts of the case. You could easily spend
> ninety percent of your time as a criminal lawyer without looking at a
> law book [whereas] . . . in my civil law cases, I look up law on a more
> regular basis.

Even where there is a defence being offered, the range of possibilities seems to
be quite limited. One barrister told us:

> . . . you will also know the defence – or will do when you talk to the
> client. There are two main types. One, the guy says he wasn't there and
> knows nothing about it. That may involve an alibi – evidence that he
> was somewhere else. . . . Or [secondly], he was there but he didn't do it
> – either because the person was mistaken or he did do something but it
> didn't amount to what they are alleging. . . . It's all facts, a store
> detective says 'I saw you' and he says 'I didn't do it' or 'yes I took it but'
> – there's some story [to explain it].

It seems that facts more than law are what the barrister must evaluate. Of
course, this can be difficult depending on the nature of the case. One senior
junior told us:

> I'll get my papers for tomorrow at half past five. There'll be no trials
> tomorrow, it'll be all guilty pleas. Some cases may take me half an hour
> to read, assimilate and write out a few notes: another case may take me
> two hours. It usually depends on the volume of papers and if it's a
> multi-handed one [more than one defendant], then you've got to work
> out as well, not losing sight of your own client's case, what the other
> defendants are likely to say, or, if you're a prosecutor, have said about
> your chap.

Another barrister, who worked almost exclusively on the prosecution side,
was certain that the job could be difficult:

> You could get a trained chimpanzee to prosecute a case in the crown
> court or the magistrates' court . . . [but] to do it properly actually takes a
> bit of skill, a bit of thought and a bit of hard work. The job, to be done
> properly, entails you thinking long and hard about it, as long as it takes.

The sort of thing that must be thought about, on both sides, relates to how the case might look as a contest in court if it were to get that far. This depends on what is available to support it. A defence advocate told us:

> ... you have the prosecution papers, you formulate a view of the overall case, the picture that is going to be presented ... and you cannot ... start running a case contrary to your case and to your witnesses.

Evaluating the witnesses and their reliability is important. An experienced prosecutor told us:

> I get a picture of what went on from the papers and it's my job for the purposes of prosecution to convey that picture to the jury ... although very often it's proved wrong by the witnesses that you then call ... they depart intentionally, or more usually unintentionally, from their witness statements ... it usually comes across much more lamely.

Such factors may be significant when it comes to negotiating over the level of charge that will ultimately be preferred. Of course, in contrast to civil practice, where a case supported by only poor witnesses might be bought off or dropped, this option is not generally available to the prosecution barrister who must follow the instructions from the prosecution authority. As one of the prosecutors we talked to complained, 'if you think that your prosecution witnesses are so incredible that they are literally not worthy of belief then that's tough, all you can do is get on with the job which is to make out your case'.

Sometimes, indeed, the problem is not with the quality of the witnesses but with producing them at all. We heard on several occasions about the difficulties that are sometimes experienced in getting hold of witnesses who agreed to appear perhaps twelve or more months before but who are now difficult to contact or trace. On the defence side, the defendant must be considered too. Sometimes this can be a positive factor if he or she is more sympathetic, credible or apparently law-abiding than usual. However, the defendant is usually measured in negative terms as a witness. For example, we were told:

> ... defendants are notoriously hopeless witnesses. There's a saying at the bar that the defendant's case is at its highest at the end of the Crown case. Once he gives evidence it usually goes downhill ... [defendants] say the most outrageous things, blatant lies.

As we have indicated already, the judge is very important even at the stage of evaluating the brief. Because decisions about how to plead are often left to the very last moment, counsel will generally know who the judge is. This will crucially affect the way in which a case is perceived. Sometimes this will be at a substantive level; as we shall see later, arguments are often tailored to fit the idiosyncrasies of particular judges. However, for the most part when the brief is being evaluated, the matter that is of key importance is what the judge is like when sentencing. As one advocate put it:

. . . it doesn't make any difference to me apart from the question of sentencing, who the judge is. I don't mind doing a trial for example, in front of judge X and fighting it and losing it so long as judge X is not going to be the sentencing judge.

Indeed, as one practitioner succinctly put it, in matters other than sentencing, 'the fact that there's a jury there always gives you a chance'.

However, the presence of a tough or a lenient judge will crucially determine how the case is evaluated in terms of advising on the plea. One barrister working in Belfast's criminal courts, after relating a story of how a minor, non-active terrorist received only a suspended sentence for possession of firearms from a particular judge as opposed to the seven-year custodial sentence which he estimated would have been handed down from another judge, declared simply that, 'the paying public just wouldn't credit the difference a judge can make'.

The presence on the bench of a particular judge, whose reputation is well known, will strongly influence the decision about how to plead and whether to abort or 'crack' a trial that is already set. One barrister explained it this way:

If he pleads guilty it is usually to get him dealt with there and then . . . just hear the plea in mitigation. . . . If it is a reasonable enough judge, someone who you know is lenient, then the pressure is on to get him to plead guilty. And vice versa. If it's a bad judge you get him to plead not guilty on the arraignment and the case is then put back in the hope that some other judge will be there when you have him re-arraigned and change the plea. You're not supposed to do that, but I mean everybody does – well, he's entitled to change his mind and you can manipulate the system to a certain extent to get what you want.

The factor of the opposition counsel, and their abilities and propensities, is of most importance at the negotiation stage. Their particular traits are, as we shall see, vital knowledge for the barrister. However, there is some scope for such factors as the ability and style to enter into the evaluation of a case, in the sense that a choice over the plea can ensure that the case is moved on to the stage where the strengths or weaknesses of the opposition can be avoided or exploited. One advocate told us: 'there are lots of times when I would go and do cases and my attitude would be determined by how good I thought the other counsel is . . . it is a very important consideration in deciding what to do.' Indeed, factors such as the identity and skill of the opposition counsel can negate other considerations. As one senior barrister told us:

. . . you know in certain cases you are going to be prosecuted hard and other cases you can tell the client 'We haven't got Perry Mason against us so don't worry. You're not going to be cross-examined properly'.

Evaluations like this may cause a barrister to view a case in a certain light and pursue a particular strategy – going either for a trial or a deal – but they cannot be completely determining, not least because there is the chance that the brief may be passed to someone else.

The question of money is not so significant in a criminal case as in most civil ones. Most defendants are publicly funded. Those that are not, generally find the money to pay for a service that is at least as good as that on legal aid. Indeed, in criminal practice, it is difficult to guess if extra resources are of any significance. One example we did come across many times was the idea of Queen's Counsel being retained to appear in the magistrates' courts for motoring offenders. Opinion was divided on the usefulness of this strategy. Some said that the £1000 or £1500 that this might cost was money well spent because the presence and authority of one of the very top senior counsel would impress the magistrate and that this would be reflected in the result. A few maintained that such a strategy might backfire as magistrates in their own courts were unlikely to take kindly to such obvious attempts to influence outcomes with resources.

Generally, however, the funds linked to a brief seem to have only a very limited input into the process of evaluating a particular case in criminal practice as compared to civil work. However, as mentioned in Chapter 2, criminal barristers often complain that legal aid rates are such that they are forced to take on increased workloads so as to maintain their incomes. On several occasions we heard reference made to unscrupulous colleagues who, in the knowledge that a contest was likely to be no more lucrative than a plea, pressurized lay clients to plead guilty in order to increase their turnover and income. It is of course impossible, or at least very difficult, to substantiate this, but we heard mention of it often enough for us to consider it a factor that some barristers might take into account when evaluating cases.

Another factor from outside the brief that may perhaps cause cases to be evaluated differently relates to the problems associated with having cases listed. The role of the listing officer is to try to maximize the sitting hours of their judges. Sometimes, it is alleged, that this results in people being pressurized into taking a slot in the court timetable when they are not ready or haven't the counsel of their choice. Indeed, as we write, there is a minor row brewing between the Lord Chancellor's Office and, unusually, both the Law Society and the Bar Council jointly over how court time should be efficiently allotted (see *The Times*, 15 December 1990). The practitioners maintain, in response to the Lord Chancellor's criticism over wasted public money, that current listing practices may lead to clients' cases being repeatedly put back to a point where a plea of guilty becomes a more attractive option than returning to court perhaps with a different counsel. One can imagine how logistical factors of this sort might well enter into evaluations made by barristers anxious not to prolong the ordeal of their clients or lose the brief.

Looking at how both civil and criminal cases are evaluated prior to the decisions that have to be taken as to strategy, it can be seen that there are a wide range of matters beyond the basic legal position to be taken into account. Having received instructions from a solicitor, a barrister must identify the real problems of the case, what the client wants and can afford, and then make a prediction about the likely outcome. On this basis, the vital decisions about whether to fight or withdraw, make an offer or seek an accommodation with the other side, plead guilty or not guilty, fight the case or look for a bargain over the charge must be made. These are the difficult questions. As one barrister put it:

> The biggest problems that face a barrister are the decisions that have to be made about the tactics of a case . . . it's not the question of how you run the case: that is easy. If you're in a case and the other side don't make any offers it's simple. You put your man in the box, call the witnesses, etc. . . . it happens by itself.

Most cases, of course, require more than just a mouthpiece with the correct rights of audience for the court. The barrister's job is to take all the disparate information that is of relevance and make an evaluation that takes into account not just the purely legal issues but questions of fact and of proof. Beyond these there are matters relating to the client and what he or she wants and can afford, the character and personality of the client and any witnesses or experts, the strengths and weaknesses of the opposition case and counsel, the logistics of the legal process itself and, of course, the judge who might hear the case. All this must be weighed up in a situation where work is being competed for and careers are being developed: instructing solicitors (and lay clients) must be kept happy, while new firms of solicitors and senior colleagues and judges must be impressed.

The information that is obtained from these sources and in these conditions must then inform a choice about what tactics to pursue. As we have stressed, briefs do not arrive as court-ready cases, but as problems awaiting optimum solutions which may or may not necessarily involve legal proceedings of various sorts in different courts. Barristers must decide the way forward on the basis of this particular legal information. This is undoubtedly a different process to law students answering a problem question in an examination. The scope of information to be considered is wider and the reason behind considering it is different. One senior counsel we spoke to emphatically made the point about the difference between practice and academic study:

> . . . in an examination answer you can be discursive, you can say 'Yes, but . . .', or 'No, but . . .'. You don't have to give a bottom line . . . but in practice you have to balance it all up and tell the client what is what.

In the next section we will look further into this.

SETTLEMENT AND NEGOTIATION IN CIVIL PRACTICE

At the stage following immediately on from the initial evaluation of the brief, there are again differences in how civil and criminal practitioners proceed. In civil practice, having made a decision about whether and how to proceed based on an evaluation of a brief, barristers very often look to the other side to see if a settlement of the matter can be effected without the costs and uncertainty of going to court. In this process of negotiation, the sort of information that barristers use will, of course, depend on their evaluation of a brief that has already been made, but it will also widen slightly. It will involve knowledge of the appropriateness and value of certain procedures and tactics, but also an increased emphasis on the personalities in the case generally and the opposition counsel in particular.

In criminal practice, there may also be negotiation, although settlement as such of a criminal case is not possible. Some cases may proceed without any bargaining between the Crown and the defence. Many, however, often involve negotiation just before the hearing, which can radically overhaul the initial evaluation of the case. As we have tried to indicate, although this initial evaluation will often leave room for negotiation over the charge that will be proffered and the plea that will be offered, when this process actually commences the sort of information that supports it is again slightly different in scope from what went before. As in civil work, the personalities of the two sets of counsel are important in determining outcomes, but there may also be in particular a role played by the judge which makes him or her of heightened significance.

The literature on negotiating and bargaining is extensive (in general, see Raiffa, 1982; Fisher and Ury, 1983; Axelrod, 1984; in the legal context specifically, see Ross, 1970; P'ng, 1983; Luban, 1985; Morley, 1986; Genn, 1987; Elster, 1989). It is not our intention here to attempt to summarize the literature or to contest the insights from the best of it which, for example, maintains basically that 'an understanding of the law in action can best proceed from an analysis of the personalities of and pressures upon the personnel who administer the law' (Ross, 1970: 18). Rather, we are seeking to add a little more detail to our sketch of what it is that comprises the legal information that barristers draw upon as they perform their role.

If a case does not go to court, the client is not receiving less value or a poorer service. On the contrary, the client will save much of the cost involved in going to law and the barrister will generally have worked just as hard and used as much expertise – albeit of a different sort to that normally associated with the drama in the courtroom. As one senior barrister put it:

> You use related skills . . . instead of persuading a judge or a jury . . . you're doing the same on your opposite number. . . . I'm trying to persuade you that this is a very, very small case and there's nothing wrong with your guy. You're trying to persuade me that this is a big case. You have to be able to put it over to the other side in such a way that he is impressed.

Negotiation and settlement is an important part of a civil practice. Barristers are often required to give opinions which will back up a position taken by a solicitor in a negotiation. The barrister may not be directly involved in all or even most of the settlements. However, there is still a large number of cases where barristers do play a very active role. As one fairly senior advocate put it, 'Ninety percent of my work is settlement. You have to be a good settler as well as a good fighter.' Communicating with the opposition is a fairly basic step in running a case and one that is generally followed:

> You must always speak to the other counsel . . . we don't tell lies . . . he may have a good point which the judge is going to take on board and you're going to go down – you then say 'Give us some money and we will settle this thing'.

Even if a settlement is not at the front of the barrister's mind, it is still often worth beginning the negotiation process. As one senior practitioner pointed out:

> It's nearly always worth speaking to your opponent with the bona fide intention of trying to find out . . . what is the genuine middle ground or with the less praiseworthy intention of finding out what his points are and preparing to answer them.

As was seen above, not every case is one that the barrister would necessarily be happy to see run all the way into court. The sort of evaluations of cases that are made routinely usher in a negotiation and settlement stage. It was described to us this way:

> You know there is a risk. You say to your people 'There is a small risk here. The case is worth £2000 to deal with it. To dispose of it you might consider making a payment of £250.' You go to the plaintiff and say 'Look there is a whole litany of problems with your case, it would probably fail but there is (in the time-honoured phrase at the bar) a "buy off" value. I'm prepared because I'm generous, because my altruistic tendencies have got the better of me, to offer you £250.' Very often they will go away.

Of course, it is not altruism at all that is at work but an on-going calculation of what is happening with the case, its chances of success and the value of risking a contest. This process uses a wide variety of sources of information. These sources are, of course, similar to those drawn upon at the earlier stage, but the information that is taken from them and the relative importance of each one is slightly different.

One of the most important pieces of information for the negotiation process relates to the opposition counsel. The personality, style and tactics of the opposing barrister can crucially affect the outcome of the negotiation and settlement stage. Clearly, any information that the barrister has about the opposing counsel is of great significance. As one barrister told us:

> I don't think any two barristers will approach negotiations in the same way . . . [there are] individual characteristics . . . you get people who relish confrontation . . . will use negotiation as a chance to, like in a boxing match, 'psyche' out the opponents. You get to know them.

Another said that:

> Like in any other business negotiation there is the hard tactic and the
> soft tactic. . . . There are people who don't like confrontation. It's all
> 'We can do business here' and we all go and have coffee afterwards and
> are great pals.

Alternatively, in the words of another advocate:

> . . . when I'm against certain people, let's say [X] who is probably the
> longest serving QC [in this area], I know he is going to be asking very,
> very large sums of money. I wouldn't say he ends up getting more but
> you don't mess him about. You don't come in with £5000 in a case that
> is worth £25 000. . . . I would always bear in mind who is on the other
> side, call it fear if you like but . . .

The personality of the barrister in question is certainly important. For
example, we were told that:

> There are those who are a soft, soft touch . . . if you're paying out
> money you can offer mickey mouse money and they will take it and
> persuade their client they've done all right . . . to an extent that's playing
> on their weaknesses but that's the game.

The ability and experience of the opposition is also of significance: 'If you're
up against some dummy who isn't really at the match you tend to go in with a
very small sum or ask for something substantially over the value.' In contrast, we were told that negotiation works best when there is:

> . . . somebody, on both sides, who is prepared to see the compro-
> mise. . . . The Senior Bar, through its experience, are able to see that –
> they can even compromise impliedly, without even being seen to do it
> or expressing it to each other. Sometimes at the junior bar there is a
> feeling that your case is always as set out in your instructions.

It is also significant to know the sort of tactics that a particular barrister
generally favours. Of course, such intelligence is difficult to ascertain. As one
advocate pointed out, 'It's all highly individual but there are some people
who are known to follow a certain strategy.' Indeed, several of the practitioners we spoke to made the point that they tried to mix tactics so as not to
become known for usually pursuing a particular gambit. However, in most
cases, the form of a particular barrister will out. For example, we were told
that 'some barristers are natural settlers . . . they don't ever see the inside of
the court'. Alternatively, 'You know those barristers who you are never
going to be able to talk to in any sensible way. You don't bother even trying
before you go in to court.'

Occasionally, barristers may fall into this latter category because of their
propensity to use sharp practices. Obviously in negotiation no-one expects
the parties to place all their cards on the table, but equally it is important to the
smooth running of the discussion that each side can be confident that the

opposition is not actively trying to mislead in any off-the-record conversation. We did hear of cases where problems arose:

> For instance, if you have a case where the plaintiff's credibility is in issue the defendant's barrister might well ask the plaintiff's barrister 'Well, have you any witnesses?' I have known cases where the plaintiff's barrister says 'Yes', which of course encourages the defendant to settle the case, and where subsequently, when the case doesn't settle, it turns out there aren't any witnesses.

While such tactics may give an (unfair) advantage if used sparingly, there are many drawbacks to their adoption as a game plan. Such factors will very soon enter into people's calculations about how they approach you. As one advocate told us:

> The penalty of playing dirty is that people get to know you play dirty . . . and accordingly they treat you more warily and this may make life more difficult.

Within the game as played straight there are a wide variety of tactics that can be adopted. Bluff and counter-bluff, systems and game plans are all laid out to be experimented with and to be guessed at by the other side. These are basically variations on whether and when an approach is made and how near to the final position are any preliminary offers. As we were told:

> The information isn't just about whether they are straight down the middle and wouldn't pull any stunts . . . but it may also be [whether] as a negotiator he is the sort of person who will make you a good offer and stick to it or will he make you a poorish offer and as every hour passes will increase it.

All of this information is relevant to the advocate; indeed, it is equally relevant, or perhaps even more so, than purely legal material in the orthodox sense. The tactical decisions made and to be made are the subject of much speculation by the other side. For example, we were told that:

> Although I take the view that it's always advantageous to try and get in contact with your opposite number before the case, the trouble with that is that a lot of them think it is because you are feeling very nervous. . . . You get some of them on the phone and immediately get the impression they're thinking 'I've got him here, he's nervous about his case getting to court'. That really annoys me.

There may be some rules that are more or less hard and fast. For example:

> Generally, the defendant should be approaching the plaintiff to see if they're prepared to take money to settle the case. If they don't approach you, generally it's an indication they don't want it settled. You wouldn't then approach them.

However, much is dictated by the plays made by individual counsel. One informant made the point:

> It is an interesting thing that at the bar there are a lot of gamblers . . . there is quite serious card playing going on for quite serious money. There are a lot of people who you would regard as really quite grey on the outside . . . they get a lot out of throwing big money into the pot and backing their judgement. I think that says something about them.

This approach as it translates to barristers' professional life certainly accords with much of what we observed and were told. It seems to us that barristers like to exert control over as much as they can and, having worked out a position, commit themselves to following the view they have taken. The material that they can control, the information that it is possible and practical to obtain, will generally be weighed in the equation that lies behind a decision about how to proceed. Much of this information comes from the experience of working with a range of barristers in the past. It was suggested to us that the library systems had an advantage in this regard, in so far as people were more likely to know each other and their particular ways of working. The information exchange there is larger and more active. As one Northern Ireland barrister explained:

> What barristers here tend to do is go to court in the morning; they consult in the late afternoon and maybe they would all be in [the bar library tearoom] at . . . 3.30 [p.m.] and there will be numerous stories in circulation about that day's activities – about what X did and Y did. There's an awful lot of information exchanged . . . much of it very useful.

Furthermore, we formed the impression that in all the library systems negotiations were facilitated simply by the fact that, working in the same building, people were more likely to encounter one another. Similar facilities for exchanging information and meeting the opposition exist to a degree in England and Wales, but it does generally seem more limited. For example, we heard the complaint that 'in London you have to positively make an effort to get in touch with someone and then it's only over the phone'.

However, to counter this, we did receive a fairly strong impression that in certain types of practice and at certain levels barristers did get to know each other and one another's form. It is a consequence of how the profession is organized and how work is obtained (see Chapter 2). This is particularly true at the higher levels of practice, where there are fewer practitioners working and a greater opportunity to know more about the individual players. As one senior barrister told us: 'There are plenty of barristers around, I don't know anywhere near all of them, but the guys who are really in there doing the cases daily are restricted in number – about fifty at most.' Even in London where the number of barristers in a particular field is larger than in the provinces, there is a tendency for certain sets of chambers to attract and retain a reputation for working in a particular area. The result is that, there too, a fairly limited number of practitioners are involved at particular levels of practice – albeit that this occurs only at the higher and more specialized levels than with smaller bars.

The restricted nature of any group regularly practising in particular courts, and working for particular solicitors, naturally leads to there being a community of professional interest. This undoubtedly affects how settlements take place. This is not because the barristers necessarily like each other or get on well: it is because they share a similar view of the realities of the legal process. For example:

> The people I'm working with, [those] ... with ten, twelve, fifteen years' experience, mostly know their way around the place, they know the value of cases, they know when they have a good case and they know when they have a 'bumeroo'. Simple as that: they know how to settle cases. They know my form and I know their form.

We also heard that, conversely,

> Inexperience can make it break down, people trying to score points – personal points can make it break down ... someone who doesn't know the weakness in their own case ... and so can trying to demonstrate something to their client or solicitor or if they have some personal animus to you or your client.

However, in the particular circumstances created by the nature and level of practice that any given community of barristers have in common, this is unlikely to happen. Indeed, this is why such niches exist. Of course, the relationships here do not operate necessarily to facilitate settlements to the detriment of clients: barristers do not settle because they are friends or out of fear of offending their peers. It is rather that, as one very senior counsel declared, in the right circumstances, 'the vast majority of cases, with reasonably competent barristers, who know the range of values of cases, who know what judges award, can sit down and knock the thing out'.

We found it significant that several barristers said that if someone from outside the usual circle were to be involved in a case, they would consider information about the opposition barrister to be something that they might well take steps to find out. For example, we were told by a fairly senior practitioner:

> I might even go to the extent, that if I were negotiating in an important case with someone who I don't know the form of, of ringing somebody up and saying 'Look X is on the other side, what sort of a guy is he to deal with?' See if I could pick up some information.

There are also a number of other factors concerning the barrister that may influence the negotiation process. In contrast to what has just been considered, these relate chiefly to the pressures of maintaining a practice. They are none the less relevant to barristers on both sides in the negotiating process.

If one looks in many courtrooms in the morning before the courts are in session, there will be a throng of barristers moving from one knot of people to another, consulting with solicitors and clients. Many of the latter group may think themselves to be the sole object of counsel's attention. Often, however, as we discussed in Chapter 2, there is a perception among the bar that it is a financial necessity to schedule more than one case for each day. This remains the situation, even though there are increasing pressures for financial stringency which mean that the settlement culture, especially in the county courts, is waning. However, even yet, the system itself can only operate on the basis that a high proportion of cases will settle. It is not uncommon for a judge to look through the list at say 11 a.m. and comment that it could do with a little more maturing as further settlements are worked out. Factors relating to this may well enter into the calculations about how to bargain. As one barrister described it:

> Most busy civil practitioners are overcommitted and that may come into how you handle the case, because if you have someone on the other side who is involved in two or three actions you know he is going to be anxious for practical reasons to settle cases and it's obviously important to know if that person has got himself covered.

However, knowing if someone is covered is not straightforward:

> Most seniors will work with juniors that are ready to cover them. A senior could have maybe five actions in one day. . . . If you see the same senior and junior down to do more than one case together and they're all running then you obviously are at an advantage.

From another perspective, if a barrister is overcommitted, this will inescapably enter into the way in which negotiation is conducted.

Most judges have themselves passed through the system: they will have been in the situation where they were overstretched, and will therefore to differing degrees be amenable to the idea of making accommodations. So will other barristers who may require reciprocity at a later date. However, there is still a fear of being overbooked. If this happens, it will require the calling in of favours from other counsel and using up the indulgence of the judge. With some judges and counsel this favour may be more freely granted than with others. To avoid problems, a barrister may well feel pressure to settle or, alternatively, feel able to take a stand. There must be, however, some doubt that considerations such as these can be used routinely as an offensive measure. Often the court is so busy that it is difficult to keep track of who exactly is doing what and is covered by whom. Also, as one seasoned veteran put it:

> . . . if you try to hold out on a poor case in the belief that your opponents are overcommitted elsewhere, they may suddenly settle their conflicting cases and be free to turn their full attention on you . . . your ropy old case then appears as what it is. The original settlement figure can seem

very tempting ... but heaven help you for not taking up the main chance.

Moving on to consider the influence of other personalities, one practitioner we spoke to made the point that 'Barristers can affect what goes on outside the court very strongly because there is no restraint upon them other than their clients.' It is certainly true that to a large extent in civil work (in contrast to criminal work as practised in some areas) the judge does not play an active role at the negotiation stage. However, the client – both lay client and solicitor client – may.

Most of the barristers that we spoke to took the view that their clients had committed themselves into the expert hands of the barrister. For example, one advocate told us:

> Mostly the client says 'I'll take whatever you think is reasonable'. Of course, that puts the onus on you. ... Sometimes they will say 'A thousand [pounds] will do: that's what it's worth'. ... Generally they are reasonable and are prepared to accept your advice ... you just have to tell them that you have got the experience and they haven't.

Of course, solicitors and repeat players in the justice game may not be so passive. As one practitioner complained: 'Insurance companies are often very difficult people to deal with ... very intransigent ... they have to be talked up ... the advocacy has to be exercised on them too.' Indeed, generally, the plaintiff has to be convinced that he or she is getting a good deal while the defendant must be persuaded that they got away fairly lightly. One senior barrister we spoke to laid down this basic guideline: 'You are a pessimist to your own client and an optimist to the other side and to the court.' Only if clients (and their solicitors) are handled properly is settlement possible. As the same barrister said: 'It's up to each side to speak to their client, their confidence must be gained, he must believe you know what you're talking about and if [the offer is] not enough you will go in and fight it.'

In many ways, this is how the whole process of settlement works. We were told that 'If you have intelligent counsel on both sides, cases can settle because they depress the expectations on both sides and that leaves a gap in the middle ... where the case can settle.' Of course, it is possible that a client will not behave as required. This is highly relevant information and will affect how a case is run. For example, one barrister we spoke to took the view that 'if you get a difficult [client], sometimes it's best to just run it.'

Although the judge does not play an active role in the negotiation that goes on outside court, he or she may still be a factor that needs to be taken into account. Moreover, in contrast to the position at the evaluation stage, it is more likely, especially in last-minute negotiations, that the identity of the judge will be known. This will affect how a barrister feels about holding out in any negotiation. We were told that, for example,

> ... if I have action against the Chief Constable and I have a judge who I know will be really unsympathetic, then obviously that influences your

readiness to settle the case . . . or if you've got a really good judge and
you're prepared to go ahead then you can afford to be more aggressive.

There is no doubt that this factor is of importance: the level of the award as
well as the outcome of the case may hinge on who hears it:

Judges get reputations . . . some are known to award very large sums:
some are known to be conservative and tight with money and low in
their awards . . . that is obviously a factor, *the* factor. Some people
won't settle a case until they know who the judge is and then either
come running to you for money or they're running into court saying
we got a great deal here and then it's you tripping over yourself to offer
them money.

While the negotiation process is operating, barristers on both sides deploy
a wide variety of tactics in an effort to be in the optimum position should a
settlement not arise. Settlements are possible at any stage and often damage
limitation exercises are undertaken when the strength of the opposition case
becomes apparent. For this reason, it is important to make a good show
especially at the start. For example, we were told of a case where a well-
known senior was deployed to harangue a jury in a defamation case for two
days and use his not inconsiderable reputation as someone who gets big
awards to instil fear into the opposition and provoke a settlement.

Given that, as Du Cann (1980: 53) remarks, 'Resort to law is a form of
civilised warfare', it would require a theoretician of war, a legal Clauswitz, to
describe what goes on here. It was a quite senior barrister who told us,
'There's not much law in most of them . . . [even] the facts don't raise many
problems but there is a considerable range of options over the tactics . . . this
is where the art lies.' These vary considerably in different local conditions and
in different types of practice, but knowledge about them is vitally important.
Such knowledge can be gained only through experience. As one older
barrister told us: 'it comes with experience. In the early days one is simply
trying to keep up with what is going on . . . after a time you think about
directing things, controlling what is going on.'

Barristers must think about tactics and how things will end up in court
from the very beginning. For example, we were told that many barristers
believe that there is an advantage in being able to open and close a case. This
right belongs to the plaintiff rather than the defendant. For this reason, it may
be worth advising someone who, for example, does not intend to pay the
balance on a debt, to get in first with a claim setting out reasons why the debt
should not be paid.

It is at this level that mastery of procedure is vital. As we saw in Chapter 4,
many barristers regard procedure as being as important as substantive law.
This is because they are able to control the information that is available to the
other side. Also, a knowledge of the correct forms is important not only to
avoid the elementary mistake of beginning a case in the wrong jurisdiction,
but to maximize the benefits to the client. For example, it is well-known that

although comparatively small claims should be commenced in the county courts it may be advantageous, particularly in London and if, for example, an urgent injunction is sought, to commence it in the High Court.

There are also tactics about changing the court in which the case is to be heard. For example, it may be worthwhile suggesting that a particular case is such that it is appropriate to remit to the county court where the awards are lower and the costs more moderate. Often this is a bona fide move and is accepted by both sides. However, it is possible to use this move to exert pressure on the other side. If a case is remitted to the county court, the High Court counsel will rarely follow it down. This is particularly true on the defence side where, as we discussed in Chapter 3, insurance companies operate a fairly rigid panel system restricting who acts for them and in which courts. Because of this, it may be worthwhile for a barrister, particularly a plaintiff barrister, setting up this situation. Then, as one counsel explained to us:

> . . . it may be worthwhile phoning a barrister a few days before the hearing is scheduled to ask if an accommodation can be made. If settlement is possible – often well below £5000 [the county court ceiling] – it is still an earner for the High Court barrister. If not the brief, and the [major] fee for it, is lost to him.

To succumb to such personal financial pressure might not be creditable but, seemingly, it is enough of a possibility for it to enter into the game plan of some opposition counsel.

Financial pressures on the parties to the case is of course one of the most potent factors and there are a wide variety of tactics that can be used to make sure that the client, irrespective of the outcome, 'wins on costs'. The issue of costs can be used very potently as a weapon, especially against those of limited means. There are various tactics available. An eye must be kept on all of these during the negotiation stage, especially when this takes place at a level more formal than the chat on the telephone or in the hall of the courts. At its most simple, this will involve an offer of settlement without prejudice as to the issue of costs. If this is not accepted and a trial is necessary, this offer cannot be referred to until a judgement has been delivered. However, the power of a letter of this kind comes when the judgement of the court matches the terms offered in the letter or is something less than it. Then the opposition can be asked to pay all of your costs from the date of that letter. Even a straightforward open letter offering terms for settlement can be useful. According to one experienced civil practitioner we spoke to:

> There is a tendency for solicitors, when things get rough, to revert to without prejudice correspondence . . . which means of course that it can never be referred to in court. . . . Very often I look through a file and see a letter that seems an eminently sensible way of resolving a dispute. . . . Then I see, in block capitals, those dreadful words 'Without Preju-

dice'. . . . I think if only that was written as an open letter, then we could really have been in a position to hammer the other side for costs.

The barrister must ensure that in any negotiations that he or she enters into, such matters are better ordered.

The negotiation stage, and all the plays that are involved in it, does not last for ever. As one barrister put it: 'Not every case can be settled . . . sometimes people come along and say telephone numbers – they say £50 000 where you say £10 000. You all fall out and have to go to court.'

We are crossing the threshold: after briefly reviewing the negotiation process in criminal practice we will go into the courtroom itself.

NEGOTIATING AND BARGAINING IN CRIMINAL CASES

Although many of the skills used are similar to those employed in civil practice, the position regarding bargaining is somewhat different in criminal practice. This is because, as we saw immediately above and in Chapter 4, the system operates in a slightly different way. Cases do not, of course, settle as such, but there is scope for considerable negotiation. This will be over the plea that is offered, the charge that will be brought and the sentence that will be imposed. The opposing barristers are again important here. The client too – either the accused or the prosecution authority – is significant to perhaps even a greater degree than in civil work. Also, there is the factor of the judge taking a more active role.

The facts of life in the criminal courts dictate that there is often room for negotiation. There are certainly some trials where the parties act on instructions and the jury or judge makes a straightforward determination of guilt. However, many cases – indeed the vast majority – involve a guilty plea. This does not mean that the barrister is then only a simple mouthpiece or merely a conduit to assist the court in processing criminals. As one practitioner stated:

> . . . some barristers will perhaps for a variety of reasons take the view that if they get paid the same for doing a plea as for doing a trial they will accept . . . the plea and go home by 11.00 o'clock in the morning. . . . But very often there are good reasons for doing this.

Indeed, there is generally much work behind many guilty pleas and barristers deploy their skills very actively – although in a different capacity to where there is a straightforward fight. As one barrister put it: 'Most criminals plead guilty at the end of the day – I don't know the figures but in my experience it must be about 95 percent. Damage limitation is your role then.'

In performing this damage limitation role, there are considerable questions of tactics and in resolving these barristers must deploy various skills and draw upon information from a variety of sources. As we know from much socio-legal work (see Baldwin and McConville, 1981), a great deal of what is done here is not purely legal in the sense of academic law. We were told that 'There are very few cases that run as serious contests. . . . Cases can run really for the purposes of working out a better deal on a plea more than anything else.' At any stage up to the opening of a case, there is scope for deals to be done and for damage to be limited. This operates on both the prosecution side, where cases that are weak in respect of a higher charge can be resolved by getting a guilty plea to a lower charge, and on the defence side where the sentence can be reduced from what it might be if the higher charge were unsuccessfully contested. One experienced barrister told us:

> An enormous amount of your work is done before you go into court at all . . . the court is really the culmination of whatever negotiations you have been able to engage in with the prosecuting counsel. . . . [The] court is the public show of a fairly long process that has gone on before you walk in.

The relationship between prosecution counsel and the defence is of critical significance. There is a great deal of room for manoeuvre on both sides. However, unlike in civil cases, this does not take place for purely partisan reasons. A commonly held view was that 'On the criminal side, there is not the same scope for being devious . . . it's more of a straight fight.' Tactics such as we reviewed above involving taking advantage of advocates who may be overcommitted or anxious to hold onto brief fees do not, we found, take place. The interests of the justice system and of the defendant seem pretty well protected from the more overt sorts of gamesmanship.

Having said that, there remains ample opportunity for negotiation using a whole set of extra-legal skills and information. It was explained to us in this way:

> In this country, strictly speaking, plea bargaining does not exist. It is a phrase . . . you should never use – certainly [not] on your feet in open court. . . . In practice, of course, very often if . . . [for example] someone is charged with wounding with intent with an alternative (as there has to be in the indictment) of unlawful wounding without the intent – life imprisonment as against five years – very often the defence will come to you and say will you accept a plea to section 20? And you then have to make a value judgement, subject to, theoretically, getting instructions from the CPS, as to whether the plea is acceptable or not.

Both the defence side and the prosecution will use the evaluation of the case that we discussed earlier to inform the making of the suggestion and the response to it. Thus to a bare assessment of the strength of the case is added factors relating to the identity of the judge, the skill of the opposition, the force of the evidence and witnesses, etc.

Also, at the time the offer is actually made, the personalities of the barristers involved can make a difference. There are some on the defence side who will, depending on the facts, be readier than others to make an approach. For example, one experienced defence barrister declared:

> If I'm charged with GBH with intent [grievous bodily harm with intent to endanger life] . . . on the morning of the case, obviously I will say to

the prosecuting counsel, 'I'll not plead to that, I'll plead to the lesser one. Go and see if you can get it dropped for me'. . . . I would usually have a go.

Similarly, different Crown counsel may take different positions: it is important to know this. For example, one prosecutor told us:

I have no hard and fast rules but if someone has used, for example, a hammer or a knife or a glass then unless the circumstances are quite exceptional . . . as far as I'm concerned that is wounding with intent.

The view taken by the prosecuting authority is also important, as is the ability of the prosecutor to persuade them of the rightness or otherwise of accepting a plea to the lesser charge. There is another evaluation and negotiation process that takes place here. As one very experienced barrister explained it:

I'm the prosecutor, I have no axe to grind . . . I go to the Director [of Public Prosecutions] and say 'I have a plea to a lesser charge, is it acceptable?' He will say, 'What do you think? How do we stand with regard to . . . the higher charge?' . . . And we basically work it out between us. . . . We are still doing our duty . . . the penalty for armed robbery as opposed to attempted manslaughter is still pretty stiff.

There is no doubt that, as in civil practice, barristers at particular levels of practice know each other fairly well and can often bring such information to bear on their work. For example, we were told:

In the rather confined atmosphere and precincts of this building [the Criminal courthouse on the Crumlin Road in Belfast] 80 percent of the people here today were here yesterday and the day before . . . it's a very tightly confined atmosphere. . . . On the Crown side there are three senior counsel and two juniors who do exclusively prosecution work in this building.

While other prosecuting counsel may be brought in from time to time, they will be selected from a panel. Defence barristers similarly will be drawn from an only slightly larger pool of barristers who are regularly briefed by solicitors with large criminal practices. The position is similar in other areas and in other jurisdictions, and even in London many regulars in the criminal courts will know one another. This knowledge of other barristers is important. As one advocate said:

Depending on who it is I'll express it in stronger or weaker terms. Certain counsel you know will . . . crumble a little earlier if they don't want to run a fight, whereas I know with others I have to call their bluff right up to swearing a jury in and starting a whole trial.

While factors relating to the personality of the Crown barrister are not wholly determining, they are undoubtedly important. Another barrister remarked that the identity and personality of the prosecutor matters

only to the extent of gamesmanship. You know in certain instances
how far you can go – you know 'old soldiering' your opponent,
bluffing, psyching. You can do a lot for your case in the robing room if
you know how to go about it. . . . I'm a bit too professional to go about
it full time . . . [but] certain barristers will.

The case can be radically affected as a result of this interaction and the judge
will not be involved generally. We were told:

This conversation takes place in the robing room. They go into court
and use the form of words 'This plea is acceptable'. If they use this form
it doesn't matter . . . if the judge agrees or not. But if they say 'This plea
is acceptable, subject to your Honour's approval', they are inviting him
into the decision-making process.

There are, however, another set of negotiations where the judge has an
important role to play. This is in contrast to the position in civil practice. As
one practitioner put it: 'If a civil case is going to be settled it will be between
the parties: it just doesn't happen that the judge gets involved. In criminal
cases it happens all the time.' In several of the jurisdictions and in several of
the areas that we visited, it was commonplace for counsel to visit the judge's
chambers before a case was heard to discuss what was to follow. The idea is
that counsel can get an indication of the likely outcome in sentencing terms if
a particular defendant were to plead guilty. As one barrister described it,
what may happen is that:

The judge will think about the sentence. You go and see the judge
and see what his attitude is and, if you get a favourable indication,
then you can plead your client quite happily knowing what the outcome will be.

Such indications, although informal, are dependable. We were told that 'it's
never been known for a judge to go back on what he has indicated – as long as
things are as you say'.
What happens here is a complex process. As one barrister pointed out,
'You can't go into the judge and say "What's he going to get?", because he
would have to see his record and of course he can't see the record if he's going
to hear the case.' It is more subtle than that. We were told that 'There is a
confidentiality between the judge in chambers and a barrister. It hasn't
happened until it happens. You get an indication maybe but no promises.'
However, this indication is often enough to enable a barrister to advise his or
her client to plead guilty. Alternatively, it may help a barrister to decide
whether or not to fight a case.
Knowing which judges to approach and how to interpret their signals is a
difficult skill to master which depends on using personal knowledge about
particular conditions. We were informed that:

... plea bargaining is an art and it's all down to experience as well ...
some judges you go into easy enough, some judges are delighted to give
you an indication. You have to know by reputation, what you've
heard.

You also have to be able to pick up signals and react accordingly. For
example, we were told that:

'Most judges will say to you 'Don't go any further. This is a very
serious offence and I am thinking of a custodial sentence very seriously
and anything that can be said for him should be said in open court'. ...
they quite often say that to you.

It was interesting that in several of the local bars that we visited, this
practice did not go on and that, further, it was frowned upon as being in some
way less than ideal. Indeed, in one area, we were told how a case had been
appealed from the local courts and how this had resulted in the appeal judges
admonishing both the local bar and bench. There, we were told: 'We're not
allowed to do it ... in 95 percent of cases in front of the vast majority of
judges it is true ... there are still one or two who call you in for a chat ... but
only a few.' In contrast, in the areas where the practice was commonplace,
there was surprise expressed when we relayed the situation elsewhere.
Indeed, one senior barrister declared that without this practice 'the criminal
courts could not process as many cases as they do or as quickly'.

However, the lack of an informal mechanism did not seem to make all that
much difference. The existence of what we described earlier as a professional
community of common interest, has the effect that very similar results are
achieved without following exactly the same procedures:

With a judge who you appear in front of regularly you get used to the
way his mind works and the sort of tariffs ... so I can say to the lad who
is on a Section 20 wounding and who is stupidly in my view ...
pleading not guilty when the evidence is overwhelming, I can say to
him, hand on my heart, 'If you plead guilty on your first occasion in
front of Judge ... [X] ... you won't go down'. ... I know, as if I had had
the message whispered in my ear, that that will happen.

Of course, the question remains as to whether generally this informal
process takes over from what happens in the public court. As we will discuss
more fully in the next chapter, there is still a need for barristers, if necessary,
to back up in court all that has been said about the facts surrounding a
defendant and his or her character.

Finally, even when a barrister has negotiated on behalf of his or her client,
there may still be a need to exercise skills of persuasion. As with settlements
in civil practice, the system can work only if the client is reasonably happy
about what has been secured on his or her behalf. As in civil practice, this
often involves depressing expectations. We were told that:

You always give the client the worst prognosis ... there is not a
barrister at the criminal bar who has not learned that lesson by under

estimating what the client would get and then getting the shock of his life . . .

There may be a great deal of persuasion required in talking to the client. As one barrister explained:

Very often you get the client wheeled in . . . at 10.00 o'clock on the day of your trial . . . I advise people as to the chances of their success and, I confess, like probably most conscientious and competent barristers, I put as much pressure upon a person as I fairly can. And I sleep easy at night. I have no hesitation doing that.

Indeed, all the barristers we spoke to were vehement that what they did was in their clients' interests and with their consent. For example, we were told that:

Baldwin and McConville brought out the unsavoury side of it, being forced to plead guilty to facilitate counsel . . . you need to be careful . . . you must make it clear that there is a decision of your [the defendant's] own, you need to make sure the solicitor is there beside you.

Although such persuasion of clients takes place, the barristers we spoke to were anxious to stress that this was not for the convenience of the bar. As one put it, 'we don't make them plead guilty so as to be out on the golf course as near to 11.00 o'clock as possible'. Indeed, the most convincing refutation of such an idea came from the counsel who remarked:

Barristers live by their reputation and work by their reputation and you don't get a reputation running bum cases . . . therefore the defence has less interest in putting weight on people to plead guilty if they think they've got a good case . . . counsel want to win cases and be seen to win cases and also if a case runs . . . you [may] get more money.

All of these factors – both in civil and criminal practice – and indeed all the various roles that the barrister must play, are important at this crucial stage. If we understand this, then we can begin to move yet further away from the model of the barrister operating in an asocial way in the courts only and using only purely legal skills and orthodox legal information.

6

RUNNING A CASE IN COURT

If and when a case comes to be argued in court, it is at the end of a much longer and more complex process. The information that comprises the case will have been selected and negotiated, the issues will have been isolated and refined and the outcome will have been predicted and calculated. All this takes place as a complex and social interaction set against a background dictated by the struggle of trying to maintain a living in a particular professional milieu.

Indeed, much of what we have said so far is intended as a corrective to the view that a barrister's performance in court is of paramount significance. A barrister's eloquence, forensic skills and ability to display a mastery of arcane legal knowledge in the courtroom is not the most important aspect of his or her role. In his entertaining and practical *Advocacy: A Beginner's Guide*, Evans (1985: 132) repeats some received wisdom about the importance of advocacy:

> It is said that most cases win or lose themselves. The old (and exaggerated) adage goes that ninety per cent of cases are unaffected by advocacy. Five per cent are lost by bad advocacy, three per cent are won by good advocacy and two per cent are totally wild.

Allowing that advocacy here refers to performance in court rather than the much wider view of advocacy that we take, this suggests that the usual emphasis on what an advocate does in the courtroom is misplaced. We would endorse this rebalancing of the importance of actual courtroom performance, so long as it does not suggest that advocacy in the wider sense of the matters that we have discussed so far is in any way peripheral. We were told many times by the barristers who we interviewed that actually running a case in court was fairly straightforward once the evaluation and tactical decisions discussed earlier have been made. Even before that there are, as we saw in earlier chapters, issues relating to the role of the barrister, and in particular his or her relationship with the solicitor, which exert an influence on what occurs in the courtroom. Not least among these influences is the sort of information that a barrister receives in the brief which constrains him or her within certain limitations (see Chapter 4). Much of the information relating to the particular case that the barrister has is mediated by the solicitor through the brief in accordance with professional roles and relationships. However, as we have stressed before, this does not mean that the barrister is merely a mouthpiece possessing the correct rights of audience. As one barrister put it: 'The solicitor may give you all the building blocks and the stuff to put them together, but it's up to you to make something of it when you get into court.'

In making something of a brief, in making it into an adequate claim or useful exercise in damage limitation that will work in court, barristers bring together much of what they have had done earlier. As we have pointed out, the prospect of ending up in court orientates much of what has already been done to the brief. Thus factors whose influence we have seen already in other, earlier contexts will be of importance here too. Not only is there the importance of the case itself, with its issues of law and fact as presented in the brief, but there are factors relating to the opposition, to the witnesses and, above all, to the judge. In addition, there may be a jury and this requires special handling. These are all significant in terms of what goes on in the courtroom and the successful advocate will understand the relative importance of controlling these factors as compared to the deployment of forensic skills or eloquence.

COUNSEL

Turning first to the issue of the opposition counsel, it can be seen that although it is at the negotiation stage where this factor reaches maximum importance, it can still be of significance in the courtroom. We have referred already to a tendency that we noted generally for barristers working at a particular level to know one another and for this to facilitate informal negotiation. Indeed, we have mentioned how there is a tendency for communities of professional interest to form. These are based on shared expertise and experience and perhaps even a feeling that the law should be implemented to give solutions rather than technical 'wins'. We first noticed this in various family courts and in Belfast's criminal courts. There the relatively small numbers of regular players resulted in the development of informal working practices designed to facilitate the efficient working of the system and to assist those caught up in the legal process. The existence of such localized communities of professional interest with their (often sharply contrasting) informal practices relating to, for example, plea bargaining, talking to judges in chambers or dampening down client expectations, has an effect in the courtroom also. Certain accommodations and arrangements over matters such as avoiding clashes in timing are of course made, but there are more substantive effects. The professional identity, as interpreted by specific local conditions and traditions, may lead to the development of mutually beneficial working practices and to a certain relaxation in formalities, especially if the judge is prepared to countenance them.

For example, this is especially true in relation to organizing on what issues the contest will focus. As we have stressed throughout, facts and legal information are not immutable. Cases do not come 'court-ready' with the points to be decided clearly marked out. They are real-life disputes and the legal issues are extrapolated from often very complex and involved situations. The relations between counsel, even if they do not know each other, are important in settling where exactly the conflict lies. In any argument, even outside the legal world, the disputants must *agree* about more than they *disagree* about: they must agree about the basic terms on which the sides meet and interact. In the legal context, and in court in particular, there are a host of informal mechanisms and shared understandings which make practical and workable the bare rules of procedure and evidence. For example, we were told that:

> . . . the signals that are given between barristers . . . are very important to the way litigation is conducted. . . . What you refrain from doing, as much as what you actually do, is often a clear signal.

The process of gathering evidence and cross-examination in a case places an obligation on, for example, a defence lawyer to always put an aspect of the defendant's case to the witness. The idea of 'putting' something has a technical meaning where strictly speaking it means that counsel intend to call a witness to prove what is being put. Alternatively, a point may be merely 'suggested' and in that situation there may not be any proof available but a reaction from the witness is sought. If something is not put, it is usually taken to amount to a concession on a point. However, because of defence counsel's obligation to put things to witnesses called on the other side, it is very important to know, or at least to have an idea about, how the case is going to unfold, so that the barrister can efficiently organize how and to whom matters are going to be put. (There is not much point in putting a whole series of conflicts to a witness who is secondary if a more primary witness is going to be called.) It is for this reason that barristers will, with various degrees of formality, make concessions and accommodations with one another in order to structure the case efficiently. These informal signals and processes do not only have the effect of making their working lives easier but, indeed, allow the points at issue in a case to become clear and facilitate the adjudication process. The importance of the activities of barristers at this level should not be overlooked. As one advocate remarked: 'there is nothing worse than being against someone who feels that they have to take every bad point . . . [and] obstruct all along the way'. Indeed, sometimes (although rarely apparently) a barrister will deliberately manipulate this process. The reaction to such a tactic perhaps indicates how important the normal process is:

> Sometimes in the course of a case you get . . . a problem where you say to the other barrister 'Are you calling X?' and he says 'Yes'. You

modify your process of cross-examination of another witness because
you have been told that X is being called. Then he doesn't call him . . .
you get bloody annoyed if that happens . . . and you make sure everybody knows what he has been up to.

Even beyond the process of information gathering and exchange there is a
role for counsel on each side to help along the litigation or trial process.
Agreement over not only what the issues are but how they should be viewed
is important. Merely because barristers accept common ground in a case does
not mean that they are neglecting the interests of their case. It is rather that
poor arguments or spurious ones are not useful to a case. Also, barristers in
regular practice are able to benefit from appearing reasonable. As one put it,
'If you have a bad point and you concede it it is helpful. You've lost nothing
and maybe next time if you say "I have a good point" you'll be believed.'
There is no doubt that the regular performers in particular courts develop
working practices that benefit and facilitate how they perform their roles. As
one experienced barrister described it:

> . . . in all cases there will be times when you can make life difficult as
> opposed to making it easier. Between two barristers that get on with
> each other it is quite noticeable in the running of the case that things can
> be done without rancour . . . and simply . . . appropriate concessions
> can be made with ease and things move along pleasantly and
> quickly. . . . If there is a clash of personalities . . . things can get very
> sticky indeed . . .

It is mainly in these sorts of ways that the opposition barrister is important
at the court stage. The expertise or personality of a particular counsel is
perhaps of less significance here than at the earlier stages. For example, we
were told that 'generally you meet people at the same level of experience or
the cases are such that experience doesn't make that much difference – after a
certain level'.

Having said this, however, there is scope for the really good barrister to
make a difference in a case. A question which we explored with many of our
interviewees was whether it was worth paying the additional cost for a really
top barrister as opposed to one with merely a good reputation. Almost
without exception all of the informants took the view that the additional
expenditure was justified. As one said:

> . . . if a relative of mine were seriously injured, whatever you pay the
> top man is worth it . . . the top man can make a difference of maybe
> £20 000 to £30 000 . . . the brief fee weighed against that isn't much.

Interestingly, when expressed in this way, most barristers were fairly clear
what they would be paying for:

> . . . on the whole, you have to say yes, it's worth it, if you want a case
> well done you have to pay the top practitioners . . . they bring in their
> experience, their knowledge of the system . . . yes their legal skills but

also their knowledge of the judge (the top QCs would know all the judges). . . . [They know] all the little things that can be of assistance in a variety of ways . . . you're paying for all this when you bring in the top man . . . basically they know their way around, they know how to make things happen.

Of course, much of this expertise is deployed in the stages before a case actually gets to court. However, even in the courtroom, an appreciation of the sorts of abilities discussed in this chapter that a very experienced barrister may have can make a difference.

WITNESSES

By the time a case comes to court, the barrister should have evaluated the witnesses. The task now for either side in making out the case or outlining a mitigation, is to deploy these witnesses in the most effective possible manner. This will involve highlighting the good witnesses on one's own side and protecting the poor witnesses, while at the same time attacking the weaker witnesses on the other side and limiting the damage of their stronger ones. One barrister even suggested that 'good advocacy is knowing the right witnesses to call and getting them to say the right thing'.

Control of all aspects of a case – even over something as relatively unpredictable as witnesses – is what many advocates aim for. This theme of control was one that we frequently found. It was expressed most graphically by the practitioner who claimed that:

The barrister is like a stage manager or director. . . . He decides which things to highlight, the level of lighting on the actors and witnesses, which actors to spotlight, which aspects to play down, almost what words to put into their mouths . . . you are directing the performance.

Even in criminal cases where a guilty plea has been entered, it is still important to make the most of witnesses. As one barrister explained it, when a person pleads guilty,

. . . what's really on your mind then is the sentence – what is the best result for this guy? If he has a bad record, then it's unlikely that a probation report or a community service report will be any good . . . you know he is going to get a custodial sentence, so maybe you aim to get it suspended. Then this is your target. . . . [But] if he is a first offender you get all the reports you can.

Whatever target is being aimed for, any relevant witnesses must be displayed to good effect. As one barrister saw it: 'You must bring out [the best aspects of the defendant's case] with investigating policemen, the probation service, the psychiatrist (if you have one) and various other character witnesses.'

All the time the barrister is attempting to limit the damage to his or her client by persuading those involved to emphasize any positive aspects of the defendant's behaviour. This process must be gone through even if the guilty plea has come about as a result of conversations in the judge's chambers about the likely sentence that would reward a saving of the court's time in hearing a contest. As one barrister said, 'You can't go into court on the basis of what has been said in chambers and do it all on a nod and a wink.' The judge must be convinced that the information provided in the earlier conversation and on which the judicial indication was based is true. We were told:

> You have to justify what you said [before] in open court. If you've said the police are satisfied that this individual has been put upon in these circumstances, it's an isolated act on his part, he's not known to the police, it's out of character . . . then you have to draw all this out in open court. You have to call the policeman . . . get testimonials from respectable persons in the community. . . . You have to draw out the important points. Unless the judge indicates that he doesn't need to hear it . . . you're there to make the case.

In the context of a contested case, either in civil or in criminal practice, the position about witnesses is more complicated. In such a case, controlling and evaluating witnesses is an on-going process: a good courtroom technique involves flexibility about revising earlier evaluations. As one practitioner put it:

> You know how your case is going and if a witness isn't strong you pull him out. . . . If I had a witness who was not credible I would try not to use him at all – even if he were giving the same evidence as everybody else.

Decisions about who to call and who to leave out are made on the basis of a whole variety of criteria. There is the structure of the case as negotiated with the opposition in the way we discussed above, the question of how a particular witness will commend himself or herself to a particular judge, the apparent strength of the opposition case, etc. Of course, sometimes other factors overrule a desire to omit a particular witness. The client, particularly in criminal cases, but in civil cases also, may want a day in court and the chance to put his or her side of things. Although the barrister may aim for complete control over the case, this is not possible.

Given that weak witnesses must on occasion be used, barristers are concerned to protect them as much as possible. There are differences in the formal etiquette about speaking with witnesses before the trial among the jurisdictions we visited. However, we found that notwithstanding any formalities proscribing the practice, it was commonplace for barristers to take witnesses through their testimony. For example, one barrister told us: 'If I have a witness I am worried about I would take him through his evidence in some detail . . . I would try to get him "match fit" or maybe even pumped up a bit, ready to perform.' Of course, this can be overdone. As one barrister pointed out:

If it's too perfect it sounds contrived. . . . The judge may even say 'This case has certain inconsistencies in it but in my view this is a badge of authenticity: if it were too perfect I would suspect it to be tutored and contrived'.

Maurice Healy, in his account of *The Old Munster Circuit*, tells the story of a case brought under the Sale of Goods Act against a shop which, it was alleged, had sold crab meat and warranted it to be fit for human consumption. He recounts how the lady companion to the plaintiff gave her evidence, saying:

> . . . I know that Russell's had cooked crabs; so I went in there, and asked the shopman for a nice cooked crab, telling him I wanted it for Mrs Wallace's supper, so as to make known to him the purpose for which it was to be used . . . he looked at the crabs, and he selected one and gave it to me. So I, relying on his skill and judgement, took it . . . (Healy, 1939: 199–200).

The story of course is dependent on the unlikeliness of the plaintiff's friend being in command of the relevant legal language.

In a contested case, these decisions about deploying and protecting one's own witnesses have to be considered alongside matters relating to the opposition witnesses. Barristers will be looking not only to protect their own case from strong witnesses but to attack any weak ones. There is no doubt that there is a role for the barrister's forensic skill in cross-examination. As one counsel pointed out, 'no-one has 100 percent recollection, so you can twist it and play on it'. Another expressed the view that:

> . . . good barristers can make honest witnesses seem liars . . . if you're dealing with a person who is very nervous and not very intelligent and you're a good cross-examiner you should be able to make quite a bit of ground.

Of course, the circumstances must be right for this to happen. It is not the barrister's skill *per se* that produces results from cross-examination, but the barrister's ability to deploy that skill in favourable circumstances. As one barrister pointed out:

> You have to have a case . . . you don't just go in and have a rattle at a witness for the sake of it. . . . There is no point in cross-examining him and getting him to say the car was going at twenty [miles per hour] rather than fifty . . . if your driver comes in and admits he was going at fifty . . . the judge would go through you.

There are a number of factors which must come together to enable even a good cross-examination to be useful. In particular, the witness must seem fragile and this view must be shared by the judge or communicated to him or her. For example, as one barrister told us: 'Plaintiffs will not concede points that they should and you can make a judge feel unhappy about them. . . . You need the judge's assistance or indulgence – he must think they are dodgy.'

In thinking about whether or not to pursue a point in cross-examination, the barrister must remember that, as one advocate put it, 'a judge is in a difficult position . . . if a person gets the story reasonably right . . . there is often no evidence to directly contradict what someone says'. Given this, it is the role of the advocate to communicate to the judge within the first few questions a feeling of uncertainty about a particular witness. As one barrister described it:

> You signal this doubt to the judge. . . . You are trying to give the judge an insight into someone. Maybe the whole case depends on one witness. . . . You make evaluations that in ordinary life would take years . . . and you [have to] act on them.

Although such matters are the subject of academic and practitioner writing on the subject of 'credibility', in practice it is often regarded as yet another instance of barristerial and judicial instinct. It is important that this instinct be shared, as cross-examination will generally be permitted by the judge only when it seems likely to bear fruit and if it does not the barrister will not enhance his or her reputation. We were told that:

> . . . credibility fights are tricky. . . . As a barrister you can die a terrible death doing that sort of case, although you can look good . . . usually you only get about ten minutes to have a go and you need a judge who will indulge you.

If the barrister is given the opportunity to pursue a credibility fight, it is then that forensic skills can be important. There is undoubtedly a technique to be mastered in order to cross-examine properly. One senior criminal barrister maintained a fairly low view of how the art was practised by some of his colleagues:

> Some of the prosecutors that I now defend against are pathetic . . . they don't prepare the case, they haven't got the wit . . . their cross-examination goes along the lines of 'I suggest to you that you did this'. 'No I didn't'. It's like a pantomime. 'Oh yes you did'. 'Oh no I didn't'. That's not the way to do it.

However, it is not cleverness in the style of the advocate in literature or on television or film that is necessarily required. An ability to ask a devastating question is not always as likely to be productive as other skills. One barrister saw the job in more mundane terms: 'you must chip away, building up the detail and not allow yourself to be deflected'. Mastery of all the routine detail in the brief is essential. Information relating to the system generally is also important. For example, we were told that:

> In cross-examining policemen [the most effective barristers] will know what sort of forms they record things on, how they use them, when they get them, etc., etc. . . . they use all this – maybe to show how a previous statement is inconsistent . . . or to set up a suspicion that a witness is unreliable.

We were offered many 'golden rules' for the effective examination and cross-examination of witnesses. For example, a major issue seems to be about how far to push and when to withdraw in a line of questioning. We were told that 'with experts you can concede lots. . . . As long as you can hold on to what you need the periphery can go.' Although it is sometimes necessary to pursue something unrelentingly, there are hazards: 'witnesses may get stronger as you press them . . . 'Is that the man?' 'Yes'. 'Are you sure?' 'Yes, I am certain'. You can easily make things worse.'

An important rule, and one which is stressed in the textbooks, (see, e.g. Evans, 1985: ch. 12; M. Stone, 1988: 80–86), is not to ask one question too many or a question to which the barrister does not know the answer. As one informant put it: 'You don't say to the store detective "Why did you keep an eye on him?" You'll certainly get the answer "Because I saw him shop-lifting before!".' Such advice reinforces the idea that the barrister's job is to try to exert as much control as possible over what is given up to the court. It is the barrister's role to know what is going on and if there are any surprises to be sprung they should, if possible, be directed from barrister to witness. As one barrister advised:

> . . . try to approach the defendant from a totally unexpected angle and if you can get in to him or her with two or three or even seven questions you can sometimes rip their case wide open – even in a simple straight-forward 'I wasn't there' case.

This element of the unexpected does seem important. Indeed, many of the classic accounts of advocacy respectfully reproduce transcripts of the finest moments in the careers of such luminaries as Marshall Hall, Rufus Issac, Edward Clarke etc. (for example, Birkenhead, 1926; Birkett, 1961; Massery, 1978; Hyam, 1990). These regularly show the deployment of the surprise question. There is Carson's sudden question 'Did you ever kiss him?' in the Oscar Wilde case, which provoked Wilde's indiscreet reply that 'He was unfortunately very ugly' (see Marjoribanks, 1932: 225). Also, there is the time when Birkett unnerved the expert engineer by inquiring 'What is the coefficient of the expansion of brass?' and received the answer 'I don't know', which then allowed Birkett to ask 'You *are* an engineer?', getting the weak reply 'I suppose so' (Evans, 1985: 162).

These and many other examples of cleverness, along with references to the art as described in ancient times by Quintilian, represent within the textbook view, the ideal of advocacy. Our impression is that such techniques may be significant on occasion, but only within a very limited range of cases. In the same way as we argue that advocacy is wider than courtroom performance, so we maintain that courtroom performance is more than the clever question. According to one barrister:

> It's the answers you get that are important . . . juries don't acquit because you're a clever cross-examiner . . . it's what you get out of them, what you can say at the end. . .'. You heard the witness say that he wasn't so sure now.

This is not a how-to-do-it book about courtroom technique, but it is perhaps worth including just one of the many examples we came across in order to demonstrate the sorts of techniques that the barrister must use.

A barrister described how he had acted in a case where two men were charged with attempted robbery. The victim had been drinking with them and had been beaten up and the two were arrested by a passing police patrol. Medical examination confirmed that he had indeed been badly beaten up, and he had sustained concussion and multiple injuries. He now claimed that in the assault the men had jumped on his hands and attempted to steal his rings. The two men interviewed separately had both admitted assault, but denied the serious charge of attempted robbery. As witnesses they could do little to assist their case beyond simply denying the charge. The barrister recognized that his cross-examination of the examining doctor would be crucial. It would not be useful to ask him about injuries to different parts of the body. Although injury to the victim's hands was not mentioned, it would not be wise to conclude by saying 'I see there was no bruising to the hands'. The doctor might say 'Well in fact there was but I omitted to put it in my report'. The barrister, therefore, adopted a different approach and got the doctor to admit that the first thing he did was to ask what had happened so that he would know what to look for in his examination:

> The thing to do is to go through everything that he did examine . . . get the doctor to say that the reason why he did that examination was because [the patient] complained about being hurt in those areas. You then leave the rest to comment upon to the jury. . . . You say to the jury. . . . 'You heard the doctor, the doctor asked him what was wrong with him. Now he told you that these guys were jumping on his hands and trying to get his rings off . . . yet he goes to the hospital and never mentions it, never mentions his hands to the doctor, not only does he never mention his hands but the doctor gives him a thorough examination and the Crown has produced no evidence that there are any bruises on this man's hands'.

When it comes to cross-examining the injured party:

> It is the simplest thing in the world. . . . You just say 'He was jumping on your hands?' 'Yes'. 'Were your hands not sore?' 'Yes'. 'Why did you not mention this to the doctor?' . . . You just wouldn't be able to explain that . . . and of course once you have you don't let him go . . . you keep at him.

Although it may be more prosaic than the examples provided in the classic textbooks of advocacy, this illustration provides for us a fuller explanation of much of what is important about the barrister handling witnesses in court. It shows the element of control that must be exerted whereby the witness is not encouraged to develop his or her testimony; it shows an awareness of how to relate the outside world to the legal forms and procedures; it demonstrates how the barrister must always orientate what he or she does around how it will look in court and how the elements of the story must be shown to the court. In short, it shows how the barrister must know his or her way about and be able to deliver what works in a particular context.

THE JUDGE AND JURY

We have already noted the significance of the judge as a factor at the earlier stages on the way to the courtroom. At the point where a hearing takes place, the importance of the judge and the impact that he or she can make reaches a high point. As one barrister saw it: 'I would think about the case but I would think about the judge just as much.' There is no doubt that the character and approach of the particular judge in any case is highly significant: it is the judge who controls almost every aspect of how the case is run in the court. We were told that 'the client's fortunes lie very heavily with the personality of the judge.' If, as we suggested earlier (see p. 44), the legal profession has similarities to the public school, where senior counsel are prefects or members of the First XV, then judges have at least the status of a headmaster. Indeed, one advocate who is by no means young or impressionable, declared simply 'Judges are gods'.

It is certainly true that most barristers do not underestimate the influence of judges. For example, one senior practitioner with a mainly criminal practice said:

> ... the approach varies very much from judge to judge ... if you're talking about law proceeding on a fairly logical basis ... law ... proceeds on an entirely pragmatic basis which is related to people's personalities ... and especially to the personality of judges ... everything depends on who the judge is and when the judge is going to sit – that sort of thing.

Of course, there may be a jury which, in certain cases – ordinary criminal trials and defamation actions – will be entrusted with making the adjudication. In such cases, the power of the judge is slightly diminished. Nearly all the barristers who we spoke to reported that the presence of a jury made the outcome much less certain. As one recalled:

> ... where you have a jury, that introduces a completely new dimension to a case ... I remember a murder case ... the prosecution knew it was cut and dried and made a very short speech ... he concluded, I'll always remember, 'Members of the Jury, if you believe that, you'll believe anything'. And they did.

Notwithstanding the role that can be played by the jury the judge retains a position of central significance. It is the judge who controls the flow of information and who can filter what the jury get to hear. Given the importance that barristers, in both civil and criminal work, attach to judges – even where they are acting with a jury – it is important to understand how exactly the personality of the judge and the role that he or she chooses to play will influence what occurs in the courtroom.

One important way in which the judge can make an impact is by directly controlling what happens in the courtroom. Although technically it is not the role of a judge to descend into the arena, it seems that it occurs frequently. As one interviewee commented: 'The judge is in no way an umpire, he takes a line.' In taking a line and making that line known, the judge is setting the targets and objective of the case. We were told:

> Even if there is a jury, judges are a major influence on cases . . . they ask a lot of questions, they are no longer an umpire . . . that is nonsense . . . the judge will take his own line in the case . . . he is the man that the parties have to please.

Quite frequently, the judge will do more than simply indicate what he or she thinks to be the matter of the case. Judges may actively get involved with the parties to a case. In that case, even with a jury, the judge's influence on a case is strong. For example, one barrister told us:

> I have seen judges so many times make out the case for a party who has failed to do so simply because he feels inclined to do so . . . they certainly don't just sit there doing nothing.

The judge may routinely take over the examination-in-chief or the cross-examination. Sometimes this is because the barrister involved is failing to do it properly, but often it is because old habits die hard:

> The judge shouldn't have to intervene . . . say 'Don't lead', shouldn't need to ask his own questions . . . [but] often the standard of what he is faced with isn't very high . . . [and] he's done it all before, and probably pretty well or he wouldn't [be on the bench].

We heard several stories about judges who, it was reported, placed a notice in front of themselves reading 'Shut up'. However, although the story was related fairly commonly, the practice it illustrated seemed to occur less often. Deputy judges – practising barristers with part-time judicial appointments – were frequently cited as the worst offenders. Often an active judge was thought to make a considerable difference. One barrister complained, 'in crime the judge who intervenes can almost act as a senior to the prosecution junior'. Of course, depending on the perspective of the barrister, this was not always a disadvantage: 'It can be better if judges ask questions, witnesses are less likely to lie to the judge.'

If a judge sides with a particular party it can make the life of at least one set of barristers considerably easier. One advocate offered this advice for those circumstances:

> . . . there's no need to be too obsequious . . . let the judges express their own theory, don't take their toy away. If the judge is going your way, keep your head down, if he's taking you there then you'll get home on a case.

Of course, the very fact that assistance from the judge is thought so influential suggests that the other side have their task made correspondingly difficult.

Judges may also influence how an argument is shaped and presented. Because of the enormous power which they exert over their courts, the character and approach of individual judges is something that the barrister should take into account. One barrister declared that 'one always has regard to his reputation in the way you frame your argument'. Clearly, this will affect how a case is approached. As one barrister put it, 'if you've got a nebulous argument over to a judge before, you would try it again'.

To some extent, every barrister will move carefully around a judge's foibles, eccentricities and even moods. For example, we heard that 'one judge wants to run them all very very quickly'. Alternatively, 'some judges put onus on honesty . . . if you can catch out a witness on even one small lie then it's all over . . . others are more robust . . . others are frightened of law'.

It is important to get it right in relation to the particular judge that one is appearing before. We were told:

> . . . there's nothing worse than seeing a young barrister do everything the judge hates: you do your thing and you sit down or you give legal authority or whatever . . . it depends on what the particular judge wants.

Knowing what the individual judge wants is important information and barristers often take trouble to find out. As one told us, 'I know the judges – you watch other cases for his mood'. Indeed, a favourite topic of conversation among barristers is the nature of judges. We heard very many stories and theories about judges. Sometimes these were about judges in general but more often they were very specifically focused and individualized. The variation between judges and the significance of the judge to the trial process means that detailed personal information is almost invariably required. As one barrister said: 'It is normal practice if you don't know the judge to enquire in the robing room.'

Although we heard most about the eccentricities of judges, it is not merely those with odd preferences that are accommodated by the barrister. It is important that an advocate is able to empathize with judges and their role and construct arguments that will be attractive to someone in his or her position. Appropriate concessions must be made in order for positive points to be made effectively. For example, one very senior criminal barrister told us:

> . . . if it's a serious case, my own personal approach is to recognize that it is a serious case . . . this will pre-empt him jumping down my throat when I make the points in mitigation.

One of our informants had extensive experience as a Recorder, sitting as a deputy judge in a variety of cases, and was able to provide a number of examples to illustrate this point about tailoring the argument. He told us that his experience on the bench had very forcefully brought home to him the need to think very closely about how the judge might be seeing things. For example, he declared that 'anything presented clearly is best. Often you [as a judge] jump at the opportunity given by a clear statement of the options.' His experience on the bench had also shown:

> ... the need to change all the old lines, 'two bites at the cherry' ... the dreadful 'pushing at an open door' ... the struggle is to avoid cliches and always try to find fresh ways of saying the same lines or new ways of thinking about things.

This idea of breaking up old routines and standard lines is particularly important with guilty pleas in criminal cases:

> Invariably there are certain things that crop up in 90 percent of cases – he is a married man with three children, been working hard all his life, he's been on bail and stayed out of trouble while on bail ... there are seven or eight things that appear in a lot of cases.

With material like this it is important to be alive to the best way of presenting it, given the audience who will hear it. Another barrister told us:

> Judges come up here [Belfast criminal courts] for a month at a time and you have to remember that that they are human beings ... they have heard this time and again ... part of my game plan is to change the way in which I present my plea – calling the policeman at the end ... maybe even referring to an authority ... [or] interrupting the plea with the character witness instead of having them at the start. ... Really to break up the routine that is always used and try to make it a bit more interesting ... it's only if you can get his interest that you can effectively persuade him.

Much of what the advocate does will be orientated around the reception that it is thought likely to receive from the judge. Advocacy in the courtroom involves couching arguments in such a way that they are maximally attractive to the judge, especially where the argument is one that is likely to be of limited appeal. As one barrister put it, 'the skill is in persuading the judge to do something he doesn't want to do'. This will not usually involve a spectacular display of oratory or forensic skill. Indeed, the barrister may have to take a backseat. As one advocate explained: 'the judges think that they have made up their own mind ... that it was obvious or that it was their idea ... that's the mark of a good advocate ... you plant an idea in their head'. It is the case that must be presented and not always the personality of the barrister. As one senior barrister put it: 'You're trying to convince him you're a complete nullity and your case deserves to win itself ... "as your Lordship asked the witness" ... you shouldn't notice good advocacy.'

In contrast, with a jury, the barrister can afford to engage in more obvious techniques of persuasion. As one barrister reported:

> ... you might raise your voice and become apparently angry or in another case, say a rape case with a defence of consent ... you'll probably adopt a mellow approach and not try to castigate the girl,

> although in effect that is what you're saying – that she lied, made it
> up.... [You say] 'She's an unfortunate girl, may have her own reasons
> for making the allegations', I'm not concerned with that, what I am
> concerned with is . . .

Although barristers generally took a great interest in their influence on juries,
it was accepted almost universally that, 'attempting to read a jury is a highly
dangerous exercise, a most inexact science . . . you really can never know
how good you are at making people change their mind'.

Although much of what the barrister does involves trying to accommodate
the judge, this does not mean that the relationship with the judge is all
one-way. Various sets of shared understandings and working practices grow
up between the professionals who operate regularly in the court. The judge is
generally responsible for establishing and regulating these. This is particularly apparent in relation to the level of formality in general, and reference to
formal law in particular, that is required in the court. As one barrister
complained:

> There is one judge who is eccentric to a degree unparalleled by any
> other I have seen . . . he requires everything to be given up to him. You
> can't just say 'unmerchantable quality', 'fitness for purpose'. He will
> say 'What section is that?' 'Where exactly does it say that?' You must
> have it all prepared, photocopied and ready to hand up to him. There
> are other judges who will say 'Usual principles?' and you just say 'Yes,
> usual principles – fitness for purpose etc.' and you needn't trouble with
> the law.

Indeed, the latter situation seems routine. We were told:

> So many of the legal matters are so well-known between the judge and
> the two advocates that it hardly needs to be said . . . you just say 'This is
> one where you might exercise your discretion' [as detailed in a particu-
> lar act].... A lot of cases are like that, you end up with the two
> barristers chatting with the judge and basically saying 'we all know
> where we are, whatever you think yourself.

It is the judge who shapes the way a case is presented in court as well as
creates and dictates the level of formality that is required at any given time in a
trial. Barristers talked in terms of there often being a process of signalling
between the judge and counsel. Indeed, this is welcomed by most advocates.
It was thought useful and necessary. One barrister with extensive experience
of planning work contrasted her experience there with that in the ordinary
civil courts:

> The Planning Inspectorate, until recently, used to say nothing at all....
> You didn't know where you were at all, how it was going . . . it would
> go through no matter what. If he gave indication you would know that
> you're banging your head against a brick wall . . . an indication is very
> helpful.

In some ways, a jury provides a similar lack of feedback, although many barristers did talk in terms of trying to establish a rapport, often with humour, among the members of the jury (see also Walter, 1988, who argues that addressing a jury is in fact a two-way communication). Indeed, with a jury, it may be necessary to make things very clear. As one criminal practitioner told us:

> You have to go the whole hog with a jury . . . even if it's bloody obvious you have to make sure . . . you use phrases like 'I can't take the risk that you may not have fully understood and I may be repeating things that are absurdly obvious to you but I am bound to say . . .'. You have to do it by the numbers.

The judge, on the other hand, is much more likely to make it clear what is on his or her mind and how the case is proceeding. One barrister told us: 'Lawyer to lawyer, a judge will tell you in civil matters that "I would need a lot of persuasion on that one", or "the door is open".' A judge dealing with a plea in mitigation can be a fairly reliable source of information on what remains to be done in any case:

> At its most extreme, the judge will say in a criminal case 'Now I've read the papers, this is what is in my mind. I would be minded to impose a sentence like this. Now what would you say to that, how would you persuade me otherwise?'.

Within particular levels of practice where the numbers of participants are restricted, the informality of the working practices becomes marked. We noticed this in relation to practice in the family courts and, most demonstrably, in the relatively small world of Belfast's criminal and special courts. We were told:

> There is nothing improper in it but in the Crumlin Road [Belfast's criminal courthouse] there is a much more informal approach – people in the criminal courts take a more relaxed attitude about getting things done.

In the scheduled or terrorist cases where juries are not involved, we were told that:

> It's very much more professionalized . . . questions kept very much to the point . . . directed towards legal issues. . . . Red herrings which, it's a fact of life, juries often get involved in will immediately be seen through by a judge and you wouldn't attempt to introduce any . . . [or] engage in any of the histrionics that we are all guilty of from time to time with a jury.

There is a tendency to get to the bottom line in a case without overly formal legal submissions:

> If you get a statement fight there is all this rigmarole about the statement being voluntary . . . but everybody knows that, everybody knows, even in a Diplock case, the statement is admissible . . . [unless

there is] under the new amendment 'violence or threats of violence'. But you don't get up and start quoting cases to the judge ... what you really need to show is that the police are lying ... that's the crux of a case like that and you all know it.

Undoubtedly, a community of professional interest is formed among the regular participants in these courts as in others where working practices can evolve among those who regularly operate there. In relation to the Diplock or special courts in Northern Ireland and the relatively few counsel who operate regularly there, we were told:

Because they all know the judges and the judges all know them. What has happened is that there is a fairly informal system worked out as to what would be in the best interests of the client. . . . It's not much to do with the law in the formal sense but with the pragmatic disposing of cases.

This phenomenon exists everywhere to some extent, but is most noticeable where regular contact allows relationships to be built up. It was in another jurisdiction that we were told by a criminal practitioner that all the technicalities are not always necessary in the context of a good working relationship: 'The big thing is the trust they have in you. Judge [X] knows that if I say my client is in employment then he is ... even if I haven't got the letter or his employer to call as a witness.' Such informality is possible because of assumptions that are made about the competence and ability of the parties involved. Indeed, we heard that in the Court of Appeal and the House of Lords the conversational tone of the proceedings reaches its height.

CONCLUSION

In this chapter, we have considered the role of the barrister in the latter stages as a case comes to be heard in court. The matters which the barrister must take into account as he or she evaluates the case and negotiates with the opposition have been outlined. The nature and range of these factors, and the variety of skills that the barrister uses, must surely confound those who see the barrister as merely arguing points of law in the context-free isolation of a neutral courtroom.

All this must be set against the background that we outlined in the other chapters in this section. There it was seen how the barrister's role and career and the barrister–solicitor relationship constrain and control what the barrister does. It was seen how legal information – a much wider concept than simple law applied to fact – is subject to a whole host of practical, personal and professional exigencies. All of this argues for a greater appreciation of the role that the barrister plays and a better understanding of the complexity of advocacy.

Barristers themselves do have an appreciation of the richness, complexity and social nature of the practice of law. It is this insight that we have sought to communicate in this part.

PART III

THE THEORY OF LAW

Introduction to Part III

One major problem with most studies of the sociology of law is that the sociologist stops short of the final (and logical) step from sociology into law. There is a fear, almost, of treading into the preserve of the academic lawyer: the black-letter or substantive nature of law. It has been said before that sociologists are every bit as reluctant to see through the 'majesty of the law' (and its other myths) as are members of the general public.

This problem has led to the distorted position where we have substantial amounts of sociological research into law which tell us much about the behaviour of juries, plea-bargaining and such like, but which are never put into any *legal* context. Thus most legal academics feel able to dismiss socio-logical studies as peripheral to the 'real' nature of law as an activity of heightened academic, textual reasoning. And few sociologists feel able to contradict this view.

This is not a pit into which we want to fall. Our research into barristers was carried out because we wanted to know more about law (as an academic as well as a practical enterprise), not simply because barristers are interesting for their own sake. Our goal is therefore to take the findings from Part II, and try to make intellectual and theoretical sense of them in Part III.

We begin by shooting down the traditional view of science, since this view has been used as a defence by those who wish to set law up as a science, or who claim for law a special logic. (For too long, it seems to us, all academic discussion, including that of law, has been blighted by Victorian perspectives of what science is.) We then move on to discuss the nature of the 'sociology of legal knowledge' and how our work fits this description, and how it links with other work into the study of reasoning and rhetoric. Finally, we place ourselves firmly within the intellectual framework set up by Jerome Frank and suggest that our findings are an extension of his own.

The barriers between the practice of law and the theory of law are, as we have already suggested, both thick and high. However, they are not so insurmountable that they must necessarily stand for ever. Law is too important to the operation of society to be allowed to go unanalysed, and left in the hands of its high priests – those who have, so far, resisted the developing understanding provided by the sociologist of law.

7

TOWARDS A
SOCIOLOGY OF LEGAL
KNOWLEDGE

INTRODUCTION

Much sociological investigation is concerned with the more easily observable behaviour of its subjects or with the more easily observed views which its subjects hold. We see this sort of research as the traditional view of the sociological researcher who travels with questionnaire in hand in a statistics-gathering exercise. This is one extreme of sociological research; other approaches don't necessarily take this strict empirical path, but do try to concentrate on more easily quantifiable social facts. For example, in Part II, where we looked at the particulars of the barrister's professional life, we were concerned with relatively easily contemplated factors: workload, contact with clients and solicitors, etc. Yet few other researchers into the legal profession have trodden our same path – as is evidenced by the lack of research writings on barristers. Most have tended to concentrate upon the social climate and context of the barrister. Nan Wilson, whose work on Scottish advocates was cited in support of our own findings, emphasized a different type of sociologically (in fact, anthropologically) discovered information – that to do with status, role and role preservation (Wilson, 1965). Alan Paterson (1982), though, in his analysis of the other end of the legal hierarchy – the Law Lords – tended more towards our area of interest and was concerned with the details of interaction between individual Law Lords and, indeed, between Law Lords and barristers (see, in particular, Paterson, 1982: ch. 3).

Generally, all these other approaches can be seen to sit easily with traditional views of law and legal reasoning – they do not necessarily encroach upon the view of law as a system of rules which can be applied to given facts in the courtroom; nor do they affect views of the natural law type. They can be seen to explain the context and surrounding factors which sometimes, usually incorrectly many theorists believe, take the legal process away from its true path.[1]

We shall look below as to whether more can actually be read into these more limited approaches (and argue that it can). However, even as they stand, these approaches are all insightful and do demonstrate what has been termed the 'debunking' facility of sociology.[2] That is, to get behind the professional's own façade and ideology, and present a more true picture of the activities and behaviour of the barrister/Law Lord, etc., even if it still leaves a picture of law as a mainly deductive and/or logical process. For example, the approaches that we are talking about here are able to demonstrate the fact that although barristers are so closely constrained by the solicitor–barrister relationship, this does not *necessarily* mean that substantive law and legal research are not important elements of the barrister's work. Rather, it can be taken to mean that those who have better relationships are better placed to have the opportunity to carry out this work. In other words, the practice of substantive law can only be carried out if the barrister has a brief in the first place. As Wilson (1965: 175) put it:

> ...the esteem of solicitors is for an advocate the most important [consideration] for success. To gain that esteem he must have adequate opportunity to show his skill in practice, and this has been notoriously difficult for certain groups at the Bar. An advocate who has the backing of influential interests, such as a relative in a solicitor's firm which does a great deal of court work or an uncle in an insurance company or a father on the council of a local authority, may expect to have an opportunity to prove his skill reasonably soon.

However, these kinds of contextual understandings are not the only fruits which can be got from such sociological investigation. They are, perhaps, the kind which are best got from the anthropological study of law and lawyers.[3]

We argue that such sociological and anthropological approaches begin to allow us to think and to theorize in much deeper ways about law – not only about lawyers: for example, what is legal information, and what role does substantive law have in the notion of legal information? This was the major thread of our argument in Part II. In this chapter, we will begin to show how our already developed notion of legal information can be pushed further. We shall try to develop a *sociological theory of legal knowledge*. We will try to make the connection between sociology and law seem to be so intractably linked that they cannot thereafter be pulled apart. Accepting our argument means that no longer can sociological study simply give the context for law: it will be seen to be at the very heart of law.

Naturally, not all lawyers agree with us in this belief. One criticism which is made of sociological investigation in law is that it is only dealing with the *least* legal part of the entire process, i.e. the extraneous context. Critics of sociological approaches to law would suggest that such studies do not tell us about the *real* nature of law at all and since they do not tell us about this, law must not actually be amenable to sociological investigation. For example, one critic Wilson (1990: 227) stated: 'But sociology of law is not legal theory; not even a substitute for it.'

It is easy to understand why this view is taken: it can be seen that the primary focus of most sociologists is rarely that of the interpretation of acts, case reading, etc., which are traditionally what law is taken to be about. The same point can be made about Wilson's thesis, since it concerns the social roles of the advocate, not the interpretation of law. Alan Paterson's study is less receptive to this criticism because he does, as he suggests, try to ascertain how difficult questions ('hard cases') of law are actually debated by the actors in the legal process:

> ... what is the role of a Law Lord when confronted with an appeal where there is legitimate room for debate between the parties as to the existence, scope and applicability of one or more common law rules or principles? In such 'hard' cases how do the Law Lords demarcate their province from that of the legislature when it comes to 'developing' the common law? (Paterson, 1982: 2).

However, there are whole fields of law where Law Lords never tread, which critics of the sociological approach will suggest are relatively, or entirely, free from sociological insight – those which are not, in Paterson's terms, 'hard cases'.

Critics of sociological investigations into law thus feel able to marginalize the sociologist with a simple, 'but they are not talking about *real* law'. The argument is that, while the results of the investigations might be valid and show us where the legal process is going wrong, say, so far as understanding the laws of tort, or contract, or whatever are concerned, sociology is no help at all.

Even in legal education, it is easy to see how effective the anti–sociological position is. No matter how many studies, especially in the USA, are carried out into jury behaviour for example (see Hastie *et al.* 1983; Siemer, 1984; Hans, 1986; Walter, 1988), all these are pushed aside and considered not to be useful in the teaching of the law of evidence or contract. Law is mostly taught as a series of rules and principles extracted not from real life, but from the texts on the bookshelves of the law library.[4]

The very manner in which 'real' law is talked about is instructive. It is termed *substantive law*, and we are led to think of it as a *concrete* body of rules and principles. The term 'substantive' gives the physical feeling of weight and substance to the hearer (substance/concrete/weight are all related by terminology and sense). Discussion between sociologists of law and lawyers always meets this substantive law barrier – and it is, of course, set up partly as a means of keeping sociological insights into law at bay. Unfortunately, this has been a highly successful strategy, and sociology does not affect legal understanding in a way which we – as the sociologically inclined – might wish. Even many sociologists feel that the barrier between substantive law and sociology of law is real. We do not.

The result is that we have two camps of knowledge – substantive knowledge and sociological knowledge – which find it difficult to interlink. Using other terminology, we can also refer to this dichotomy as that between formalism and non-formalism (Shklar, 1986).

In the rest of the book, we shall try to create a bridge between the substantive and the sociological views of knowledge. We shall do this by looking to notions of the *sociology of legal knowledge*, as a continuation and development of our sociology of professional legal behaviour and legal information which was presented in Part II. A sociology of legal knowledge will thus need to look at that body of knowledge which is described as substantive and try to ascertain how it links in with, is affected by and is parasitic upon the sociological knowledge which we have described earlier. Thus, for example, a sociology of legal knowledge will have to discover where the notion of rule fits into legal behaviour, or how the reading of legal texts is affected by a 'non-legal' context. By doing this, the charge that sociological views of law are irrelevant to understanding the nature of law, can be met head on.

Before we do this, it is necessary to look at other developments which have been happening in non-law fields. This should be instructive, especially since – as Posner has contended – the nature and staffing of law schools has meant that most of the insightful ideas about law have actually had to be imported from other disciplines (Posner, 1988: 363–4). We shall be importing ideas which have arisen in the study of science.

THE SOCIOLOGY OF KNOWLEDGE

The inception of the sociology of knowledge is usually attributed to Karl Mannheim, who suggested – contrary to Marx's view that the class system was economically determined (and thus deterministic) – that an individual's view of his or her position in the class system was determined as much by ideological factors as by economic factors. As Marx stated in his *A Contribution to the Critique of Political Economy*:

> The mode of production in material life determines the general charac-
> ter of the social, political and intellectual processes of life. It is not the
> consciousness of men that determines their existence, but on the con-
> trary, their social existence determines their consciousness (Marx,
> 1970: 11–12).

Mannheim suggested that while sociology might well concern itself with the economic position of its subjects, there was also a 'style of thought' which sociologists had to take into account – how people see themselves in the world and what their values are, etc. People might thus see themselves as part of groupings which transcend the more elementary ones of class (e.g. the Conservative-voting, blue-collar worker). This style of thought, in its widest vein, is the subject matter of the sociology of knowledge. In the nineteenth century, of course, Durkheim had been positing with regard to primitive cultures that the social make-up of a society was reflected in the classificatory systems of that primitive culture. But, given that Western cultures were supposedly more scientific and their knowledge based in scientific truth, it was a large step to suggest that Western thought was as prone to being dominated by social structure (and hence error) as these primitive tribes. Therefore, the move towards a sociology of Western knowledge was not immediately taken.

What sort of questions are relevant to a sociology of knowledge, anyway? These can be diverse – from those of what influence does occupation, group structure, historical situation have on the kind of thoughts which individuals have, to how are these thoughts transmitted from individual to individual within the group. For example, in a sociology of legal knowledge, one will look as much at the 'thought styles' of barristers (and how these differ from non-barristers) as well as at their social position and background and see how the two interact and integrate. The ideological aspects of law become areas of study, too. Importantly, one will also look at how the knowledge about law which barristers have will be transmitted, held and handled. This latter element will be the one which we emphasize in Part III.

It is important to recognize in this field that both traditional and knowledge-based sociology are compatible. Neither cancels the other out – traditional sociological investigation (e.g. Abel, 1988) does not necessarily conflict with an approach concerned with knowledge. The more recent is simply a development of the earlier discipline.

While anthropologists who investigate various cultures would argue that they have always been looking at the way in which knowledge is socially constructed, in Western society it has really only been in the past fifty years or so that the field of the sociology of knowledge has developed. The material for study in the field has been described in this way:

> It is primarily concerned with the relations between knowledge and other existential factors in the society or culture. General and even vague as this formulation of the central purpose may be, a more specific statement will not serve to include the diverse approaches which have been developed (Merton, 1968: 510).

Most of the interesting work has been carried out in the area of science and mathematics (including the latter's sub-field, logic). It is not an accident of chance which has led to these being the main areas of research. Rather, it is because they were previously seen as being incapable of succumbing to sociological investigation (as many believe legal theory to be now). Durkheim, while believing in the power of sociological investigation, explicitly exempted science and mathematics from his list of fields which were so amenable. Thus, given the view that they were the hardest cases for sociological insight, they were chosen to prove that even the most difficult fields are receptive after all.

It is important to highlight here that law and legal theory have been much influenced by the concept of 'science'. Many theories of fact-finding in court are mirrors of classical theories of scientific fact-finding. The positivist theory of law as a deductive, rule-processing act owes much to the classical theory of science as a logical (both deductive and inductive) process. Hence, our look at the sociology of scientific knowledge does two things for our argument: it demonstrates how knowledge is socially constructed and it demonstrates how the assumptions which underlie traditional legal theory are being disproved. We therefore make no apologies for this diversion.

THE SOCIOLOGY OF SCIENTIFIC KNOWLEDGE

One of the main reasons why Durkheim exempted science and mathematics from sociological analysis is that they seemed to deal only with hard physical facts; they were objective rather than subjective. Also, they seemed to have a clear (and very successful) method which set them aside from the more wishy-washy areas such as economics and the other social sciences. In essence it seemed, to the scientifically oriented Victorians, that science was getting them closer and closer to the ultimate truth, a truth which they were being denied in other areas. It became relatively common for other subjects to emulate the methods and procedures of science, hoping that this would allow the scientification of their knowledge. We can still see this clearly in, for example, the attempts by psychologists to model their studies and their experiments on the scientific experimental technique, but many others followed this path – phrenology is one obvious example. Even philosophers attempted to follow the scientific methodology in, for example, logical positivism and logical atomism.

In the sociology of scientific knowledge, which has developed in critical response to Durkheim's position, researchers have tried to show that science and scientific development are affected more by social factors than by the 'scientific method' so promoted by philosophers of science and scientists themselves.

This is, of course, difficult to accept within the popular view of science. Here science is supposed to be a study of what is true everywhere and at all times. The stuff of science is taken to be phenomena that are repeatable rather than historically contingent. If something happens only every so often in one way and at other times in a quite different manner it is, within this view, not science but history or storytelling. Thus physics is clearly a science because it deals in universal assertions such as, for example, all planets move in ellipses. The shape of planetary orbits is a necessary consequence of the relations of the motions of objects in a gravitational field. All existing planets and all possible planets will behave in this way and, because this is certain, physics often provides even philosophers with an example of a true science.

However, Thomas Kuhn's (1962) work, *The Structure of Scientific Revolution*, suggested another view of science and scientific advance that was quite different from the one commonly held. Kuhn's thesis is now held by a large number of scientists. In this theory, scientific advance consists of an episodic succession of professional dominant thought-frames. It was the succession of these paradigms, rather than a step-by-step evolution towards some better reality or truth, that marked the development of scientific progress. Since

Kuhn, a whole series of other researchers have taken up science as the object of their study and have pushed this idea further. Thus science, in this view, is not about *absolute* truths, but rather about relative and developing truths.

In the history of science, the emphasis is on questions of dominance and the focus is on power struggles over resources and reputations and among organizations and disciplinary elites. In philosophy, although there are still those who adhere to an idea of nature or 'the way things actually are' as the beginning and end when it comes to knowing, there has been a reaction against permanent principles and inherent essences there too. The trend is now towards a plurality of perspectives, including the sort of approaches provided by language games, rhetorical styles and practical outcomes that are beginning to filter into legal theory.

Some diverse examples might illustrate some of the ways in which this social constructionist conception of science can operate. The common view of medical research in general, and pathology in particular, is as a process of straightforward development and progress. However, it is clear that social, technical and paradigmatic factors have had an influence.[5] For example, factors such as the incidence of infection affected the development of the discipline of pathology. Prior to the advent of antibiotics, infection produced gross lesions and the florid presentation of these encouraged the view that diseases were actually caused by infection. The dominant German school at the beginning of the century even explored seriously the idea that very complex conditions such as cancers were produced as the result of infection. This paradigm was orientated around structure and the changes in structure that could occur. The practical responses that arose from this way of thinking centred around the search for infecting agents and, in particular, bacteriology emerged as the significant sub-discipline. In contrast, after the Second World War, the period of development and widespread use of antibiotics, there was a change in the symptoms presented and a re-orientation of the paradigm from matters of structure to questions of function. Now research is centred on matters such as immune mechanisms and allergies and is dominated by the sub-disciplines of biochemistry and immunology.[6] Kuhnians would suggest that what operated here was a paradigm shift between the two periods where different knowledge assumptions were made.

A more extreme example, and one stressing the social and professional factors, can be found in the field of evolutionary biology. In 1909, the prominent palaeontologist Charles Doolittle Walcott discovered the Burgess Shale. This was a deposit of fossil-bearing rock in Yoho National Park in the Canadian Rockies. At the time, the discoverer saw the Burgess Shale fauna as a collection of conventional organisms. However, the fossils found there are now known to be highly significant to ideas about the evolution of all life. This conclusion was arrived at after much painstaking reconstruction work by three scientists in the early 1970s. They were able to demonstrate that this very small quarry contained a collection of invertebrate fossils that showed a diversity of body plan that surpasses all living marine invertebrates. The fossil record suggests that a diversity of animal types, including all the basic

body plans of the invertebrate animals now known, appeared almost instan-
taneously (in geological terms) at the beginning of the Cambrian Period
about 550 million years ago. Before this crucial period, there were relatively
few forms and a short period after (about 500 million years ago) much of the
diversity of form that had appeared was lost.

In his book, entitled *Wonderful Life: The Burgess Shale and the Nature of
History*, Stephen Jay Gould (1990), chronicles the story of this discovery. He
addresses himself particularly to the question of why the original finder
should have misread or suppressed evidence that has considerable significance for our view of evolutionary possibilities. His argument is that Walcott
was irredeemably hooked into the progressivist ideology of the nineteenth
century with its Whiggish picture of the history of life. Within this paradigm,
the evolution of life was seen as a movement from the simple to the complex.
There was seen to be a tree of life which begins with a narrow range of types
at the bottom of the trunk and slowly diversifies and branches out as the tree
grows. The modern interpretation of the Burgess Shale, and the idea of a
Cambrian explosion of life, is in stark contrast to this. Instead of a tree, it
suggests a bush with all the main branches emerging at ground level and most
of them being nipped in the bud at an early stage. Gould maintains that
Walcott 'shoehorned' the fossils into the standard classification of animals
and that he did so because of 'his deeply conservative and traditional perspective on life and morality'. His position as a busy administrator coming
towards the peak of a successful career within the orthodox tradition perhaps
left neither the time nor the inclination to undertake the process of reconstructing the damaged fossils. This was, of course, in contrast to the three
scientists in the 1970s who, Gould maintains, because of temperament and
circumstances operated outside the elite group and inner hierarchy within the
profession. For them, the political path to career success in science was
blocked. They took the career move of rebelling against the orthodoxy by
gambling on a reinterpretation of the data of that orthodoxy.

The point to be taken here is that there is an overwhelming influence from
ideology upon the process of science. Science is not objective, logical, meth-
odological, knowledge and truth and totally removed from non-science (the
latter, in this view, merely opinion). Indeed, the popular view of science is as
vulnerable as is, in our argument, the popular view of law.

As another example of the sort of insights which are being provided into
science, we can look at one which we have used before (Leith, 1990). It has to
do with the debate in science over whether there is a scientific *method* for
ascertaining the truth or falsity from experimental data. This is an important
point because, as we have mentioned, right throughout the nineteenth century (and even today), this was the view held by many active scientists. It was
believed that science had such a method, and this was one of the main reasons
for science being successful (and the social sciences unsuccessful). This viewpoint has been termed positivism.[7] The particular controversy which Collins
and Pinch (1982) investigated was that of *parapsychology* and its attempt to
'become a science' through the investigation of the Uri Geller phenomenon –

spoon bending. In order to advance their claim, the parapsychologists were using the traditional technique of normal science – the closely observed experiment. It was here that the whole question of what is science and what is not, and the status of parapsychology, met and clashed.

One of the striking conclusions Collins and Pinch arrived at from their experiment in investigating experiments was that a set of experiments *cannot* provide a *definite* means of deciding between these two scientific world views. No matter what experiment was carried out, the two opposing groups of scientists (or scientists and non-scientists, depending upon your view) could not agree on the results of the experiment. This is not surprising to the sociologist of science. In all areas of science, there is argument and debate over fundamental knowledge and viewpoints, as can clearly be seen in the arguments and papers which appear in the journals of science.

The problem lies in the very nature of extracting from an experiment information which is consistent and factual. This is a problem which is to be found in *every* experiment (as well as every court of law, we argue), not only those of parapsychology:

> In a sense, every human act is unique. Each time the 'same' act is performed it is performed in a slightly different way, in a different environment, at a different time, by a different person, or one who is changed by virtue of being older. . . . Experimental activity, as a species of activity in general, also consists of sequences of unique acts. To make sense of these acts it is necessary to see them as not unique. Seeing them as not unique requires that most of what could be seen as happening and most features of the environment is ignored (Collins and Pinch, 1982: 125).

Thus the act of making sense in a rational way of what is happening in an experiment means that much of what is happening in the experiment has to be set aside. How do we decide what to ignore and what to concentrate upon if not by our own bias? And how, then, can we partake of a scientific experiment without our biases coming into play as a way of seeing the experiment? The answer is, of course, that we cannot. Thus the result of Collins and Pinch's work is that the whole edifice of scientific experiment is seen to be not as structurally sound as scientists often argue. Rather than there being some method which can be applied in a mechanical way to distance the scientific observer from the experiment, the results of the experiment are intimately bound up with the scientist's own perspective and bias.

Not only did Collins and Pinch draw attention to the difficulty of getting clear experimental results, but they also suggested that the physical and cultural environment in which the experiments took place affected the views of the researcher. This, again, is hardly what is to be expected given the idealistic view of science which is so prevalent:

> Our beliefs tended to change as a function of the nature of the latest period of prolonged exposure to scientists. Long exposure to critics

made their point of view seem to be the only sensible one, and seemed to make the believers appear hopeless cranks and even charlatans. On the other hand, prolonged exposure to believers – for instance, in the remarkable cultural climate of the West Coast of the USA – made paranormal phenomena seem to be an obvious fact of everyday experience which only the most pig-headed could fail to perceive. In the latter circumstances it was the sceptics who looked like dense, dishonest and antediluvian conspirators battling tenaciously for a lost cause (Collins and Pinch, 1982: 23).

The fact that science does not, if Collins and Pinch and other sociologists of science are correct, live up to the idealistic view of it as a completely objective and certain set of methods and beliefs, does not mean that science is in-effective – quite the contrary. It does mean that science is marked by much more debate and uncertainty than many have suggested; in other words, scientific knowledge is marked by the human factors of indecision, argument and uncertainty.

In Chapter 8, we will look at some of the points which Collins has made about the textbook tradition in science, since it too is important to our argument about substantive law. But briefly, he suggests that science in practice is different from science in the textbooks, and that there are tensions between the two kinds of knowledge which cannot be successfully brought together. This, we will argue, is the scientific corollary of Pound's thesis concerning law in textbooks and law in practice.

There are a growing number of texts on the area of the sociology of scientific knowledge which provide potential illuminatory material. The common thrust of all these studies are to demonstrate that scientific knowledge is a more complex phenomenon than is suggested by the traditional, classical view.

A note should be made here about the writings in the philosophy of law on the nature of law which advocate it best being seen as a 'science' (e.g. Kelsen, 1967). These writings all suggest that law should mirror the traditional view of science – as decisive, clear and certain (e.g. the positivist school). However, if we accept the findings of sociologists of scientific knowledge, then we have to be suspicious as to whether law can mirror such a traditional view, for if science cannot be these things, surely law cannot either.

THE SOCIOLOGY OF MATHEMATICAL AND LOGICAL KNOWLEDGE

The examples above come from the physical and biological sciences, but sociology has also made inroads into understanding mathematical knowledge which, like the hard sciences, was seen previously to be outwith the compass of sociology. We shall not look into mathematics here, but simply note that the philosopher Ludwig Wittgenstein's later theory, which is of much interest today, can be seen as one which posits a social theory of the development of mathematics (Phillips, 1977). Such a view suggests, for example, that mathematical entities are not discovered but are invented – they are social constructions, rather than reflections of reality. Given the long history (from Plato, at least) of the belief that entities such as triangles, circles and prime numbers do exist (rather than being simply ideas in the heads of mathematicians), the argument that mathematics is socially constructed is hard for many to accept (see Kline, 1980, on this).

However, an interesting study into the development of a geometrical object – the polyhedra – was carried out by Imres Lakatos. In *Proofs and Refutations: The Logic of Mathematical Discovery* (1976), Lakatos represented the historical development of the concept of the polyhedra as a debate over the meaning and the borders of the concept. It is an illuminating example of just how, over time, a mathematical concept can be seen to alter and change as social and intellectual climates change. Lakatos is interested in the social nature of mathematical proof, and how it is impossible to define a mathematical object so precisely that the object is proof against 'concept-stretching' as each new generation of mathematicians alter and change the concepts they take from their predecessors. Lakatos' point is that mathematics does not develop in a neutral, logical manner; rather, it develops as each new generation finds new problems to apply it to.

However, while the general area of mathematics will not concern us greatly here, a sub-area will. This sub-area is that of logic. Logic, as we shall see later, is an important area for those in law to understand, since the relationship between logic and rhetoric has defined our present view of what law is, and what kind of reasoning is 'proper'.

Logic and law have been seen to be close neighbours for centuries, and even now there is still a powerful lobby for the fact that law both should be and is logical. This belief has had substantial support recently from research into computers and law, where many researchers are convinced that law (as a logical system) should be easily handled by computer – as the logical machine, *par excellence* (see Leith, 1990, 1991, for fuller information on this). The first writer of a textbook on the subject of logic and law, Abraham Fraunce, put the intimacy of the connection as far back as 1588. George Boole, suggested by many as one of the founding fathers of modern formal logic, used Jewish dietary law in examples in his formative work. Others, for example Ilmar Tammelo, have taken up this view and made it more modern (Tammelo, 1969). This general view relies on the assumption that logic offers a firm foundation for legal reasoning. Indeed, it is logic which is seen to be the only real constraint upon the efficacy of the justice system: without logic, in Tammelo's view, there would be no justice. Many other writers on jurisprudence have taken a similar view to this. MacCormick, in his *Legal Theory and Legal Reasoning* (1978), postulates just such a view when he argues that logic provides a firm footing for the 'deductive justification' of a judicial decision.

We might well say that the orthodoxy current in law at present is that logic has something (or much) to offer both law and legal reasoning. The notion that technical logic is useful to law, and that it reflects real reasoning processes, has even brought a situation about where everyone claims to be being logical, or that certain legal decisions are logical/illogical, without feeling the need to explicitly relate these views to technical logic. For example, one constantly sees non-technical discussion of the 'logic' of a case or decision which seem to imply that there is some formal logical rationality behind their opinion on the case, even though the formal logicality of the case is never described. It is a situation in law where the very idea of logic is seen to be an all powerful tool for thinking, and everyone claims this logicity for themselves but denies it to their opponents.

Unfortunately for this logic bandwagon, the sociology of mathematical knowledge does not support the view that logic provides a clear method for deciding the truth or falsity of statements, arguments or premises.

There are several arguments against the logical perspective which have come from looking at the history and the social background to mathematics. One looks to the fact that logic itself is not a single coherent idea. For example, there are many different schools of logic, each of which suggest that the logic they use is valid, but that those of other schools are invalid. When we look at the history of logic, we see that this battle over just what logic is has lasted for many, many centuries. Yet, most lawyers with an interest in logic seem to believe that logic is a relatively simple and consistent discipline. An early attempt to bring logic together into such a consistent body was carried out by Cohen and Nagel in their *An Introduction to Logic and Scientific Method* (1934). They wrote that there was 'a bewildering Babel of tongues as to what logic is about' and that each of the various schools of logic 'speak different languages, and each regards the other as not really dealing with logic at all'.

The fact that logic is a subject in which there is considerable internal debate and confusion should not be taken to mean that logic, as a technical and mathematical discipline, is of no value. Rather, what should be taken from this, is that logic does not offer the certainty which many claim it can. Since it cannot itself offer certainty, it cannot offer a firm foundation for reasoning.

One of the technical problems with logic which mitigates against logic offering certainty in reasoning, is to be found at the very heart of even the simplest logic – it is to do with the meaning of the basic logical connectors and is one of the causes of the Babel of tongues which Cohen and Nagel unsuccessfully tried to subdue. Since it is relatively simple to understand, we shall give it here as an example of the problem: there are, though, many more such which litter the textbooks of logic.

Logical statements are composed of clauses which are connected by logical connectors. One connector is the logical OR, another the logical AND. In legal reasoning, though, an important one is the connector which suggests a causal connection (written as '$->$'), and is sometimes read as 'if ... then ...' as in '*if* a valid application is made *then* a grant may be paid'. The generality and importance of '*if* ... *then* ...' may be understood when we realize that we can use it with any kind of causal argument. In technical terms, this connector is called the implicative connector. It has been the source of confusion and argument among logicians for many thousands of years. It is also, of course, one of the most basic of all logical connectors.

The problem is that there is no simple way to translate the technical symbol '−>' into natural language, or natural language into the technical symbol. Some argue that it can be read as 'if . . . then . . .', whereas other logicians disagree vehemently with this and suggest that there can be no natural language version of it at all, since 'if . . . then . . .' in English means something different from '−>' in logic. For those who advocate logic in law, such a problem should cause sleepless nights; for, if we cannot translate the 'if . . . then . . .' of legal rules into formal logic due to the confusion over interpretation, can we really be sure that logic can handle law?

Given that such a basic element of logic is the cause of so much argument (it is like mathematicians not agreeing on the meaning of '+'), it is difficult to see why so many argue that logic offers certainty. And it is not only the logical connector for implication which causes trouble:

> Of the readings 'not' (of '−'), 'and' (of '&'), 'or' (of 'v') and 'if . . . then − −' (of '−>'), Strawson has remarked 'the first two are the least misleading' and the remainder 'definitely wrong' (Haack, 1978: 35).

The sociological investigation of mathematics and logic is also substantiating the view of the first British Professor of Jurisprudence, that much of the difficulty with logic is not in the formal elements, but how arguments are constructed:

> Since the syllogism can give us no new truth and since it may mislead, what is its use?
>
> I incline to think that the important part is not the syllogism. But terms, propositions, definitions (abstracted from all particular matter) are all-important. It is a great error of most logicians to consider these as merely subordinate to syllogism, which is the most futile part (Austin, 1885: 1012–13).

This discussion of logic is important for the thesis of this book, for we argue that the view of logic which is current today has radically affected the way that we view rhetoric. Since we suggest that rhetoric is fundamental to law (while logic is not), it is important to realize that logic is not the simple, certain body of knowledge that many argue. Yet, it has only really been through the sociology of mathematical knowledge that the anti-logical position has been thought through.

STEPS TOWARDS A SOCIOLOGY OF LEGAL KNOWLEDGE

We do not want to claim that our arguments are the first steps in a move towards a sociology of legal knowledge, rather than a sociology of the legal profession. Quite simply we do not want to make this claim because it is untrue – others have taken steps to look sociologically at the development of law, and to look at how law is affected by social context (most recently and comprehensively by Cotterrell, 1989).

In fact, much of American Realism – which we return to in Chapter 8 – can be seen to be involved in questions of how the social context of the court system, the environment in which law is used, etc., all impinge upon law. Pound's (1910) paper on why law in textbooks is different from law in practice is one, Hutcheson's (1929) article on the 'judicial hunch' is another. And Llewellyn's statement that he was more concerned with 'a jurisprudence for the hundred thousand, rather than one for the hundred' emphasizes that realists were more concerned with the social reality of law, than with the law as seen through the textbook. Realism is not a simple subject, for its advocates took many different positions: some even tending to advocate that the law should follow the scientific approach which we have argued against above. However, as Livingstone (1988: 151) in his introductory article to the problems of realism has suggested:

> A second front opened up by the realists was to suggest that not only did the rules control judicial decisions much less than the formalists believed but those decisions had much less impact on the lives of other legal officials and ordinary citizens than had often been assumed. The formalist cry that all the law was in the books suggested that the only thing worth studying was the decisions or more precisely the reasoning of appellate court decisions. Realists argued that the effects of these decisions were often confined to setting new problems for law school professors and their students.

Until very recently, in the jurisprudence environment in the UK, realism has been given a very poor press indeed. Livingstone's essay gives a coherent explanation of why it has not flourished well in the UK, and notes how its misrepresentation by Herbert Hart has caused it to be much misunderstood. In many ways, this text on barristers is a following on of the realist perspective and an attempt to further bury the ghost of Hart (see the various articles in Leith and Ingram, 1988, and the follow up to this in Livingstone and Morison, 1990). We will return to one realist, Jerome Frank, in Chapter 8.

Paterson's (1982) work, *The Law Lords* can be seen as a much later piece of work in the sociology of legal knowledge. Using traditional interview techniques, Paterson questioned the Law Lords on the processes they used to come to agreement (or disagreement) on the decision of a case which had reached the pinnacle of the appellate system – the House of Lords. Paterson's work clearly demonstrates the social nature of negotiation in the Lords:

> The bulk of the Law Lords in the past twenty-five years or so seem to have taken the view that group membership was at least a relevant attribute in their decision-making role. They have been prepared to argue at length with their colleagues, but usually only in a group context, for example in the corridor, the Conference Room or the Library (Paterson, 1982: 112).

Not only was the group aspect of decision making studied by Paterson, but also the relationship between advocates and the Law Lords, and from where Law Lords get their particular views of the world. All told, Paterson's study was a striking study in the sociology of legal knowledge. Unfortunately, it can be criticized for being jurisprudence for the hundred rather than for the hundred thousand – that is, that it is appellate-centred.[8]

Paterson himself uses the notion of a 'hard case' to delimit his field of interest from that of a full-blown sociology of legal knowledge. Thus, he suggests that it is legally difficult cases which arrive at the House of Lords; these are cases which are by their very nature non-conducive to traditional legal thinking. Paterson's study is thus, in many ways, complementary to traditional textbook-centred views of law; it is not an attempt at giving 'everyday' substantive law a sociological centre. It is implicit in Paterson's perspective that most legal questions can be decided in a legal manner in the lower courts – only those which are hard cases make it to the Law Lords, and they do so by being 'legally hard' rather than through any other necessary factor.

Paterson describes his hard cases as following within one of four broad and overlapping categories:

(a) Cases where there is a binding or strongly persuasive precedent whose *ratio* is clear and in point but which the court is being asked to overrule or distinguish. In such cases the 'be consistent' and the 'be fair' or the 'don't legislate' and the 'be fair' expectations may conflict.

(b) Cases where there are alternative strands of ostensibly relevant precedents or competing principles confronting the court. Here a conflict between the 'provide justification' and the 'be consistent' expectations can arise.

(c) Cases for which there is a closely analogous precedent whose *ratio* is unclear, or which fall within the penumbra of uncertainty of an ostensibly relevant rule. In such cases the 'don't legislate', the 'be consistent' and the 'be fair' expectations may conflict.

(d) Cases where there are no strongly persuasive (as opposed to merely permissive) legal rules or precedents in point in the existing law. In these situations the question whether to extend an existing rule by analogy or to create a new rule or to apply an existing legal principle may involve a clash between the 'don't legislate' and the 'be fair' expectations or between the 'decide the case', the 'provide justification' and the 'don't legislate' expectations (Paterson, 1982: 128).

These classifications can be seen to be closely related to those of traditional legal thinking. However, when published, Paterson's study was seen to be sociologically daring because he did suggest that the Law Lords do not talk about cases in terms of doctrine alone, and that there is a substantial amount of debate over the policy elements of these cases. However, in Paterson's study, there is no mention of the social conditions which give rise to cases moving onto the House of Lords (for example, the wealth of the parties or economic considerations being taken by the parties or, indeed, any of the factors we described in Part II). These are assumed to be non-problematic. Because he misses out on these various factors, Paterson's approach is better seen as a sociology of appellate judgement at the highest level, rather than a full sociology of law.

At about the same time that Paterson was publishing his *The Law Lords*, a newer approach was being initiated in the USA. This newer approach, termed the *narrative approach*, has since taken on the attributes of an avalanche and has exploded in a variety of other disciplines – philosophy, literature and rhetoric to name but a few. The narrative approach in law was developed by two anthropologists, W. L. Bennett and M. S. Feldman in their *Reconstructing Reality in the Courtroom* (1981), where they posited that storytelling was one of the major factors of the criminal trial:

> Our search for the underlying basis of justice and judgement in American criminal trials has produced an interesting conclusion: the criminal trial is organized around storytelling. . . . Our analysis of American trials illustrates how an underlying storytelling process can be detected, described, and connected to the formal justice procedures that are unique to a particular society. Even when storytelling is not the underlying basis of legal judgement in a society, there is another generalization that can be drawn from the American case: legal judgement involves more than a set of formal procedures for resolving disputes in society. Formal justice procedures (rules of evidence, uses of case law or opinions, etc.) must engage some parallel form of social judgement that anchors legal questions in everyday understandings (Bennett and Feldman, 1981: 3–4).

It is relatively easy to see how Bennett and Feldman could take such an original perspective of the legal process: as anthropologists, they would already have been heavily influenced by the social nature of thought. For, as we noted above, it is anthropologists who have claimed to be the initiators of the sociology of knowledge. We can describe Bennett and Feldman's work as the sociology of legal knowledge, since they look to social patterns of thought for the rationality of the legal process.

Bennett and Feldman's work is important, but it is, we argue, limited and thus flawed. For example, it sets criminal practice aside from civil or non-jury practice, and emphasizes too much the storytelling aspects to the detraction of other elements we would consider essential. However, it is a clear move towards a sociology of legal knowledge. We look at this work more closely in the next chapter, where we extend our own view of legal information.

A final example of the development of a sociology of legal knowledge is the more recent kind of work which has developed, in part from Bennett and Feldman, but also from the continental school of philosophy termed *semiotics*. Though many semioticians would cry out in horror at being labelled sociologists, there is a common set of working assumptions (if not language) used by sociologists of knowledge and semioticians which leads us to think of the two on parallel courses towards a common harbour, if not necessarily steaming in each other's wake.

Perhaps the most sociologically inclined of the semioticians is Bernard Jackson who, in his *Law, Fact and Narrative Coherence* (1988) argues for what we would describe as a social theory of legal fact-finding. This is, of course, an important step in the building of a complete theory of the sociology of legal knowledge. In major part, it was the finding in science that *facts* were more complex than the traditional scientist believed (or believes) which gave rise to the sociology of science; thus, a similar move in legal theory can well be described as a potential cause of the breakdown of the ideology of the rule/fact dichotomy.

Jackson argues, as we do later in this book, that narrative is important. However, he suggests that narrative is not the answer to all our theoretical problems and indeed that: 'Narrative Coherence currently threatens to become a fashionable slogan within legal philosophy' (Jackson, 1988: 18). Given the wide range of philosophers of law who have taken up the cry of narrative coherence, this is a timely warning. Most interesting of Jackson's points is that he suggests that the real aspect which distinguishes the different philosophies which use the narrative framework is how they see how these stories relate to truth in the world. The positivists and traditional lawyers are able to add the narrative element onto their theories, Jackson argues, because they have a correspondence theory of truth, i.e. they accept that storytelling happens but the most successful stories in court are those which relate to true facts which actually happen in the world.

Others, including the semioticians, who do not hold to this correspondence theory, see that facts are socially constructed and that the narrative theory is part of a sociological theory for the constructing of legal knowledge. This, broadly, is our own view. A theory of the social construction of facts is not a complete theory of legal theory, of course, but it does count as a very important element in such a theory – most certainly it is an essential element.

A word should be said about the semiotic element of Jackson's theory. We would argue that semiotics is not essential nor necessary in coming to the general position which we hold in common *vis-à-vis* the nature of facts. Indeed, Ludwik Fleck, in his classic work from the 1930s, *Genesis and Development of a Scientific Fact* (which incidentally influenced Thomas Kuhn – we prefer the Fleckian view) was able to reach a similar position without semiotic insights. However, Jackson – in discussion – has argued that semiotics provides *a*, not *the*, mechanism for coming to this position. We are, anyway, concerned that semiotics has a tendency towards formalism which might, in other hands, lead to different assumptions (Leith, 1989) as well as a taint of scientism.

CONCLUSION

We have tried in this chapter to set a context for contemporary understanding of law. We have looked to developments in the philosophy of science to begin to undermine the 'scientific' assumptions in legal theory – that technical law can be kept separate from social factors. In Chapter 8, we will follow this up by suggesting that technical law itself arises from the social negotiation which is the legal process. We will do this by recourse to the data we presented in Part II.

It is important to realize that the rise of sociological approaches asking the question 'What is law' runs counter to the view that a sociology of law is not a theory of law. But such a 'paradigm shift' is not easy to make. Given the power of the substantive law ideology, it is not surprising that the ideology has lasted for so long, even though realism in the 1930s put so many effective arguments against it.

In the UK, it has been particularly obvious that anti-sociological approaches have been the norm in both legal education and in the philosophy of law. For some thirty years, thinking about law has been under the cloud of positivism, epitomized by Herbert Hart (1961) in his *The Concept of Law*. This was a 'sociology of law' (as Hart claimed it to be), which was basically anti-sociological and middle class. It did nothing to take ideas which were happening outside of Oxbridge philosophy and apply these to law. Thus, while in the philosophy of science and mathematics, the distinctions between fact and procedure and rule were crumbling, it was still possible for the orthodox view of legal reasoning to follow almost exactly that of Bentham (Leith and Ingram, 1988), who suggested a Platonic view of reality and knowledge.

It is only within the last few years that unhappiness with the Hartian view of law has grown. Our research into the barrister's world and the nature of legal information is one push further down this anti-positivist road.

NOTES

1 The well-known work of Baldwin and McConville (1981) on plea-bargaining provides an obvious example of what we are talking about here.
2 We refer to the views of Berger and Kellner (1981).
3 As noted by Wilson (1965), Reisman (1951) suggested that all sociologists and anthropologists have a problem in researching lawyers because they believe in the magic of law (see pp. 1 and 139 of Wilson's thesis, and elsewhere.)
4 Even the two relatively recent 'Law in Action' or 'Law in Context' approaches mean law in action on the bookshelves or in the context of the library (though this may mean the bookshelves or library of political science or social studies).
5 See also Foucault (1976), for the related but separate issue of medical practice as opposed to medical research.
6 The availability of research funds for projects related to AIDS and to cancer has influenced the flow of much research recently.

7 And, as we have intimated, is closely related to the positivist school in legal philosophy (see, e.g. Hart, 1961, and criticisms of this in Leith and Ingram, 1988).

8 A similar sort of work to Paterson's (though much criticised for its journalistic approach) is Woodward and Armstrong's (1981) *The Brethren: Inside the Supreme Court.*

8

ELEMENTS OF
ADVOCACY AND
LEGAL INFORMATION

INTRODUCTION

In Chapter 7, we began to discuss the idea of a sociology of *legal* knowledge, and suggested that in order to achieve this we must, broadly, follow the paths laid out by the sociology of science and accept that knowledge is socially constructed. To say that legal knowledge is socially structured means several things.

First, it means that legal knowledge cannot be fixed and immutable since it is merely a product of certain social and intellectual conditions. Thus on the macro level, 'contract' has no firm or fixed meaning which lies outside its usage; and on the micro level, all the 'facts' in cases and courts are contingent upon a process of negotiation and agreement which take place within the particular conditions set by the social organization of the profession.

Secondly, it means that the transmission and understanding of this legal knowledge is social and interpretive, rather than 'scientific' (e.g. there are no procedures which can provide a single correct understanding). Also, the passing of this knowledge from one to another mitigates against certainty and clarity due to the nature of person-to-person communication being also interpretive.

Thirdly, legal knowledge cannot be divorced from the environment which provides the time, desire and the effort to construct and maintain it. Thus legal knowledge can be refined and well-worked, hasty and rough, or almost non-existent depending upon the situation in which it is constructed – there is no one qualitative level of this knowledge which sets it off as being 'legal' apart from the fact that it arises from the legal community.

Fourthly (and perhaps consequent on the others), legal knowledge is constructed to a specification that is drawn up in close relation to the context in which it is to be used. A good legal argument is one that works, one that achieves the result required, even where this may differ from what could be achieved if doctrinal integrity was what was being sought.

All told, these four aspects can be described as anti-formalist. They hold that it is not enough to posit that law can be viewed as a coherent and formal system of rules, principles and such like for, unlike a formal mathematical or logical system, formal coherence and formal consistency are not typical facets of socially based systems. It is important to note that there are many who hold that it is possible to subscribe to both a formal view of law and, at the same time, a view that allows this formal body to interact with political and moral standpoints (Dworkin being one example of this view). A theory of the sociology of legal knowledge cannot accept this division of law into part formal and part informal system – both, to it, must be informal.

The major thrust of these elements seems to be towards a highly relativistic picture of legal knowledge – a type of knowledge which turns to dust in the hands. They appear to be relativistic since they give no firm foundation upon which we can base our reason and our thinking. Indeed, to a degree, we are arguing for this relativism, even though we realize that relativism has been attacked from all corners by all comers (see Feyerabend, 1978, on this), since it seems to offer only anarchy and irrationality. To Ernest Gellner, an opponent of relativism, the only solution is finding the universal truth which stands apart from cultural relativism:

> A spectre haunts human thought: relativism. If truth has many faces, then not one of the them deserves trust or respect. Happily, there is a remedy: human universals. They are the holy water with which the spectre can be exorcised. But, of course, before we can use human universals to dispel the threat of cognitive anarchy which would otherwise engulf us, we must first *find* them. And so, the new hunt of the Holy Grail is on (Gellner, 1985: 83).

Some might suggest that the hunt is not new, that the search for 'human universals' has been on for a very long time. At present, of course, times are hard for those engaged in this enterprise. As Fish reports:

> . . . in discipline after discipline there is evidence of what has been called the interpretive turn, the realisation (at least for those that it seizes) that the givens of any field of activity – including the facts it commands, the procedures it trusts in, and the values it expresses and extends – are socially and politically constructed, are fashioned by men rather than delivered by God or Nature (Fish, 1989: 485; see also Vickers, 1988).

In law, there has recently been some evidence of such a turn,[1] but generally the relativists have been in decline since the demise of the Realist movement. The main schools in the Philosophy of Law have been the natural law approach, which was an attempt to discover universals that can act against the threat of irrational law, and the positive approach, which looks to logic as a human universal to overcome this same threat. We would argue that, like the original Holy Grail, this second one too will elude discovery.

We must declare ourselves to be, in Richard Lanham's classification, something akin to *Homo rhetoricus* who holds that the truth is individual and temporary rather than universal and lasting, that it is indeed contingent. This is in opposition to *Homo seriosus* who fears the invasion of the citadel of essence by the negotiable, the protean and the unpredictable. This species instead holds that

> ... every man possesses a central self, an irreducible identity. These selves combine into a single, homogeneously real society which constitutes a referent reality for the men living in it. This referent society is in turn contained in a physical nature itself referential, standing 'out there', independent of man (Lanham, 1976: 1).

Language, developed to communicate facts and concepts about man or nature or about feelings, can for them be measured by its clarity or sincerity as compared to the reality thus envisioned. These two positions are constantly in opposition and are irreconcilable. Fish (1989: 484) points out that 'the history of Western thought could be written as the history of this quarrel'. Our concern is that in the context of law this history has been particularly mistold.

Our view of law and the legal process, though, is not of anarchy and irrationality at work. Instead, as we saw in Part II, we see – at least from the barrister's perspective – that the world is relatively constant and clear, and that there are similar problems met by similar barristers in different cities, in different areas of law and at different levels in the court system. This is not a picture of anarchic confusion, but one of a highly constricted and constrained world. So, how is it possible to hold a philosophy where knowledge is seemingly at the whim of social and uncontrollable factors, and yet also view the actors in the world as tightly restrained? The answer is simple: it is that though knowledge is potentially in a constant state of flux, it is held reasonably stable through the medium of social interaction. Thus the very cause of the possible chaos (the social nature of knowledge) is actually that which holds the chaos at bay. Essentially, the legal world gives legal knowledge the impression of being fixed because it acts as a *community* which must work together.

Barristers, as actors in this potentially disruptive and confused world, *have* to come together and work together (along with judges, solicitors and clients) in order to get through working life. Though it is not essential to be in total accord all the time with all one's colleagues, it is necessary to let oneself be constrained by the pressures of barristerial life in order to be a barrister: those who are not constrained do not manage to remain in the community. While the constraints are of various sorts (economic, social, etc.), *there are also constraints on thinking about law* which are just as important. Therefore, the answer to those who look for the seeming stability of legal practice among the rules of law is to suggest they look rather at the social conditions which give rise to those practices rather than on the bookshelves of law at the rules themselves.

In this chapter, we will further examine the findings we presented in Part II in the light of the social nature of legal knowledge which we introduced in Chapter 6. Our attempt is to demonstrate that legal knowledge and legal information are a matrix of practices and ways of thinking which cannot be fully modelled by the textbook view of law. We argue for the richness of legal life as a host of interacting social processes. In other words, we argue for a full-blown sociology of law and legal theory (see Wilson, 1965: 139).

THE TEXTBOOK TRADITION IN ACADEMIC LAW

In Part II, we saw the role which was played by substantive law research in the preparation of a case for court. We also noted the attitude which some members of the judiciary and solicitors had towards a barrister who is too oriented to substantive law. These suggested that there were sometimes pressures against the citing of legal authorities in court. Generally, our findings were that substantive law research as an active and ongoing element of case preparation was not carried out as frequently as the traditional view of the barrister's task would expect.

However, we do not think our interviewees argued for a world free of substantive law. Rather, they seemed to suggest that most of their legal knowledge is routinized and garnered from practice and experience, not from constant exploration of textbooks. Further, court practice and procedure is highly significant and important to the barrister; we might consider this to be every bit as 'legal' as citing legal authorities, since much of these procedural elements are derived from past litigation and legislation. To the practising barrister, neither of these is of greater 'worth' than the other. To the typical legal academic, however, the substantive law element is of much greater import than the procedural, as can be seen from the writings in the various academic journals.[2]

Our findings can thus be seen as highlighting Pound's suggestion that law in practice is indeed different from law in the textbooks. Our barristers did not deny the use of substantive law, but seemed to indicate that it was treated in a different manner from that of law schools and law academics: that the kind of interpretation that was used was different.

Legal academics have a very textual, that is written, view of law. This is very easy to see. Not only can it be seen in the traditional concentration upon legislation and case report, but it can also be seen in the current interest in 'law and literature', for literature is of course an entirely written medium. Posner is one who has suggested, in his *Law and Literature: A Misunderstood Relation* (1988), several important connections between law and literature. Some of the connections he highlights are:

2. Both legal and literary scholarship are centrally concerned with the meaning of texts. In the case of law these are constitutions, statutes, judicial and administrative rules, and judicial opinions. And legal scholarship, like literary scholarship, consists to a significant extent of

commentary on texts temporally and culturally remote from the commentator . . .

3. Many legal texts, especially, judicial opinions, resemble literary texts in being highly rhetorical rather than coolly expository. Judges and other lawyers resemble literary artists in the close attention they pay to the choice of words in which to express themselves, as well as in the fondness for metaphors and similes noted earlier . . .

5. The legal process, especially the adversary process of Anglo-American civil and criminal jury trials, has a significant theatrical dimension. This is one of the reasons why trials are a staple of literature and why writers of fiction . . . have turned their talents to the description of actual trials (Posner, 1988: 8–9).

While the last is, in our view, an argument against the literary nature of law, since it emphasizes that law (in courtroom practice at least) is used parasitically by writers because it is non-literary and offers itself to the writer as a source of drama, it can be seen that the legal text is held by many, if not most, lawyers to be of prime importance to the lawyer. Indeed, it can be said that most academic lawyers would argue that the written document is the most important element in the legal process – certainly, the academic process emphasizes the written above all else.

Our findings point to a different view of law in action, and one which is much closer to the historical idea of the 'common lawyer' who, rather than using the techniques of literary analysis, uses law found in the common body of knowledge held at the bar and the library. Law in this view is, to use Jackson's (1988) term, 'hearsay'. To be sure, there is a degree of interaction: our lawyers did not claim never to look to legal texts, nor did they seem to underestimate the substantive law element in their education, but what they did emphasize, over and over again, was that the substantive law was only one part of the story – the context in which that law was to be used was the other.

Contrary to this, we might say that the overriding concern of the academic lawyer is freeing himself or herself from the context of law. From masses of case reports and piles of contradictory legislation (different Acts brought in by different governments in different political climates, etc.), academic lawyers try to stand back and put some principle and fundamental meaning to their area. In order to do this, of course, the context has to be dropped, for that very context with its confusing facts and *obiter dictum* would hide the trees of principle in a forest of particular litigations. Sugarman has described this process of escaping context as the *textbook tradition*, a direct result of the common law tradition in legal education:

The common law frame of mind continues to overshadow the way we teach, write and think about law. Its categories and assumptions are still the standard of most first-year law students; and they continue to organize law textbooks and case-books. Stated baldly, it assumes that although law may appear to be irrational, chaotic and particularistic, if one digs deep enough and knows what one is looking for, then it will soon become evident that the law is an internally coherent and unified body of rules. This coherence and unity stem from the fact that law is grounded in, and logically derived from, a handful of general principles; and the whole subject – areas such as contract and torts are distinguished by some common principles or elements which fix the boundaries of the subject. The exposition and systematization of these general principles, and the techniques required to find and to apply them and the rules that they underpin, are largely what legal education and scholarship are all about (Sugarman, 1986: 26).

It is, of course, not only in law that we have a textbook tradition where principles are systematized and handled without need to look back at the context. In all areas of science and technology, that same need to extract theory from the complexities of practice is found. For example, one of us with a background in computer science has found this to be prevalent in that area too. In fact, computer science is a good example for what we mean. A computer program is a very complex artefact, and those programs called operating systems – which make the computer hardware 'work' – in particular, are very complex indeed. They can be many tens of thousands of pages of program code in length and can take up to 10 000 man years of effort to produce. Programs of this complexity cannot be dissected and examined with ease. Also, there is an organic quality about these programs, since they are forever being altered, extended and changed (just like legislation and case law). Therefore, in the textbook tradition of computer science, the attempt is made to stand back from the actual programs and discuss them in terms of principles and abstract procedures. One textbook on operating system design describes the nature of the abstracting task:

> It is important to realise that real operating systems are seldom static in design. They continually undergo changes and alterations, thus making up-to-date, comprehensive description difficult, if not impossible, to undertake. For this reason the following case studies should be viewed merely as examples of the kinds of resource management techniques and algorithms that are likely to be found in real systems. These examples should serve not only to broaden the reader's experiences and insight but also to provide a perspective for the study of other systems and a conceptual starting point for a deeper study of the systems outlined (Madnick and Donovan, 1974: 512).

In computer science, then, the abstractions of the textbook tradition are used to provide insight into complex programmed systems. No-one in computer science, it might be supposed, actually believes that the descriptions used in textbooks are close descriptions of reality, since the divergence between a description which takes a few pages in a textbook and a few hundred pages in the text of a program is too vast to encourage the belief that one is an accurate model of the other: it is merely seen as an abstract picture of reality.

But this same view of the limited nature of the textbook description does not transfer across to law. There, in the textbook tradition, there seems to lie the belief not only that the textbook is a model of reality, but that the textbook provides the reality itself. This is indeed a striking difference: theoretical, abstract and acontextual law is viewed as 'real law', whereas practical, court-based law is viewed as sociological divergence from that real, substantive law. In this book, we are actually arguing against this view of law as an abstract system of textbook knowledge, and suggest that written law stands in the same sort of relationship to law in practice, as does computer science theory stand to computer science practice. That is, substantive law is a more practical activity than legal academics believe.

We can look at an example from another scientific discipline which illustrates some of the problems of the textbook tradition. Coming from the scientific area, it supports the picture we presented in Chapter 6 that science can no longer be seen in the traditional, classical light. Our example is one of 'crystal growing', i.e. making liquids form into special types of crystals which are used in the electronics industry. The example comes from the work of Harry Collins.[3]

Collins' interest was in the taking of knowledge about the field of crystal growing and putting it into a computer so that the computer would have expertise about the area. The general field is called *expert systems research*, because it attempts – unsuccessfully as has been argued elsewhere (Leith, 1990) and in law (Leith, 1991) – to make a computer compete with real experts. The proposed output from Collins' project was a computer program which was expert at crystal growing. Collins was interested in the difference between the nature of the computer expertise and that of the human expert.

One of Collins' first findings was that there was a concentration upon *textbook* knowledge by most involved in the crystal-growing field, even though they all realized that the textbook information was not an accurate representation of what crystal growers actually do: it was as though information held in a textbook somehow had a higher intellectual standing than more practical experimental information/knowledge, even though the practical experimental knowledge was more useful to crystal growers. As Collins (1990) states:

> We have much more respect for abstract text book knowledge than for the knowledge required to achieve practical outcomes. Even our expert, when asked to describe his practice, had great difficulty keeping away from the irrelevant and incorrect text book account.

The human crystal grower worked in a crystal-growing research group where the head of the group had written a standard textbook on the subject of crystal growing. It made much of the need, in general crystal growing, to have access to high-pressure environments (i.e. pressure chambers) in order to get crystals to grow, using a technique called *crystal pulling*. While, in general commercial systems, this might well be the best way to carry out the process, by and large it is not actually done this way in the laboratory: much more simple means were actually used by the research team (which did not require high-cost equipment), yet these methods were not detailed in the textbook. The team actually had costly equipment available to them, but preferred to use these other techniques, indicating that the techniques used were not inferior, at least in the laboratory context, in comparison to the detailed methods.

The textbook, rather than the actual methods used, however, heavily influenced the knowledge elicitation sessions between the expert and the knowledge engineer. Collins' observations of the dialogues between the expert and the person trying to produce the computer program illustrated how it was difficult for the expert to get away from the formalized knowledge in the textbook:

> The text book continually took priority in Green and Draper's discussion in spite of desperate attempts to bring actual practice to the foreground. There are two reasons for this. The first is a matter of the conventional social hierarchy of knowledge types engendered in our educational ideologies. . . . The other thing, of course, is that experts are in principle incapable of speaking all that they know, and in practice, unlikely to have the degree of phenomenological self-consciousness required to say even that which could be articulated in principle. Text book knowledge is more easy to speak about precisely because its formalised and abstract nature lends it a perpetual and inescapable unfamiliarity.

The textbook, in this situation, is acting as a constraint upon the way that the team think and talk about their crystal growing. They find it difficult to explicate what they are doing in practice, without resorting back to the incorrect (at least in this context) and incomplete knowledge held in the textbook.

In computer science, just as one cannot teach operating system design by looking at every detail of how actual implementors solve implementation problems, more emphasis is given to the textbook description, even though the textbook itself notes that it idealizes reality rather than reflects it (as our quotation above shows). In this crystal-growing example, however, Collins shows us something more heightened: it is that even though practitioners are aware of the mismatch between implementation (in this case, the implementation of crystal growing) and theory, sometimes in science it is difficult to stand outside of this mismatch. When describing what they do, the crystal growers continually fall off the fence into the hands of theory, rather than practice.

THE NATURE OF LEGAL INFORMATION AND LEGAL KNOWLEDGE

It seems to us that something like this textbook/practice bifurcation is occurring in the descriptions we have of law. Practitioners, in barristerial writings, emphasize the practice of law – the courtroom drama – and downplay the theoretical aspects, while the academic lawyers emphasize the textbook theory of law, and downplay the practical and contextual elements. Neither view, it seems to us, is an accurate representation of legal reality.

It is our view that the coming together of the practitioners' and the academics' views of law can only be achieved by looking to a theory of *legal information*, and accepting that that theory must be highly charged with sociological insight. We propose this because we have already seen in Part II how constant negotiation and social interaction within a context created by particular cases and by the endeavour of maintaining a career moulds practice in law. And, of course, theory is a formalizing of that legal practice as cases move their way up the appellate system. The concept of legal information helps us to relate the practical elements and the theoretical elements together into one understandable process of legal knowledge. Later in this chapter, we will look more fully at this notion of legal information.

STORIES RATHER THAN LEGAL INFORMATION?

Having given an overview of our concept of legal information and its construction during the pre-trial and trial periods, we need to look further to theories of how this information is processed in the court. Hence, we shall briefly look at what is coming to be seen as a central text in legal theory, *Reconstructing Reality in the Courtroom* (Bennett and Feldman, 1981), which proposes storytelling as pivotal to the criminal trial. We have already mentioned that we see it broadly, as on an interesting track, but being too simplistic to provide a good and reliable understanding of the legal process. It is, as we have mentioned, already being seen by some legal theorists as something of a bandwagon, and we must be careful not to be carried along by a tide which will leave us high and dry.

Put simply, Bennett and Feldman's theory is to do with how reality is taken and translated into a form which is suitable for the ordinary person who meets the criminal justice system. This can be the defendants themselves, but more importantly the jury members who have no legal qualifications, but who are brought into the legal system to adjudicate on guilt or innocence. Since membership of the jury is open to such a wide range of potential personality types and classes of persons, etc., Bennett and Feldman suggest that there must be some simple means whereby the legal process is made intelligible to them. They note that jury studies in the past (especially those which have tried to look for the potential bias in juries) have looked to the complexity of the jury process and have used varieties of statistical techniques as part of the research strategy. Unfortunately, they suggest that such techniques have not demonstrated any forces or biases which, many commentators claim, do actually exist and which have an effect upon the jury:

> Whether one conducts interviews with participants or reads the voluminous literature on trials, the overwhelming impression is that trials hinge on a collection of narrow variables, such as: lines of questioning; lawyers' tactics; the testimony of key witnesses; judges' instructions; rules of evidence; the race or social status of the defendant; the nature of the crime; the class, age, sex, or racial composition of the jury; and so forth. The problem with such explanations is not so much that they are wrong, as that they are incomplete (Bennett and Feldman, 1981: 17).

Just as we emphasized in Part II that the legal process is court-directed, Bennett and Feldman argue the same. But they go further and suggest that the simple framework of reference which gives all the above variables meaning, is the *story*:

> The story is an everyday form of communication that enables a diverse cast of courtroom characters to follow the development of a case and reason about the issues in it. Despite the maze of legal jargon, lawyers' mysterious tactics, and obscure court procedures, any criminal case can be reduced to the simple form of a story. Through the use of broadly shared techniques of telling and interpreting stories, the actors in a trial present, organize, and analyze the evidence that bears on the alleged illegal activity (Bennett and Feldman, 1981: 4).

Stories, to Bennett and Feldman, provide the social framework which makes all behaviour meaningful. It allows jury members to decide on the reliability of a witness as well as to find, say, missing elements in the evidence which is being presented to them. The more credible the story, then the more credible the witness, is one conclusion to be reached.

There is a substantial amount of evidence to suggest that barristers do use stories in their presentation of cases. Posner, for example, in advancing his ideas about the relationship between law and literature, declares:

> . . . effective trial practice equals meticulous preparation and a theory of the case created by organising, selecting and recasting the raw events to make an intelligible, coherent and appealing story (Posner, 1988: 361).

Presumably, Posner's own experience on the bench in US courtrooms has caused him to value a well-crafted tale. Often, of course, the stories will be stock stories in the sense that although details will change the central plot will be constant. We might expect this since, perhaps, so many of the cases they handle are of a similar nature, and they cannot all be differentiated, especially in the lower level courts.[4] For example, Evans, in his text for young advocates, tells of the necessity to provide a storyline ('show them the way home') suitable for judges or juries who prefer to believe that policemen don't lie:

This ['show them the way home'] is a well-known phrase among advocates, and it is one of the most important rules of advocacy. Let me explain it as best I can. For a jury to come back with a verdict of not guilty is sometimes difficult for them. They *are* left wondering whether the defendant did it or not and so they intellectually realise that not guilty is the only proper verdict. The difficulty is that half a dozen decent-looking and decent-sounding police officers have given clear evidence of the defendant's guilt, and if the jury come back with a not guilty verdict they will be appearing to reject that police evidence in its entirety. They don't like the idea of doing that. . . . If this is so with a jury, imagine how very much more difficult it is with a magistrate. Neither jury nor magistrate like the idea of finding that the police have been less than honest. . . . You 'must show them the way home', show them how they can acquit in comfort (Evans, 1985: 80).

And just how is this to be done? Evans suggests telling 'lies' (e.g. accusing the police more of enthusiasm in wanting to do their job effectively, rather than concocting evidence), making the story acceptable to the jury and judge rather than emphasizing the truth of the lack of police honesty.

It would be difficult to believe that every barrister was capable of running each and every case in a manner which highlighted the individuality of that defendant/litigant, and that even this fact would make the necessity of having a series of stock presentations obvious. Of course, this does not mean that the decision to use that particular storyline is made and then must be followed through – as we have seen, the barrister is highly attuned to all the factors which make a case work out successfully, such as the performance of witnesses and opposition counsel, the impact of evidence and, of course, the signals given by the judge, and must be able to change strategy if required.

However, Bennett and Feldman are particularly interested in the unfairness which is presumed to exist at the heart of the legal process and suggest that storytelling can explain why some come off so badly when in contact with the legal process:

Perhaps the most significant application of the storytelling perspective involves clarifying the nature of bias in the justice process. Stories are symbolic reconstructions of events and actions. People who cannot manipulate symbols within a narrative format may be at a disadvantage even when, as witnesses or defendants, they are telling the truth. Moreover, the interpretation of stories requires that teller and listener share a set of norms, assumptions, and experiences. If witnesses and jurors differ in their understanding of society and social action, stories that make sense to one actor in a trial may be rejected by another. The biases that result from storytelling in trials are more subtle and more difficult to combat than the sort of bias that is based on straightforward social prejudice (Bennett and Feldman, 1981: 6).

The field of applying this knowledge about stories to law and, more generally, philosophy has become known as *narratology*. It attempts to reduce the complexity of information (Bennett and Feldman actually refer to its ability to reduce 'information overload') to a simple format. No doubt part of the attractiveness of the idea is that it does seem to be so general, and has so many applications where people have to meet and to communicate information.

The narrative theory has been taken up as a concept by many whose perspectives radically differ. Bernard Jackson argues that what separates the different uses of the narrative perspective in legal theory is that some see it as having a limited application. Thus these theorists (he is specifically dealing with Neil MacCormick and William Twining here) look to the narrative element in the presentation of evidence as a justifying element in the legal process when there is a lack of truth-based observation. Narrative thus becomes a process of trying to think through the *probabilities* of different actions having happened. Jackson uses MacCormick's 'Burke and Hare' example to demonstrate this:

> The police witness says he found a human corpse in a box in William Burke's house. The corpse bore marks of bruising. The juror *knows* that was said. If the juror believes that the witness is honest and has a sound memory and is remembering facts he had the opportunity carefully to observe (all of which features of witnesses and their evidence it is the task of the cross-examination by defence counsel to test), then the juror has reason to believe that the testimony is true, or more or less probably true depending on the credibility (that is, the honesty, accuracy and reliability) of the witness (Jackson, 1988: 19).

We give this example here to point to the ease which narrative perspectives can be taken up by legal philosophers, and how they can be more limiting than that of Bennett and Feldman. The latter do not see storytelling as only coming to bear as a probabilistic mechanism. Far from it. Bennett and Feldman, as anthropologists, seem to be arguing for the social nature of understanding and suggesting that stories provide the truth, rather than complement it. Bennett and Feldman would argue, in the 'Burke and Hare' example, that some members of the jury would (because of their social understanding) find stories which relied on the truth-telling aspects of police witnesses more coherent and consistent than those which other jury members (from different areas of social understanding) might. As they state:

> Does this [testing of coherence and probability] mean that juror's judgements (and most other social judgements as well) are based on objective pictures of what 'really' happened? Not at all. At every stage of the storytelling–interpretation process, both storytellers and interpreters make choices about how to define story elements, and what frames of reference to apply. In this sense, a story is a reconstruction of an event in light of the teller's initial perception, immediate judgements

about the audience, the interests that appear to be at stake, and, perhaps, most important, what has gone before in the situation in which the story is presented (Bennett and Feldman, 1981: 64–5).

Our perspective of storytelling is close to this view of Bennett and Feldman (and Jackson as well) in that we believe that 'truth' and 'facts' which come to be agreed in court are socially negotiated. The various processes we highlight as producing and manipulating legal information are part of these fact-producing negotiations. However, there are problems in taking Bennett and Feldman's position as it stands currently.

For example, the concept of 'story' is so wide-ranging that it can compromise almost anything one wishes. This is, of course, an advantage but it has its dangers. For example, it is possible to represent any information as a story: since information is usually passed from person to person, has a context which makes it understandable, and is time-oriented (i.e. things happen in a given order), all these can be represented as a story. The advantage of this is that it takes us away from those sorts of views which linger on from logical positivism or atomism, i.e. which suggest that facts which are verifiably true are understandable simply because they are so. Unfortunately, the danger is that we simply use 'story' as a blanket for all sorts of verbal/textual behaviour which is better looked at with more restricted concepts. A further danger is the possibility of reification of a 'story' in the same way that the concept of a 'rule' is constantly reified in traditional legal theory.

A second problem is that Bennett and Feldman's thesis is directed towards ordinary people who sit on a jury. It is probably due to the fact that neither of these researchers were lawyers, which makes them limit their view to that of the criminal trial – for we are given no direction as to why telling stories in front of a jury should be any different to telling them in an interlocutory matter in front of a sole judge in the Chancery Division. It seems to us that there is no reason to stop at the jury: if narrative is essential to communication, then we should expect it to appear at all parts of the legal process.

A third problem is that of emphasis. They do not suggest that the areas which other researchers have looked at (race or class, testimony of key witnesses, style of advocacy) connect in with the story-telling thesis. They do not deny any of these, but turn the traditional tables around by emphasizing the story rather than those aspects which allow stories to be told. For example, their definition of a trial shows that those elements of the construction of a case which we emphasize, are relatively neglected:

... a trial is a set of rules for reconstructing a disputed incident in a symbolic form that allows the actions of the participants to be judged in fairly uniform fashion by (in theory at least) any judge or jury who was not witness to the incident. The rules governing formal trial procedures result in the introduction of information in ways that force jurors to concentrate particular judgement skills on a key disputed action and its immediate circumstances (as opposed, for example, to judging the character of the defendant, the opinions of the judges or witnesses, etc.). Each symbolic element introduced in support of an interpretation of the central action is subject to possible disproof, resymbolization, or rejection by judge or jury as irrelevant to the interpretation of the designated central action. The judgement form that permits the most economical organization, testing, and interpretation of the information introduced within the trial format is the story (Bennett and Feldman, 1981: 165).

This is not wrong, but what it is not is a theory of legal knowledge. In fact, Bennett and Feldman are clear that there are legal procedures and such like which impinge upon what 'information' is allowable within the courtroom. However, taking their theories a step further, we can see that a full theory of legal knowledge which accepted the narrative paradigm would suggest that these same legal procedures and rules would themselves be discussible in story terms. Hence, arguing over whether or not a judge should apply a procedural rule (say, one which prohibits certain evidence from being introduced) would necessitate reasoning and debate and the putting forward of 'good reasons' in narrative form by both advocates to the judge.[5] In fact, this is just what our interviewees suggested actually happened. There was a constant interplay between advocate and judge attempting to find particular lines of reasoning (which we can describe here as narratives) which appealed to that particular judge. It is also true that we were constantly told that advocacy before a jury was different from that before a judge, in that different kinds of presentation had to be used – a situation which would be predicted and expected by narrative theory.

However, story-telling is not enough. The storyteller in a traditional oral society, or the politician painting pictures of the upright society he promises, might be able to pander to the unfettered whims of his or her audience, but this is not possible for the advocate. He or she is given and controlled by the information which arises elsewhere, and which must be taken into account in any full sociological theory of legal knowledge.

What is the connection between stories and information? The connection between Bennett and Feldman's theory and a theory of legal knowledge is actually that of the triumvirate relationship of *rhetoric*, *logic* and *logos*. We look to these in the next section.

THE CENTRAL ROLE OF RHETORIC IN KNOWLEDGE

If we really must look for someone to blame as to why we find it so difficult to connect together the narrative theory and the concept of legal information, the most appropriate fall guy must be Aristotle. For it was Aristotle who effectively destroyed the fuller concept of *logos* for his descendants and left us with a view of rhetoric which has cast it – among its critics – as the medium of false knowledge.

'Logos' as a concept has had a diverse history, but its roots can be seen in the early Greek notion of reason and expression. As Fisher (1987: 5) describes it:

In the beginning was the word or, more accurately, the logos. And in the beginning, 'logos' meant story, reason, rationale, conception, discourse, thought. Thus all forms of human expression and communication – from epic to architecture, from biblical narrative to statuary – came within its purview. At least this was the case until the time of the pre-Socratic philosophers and Plato and Aristotle. As a result of their thinking, logos and mythos, which had been conjoined were dissociated; logos was transformed from a generic term to a specific one, applying only to philosophical (later technical) discourse. Poetical and rhetorical discourse were relegated to a secondary or negative status respecting their connections with truth, knowledge, and reality. Poetic was given province over mythos; rhetoric was relegated to the realm where logos and mythos reign in dubious harmony. A historical hegemonic struggle ensues among proponents of each of the three forms of discourse which lasts to this day.

Logos then, once a holistic concept, has become the three bruised but battling disciplines of logic, rhetoric and poetic of which – in current Western thought – the latter is the most minor, but the former the most powerful. There is no doubt that poetic, as the expression of literature and drama, has import to the advocate trying to capture and enrapture the jury in a murder trial or the Law Lord trying to seduce his brethren by written argument, but it is not our major concern here. Rather, our main concern is the battle between logic and rhetoric, the two elements of logos which were specifically separated and given life by Aristotle. Logos, in the Aristotelian framework, meant the technical analysis and production of argument (and later took the title, logic), whereas rhetoric, in this same framework, became the means of enunciating and discovering knowledge when truth and falsity were not certain.

Given this split of logos, the scene was set for the belief that logic provided truth, while rhetoric could – depending upon the individual viewpoint – help clarify or confuse. Little wonder that in the post-Aristotelian history of rhetoric it has always been seen in the lesser light to logic. But, as Ong has stated, the formal logic which developed post-Aristotle is actually based on the questions which were raised by the minor discipline:

> Formal logic grew out of rhetoric and, more remotely, out of verbal combat, for formal logic came into being when the question was raised, Why is it that what you say demolishes what I say? What are the structures in play when yes and no are set in motion against one another? After it was invented by Aristotle, logic had its ups and downs. It took various turns, and much of it atrophied from time to time. In modern times it has taken on a new life such as it has not had since medieval logic. . . (Ong, 1977: 208–209).

In Chapter 7, we looked briefly at some of the problems with which formal logic is beset. Technical argument, for example, rages over the interpretation of the most elementary and fundamental meanings of the logical connectors. In the logical systems themselves, of course, these problems are not major; but when we come to translate back and forward between natural language and/or the world of social complexity and these logical systems, we find that success has been lacking. Open any textbook on philosophical logic and we see the contortions as the logician tries (and fails) to model the simplest of ideas which a child handles with ease. And these philosophical logicians never agree that each others' systems are really logical at all! Yet they firmly believe that logic offers certainty in reasoning – that logos lies with logic.

Rhetoric, since its demise in the post-medieval world, has mostly stayed in its place – subsidiary to logic – and has given logic the benefit of the logos doubt. But recently, with the validity of logic in science coming under question, and with the rise of sociological views of knowledge and mathematical knowledge, rhetoricians have been less keen to accept their minor role. One sign of this is the increase in interest in narrative: stories though persuasive and allowing communication are, of course, not logical.

The logical view of the relationship between rhetoric and logic is that rhetoric is necessary to present the facts discovered by logic. It is as though rhetoric is a skin which clothes logical knowledge, and when the logical basis is removed, there is nothing left to give rhetoric any substance. Contrary to this, the rhetorical view is now that, with the demise of the concept of 'brute fact', we see how facts rely upon rhetorical construction, e.g. the rhetorical technique of storytelling. This latter view radically changes the sceptical description of rhetoric as 'flowery speech' to the more correct one of 'socially negotiated knowledge'.

The advocate, when presenting the lay client's case in court, is not presenting a list of logical facts. He or she is in constant social negotiation with the judge, the witness, the jury, the opposing advocate over what shall, in the trial, constitute the 'facts'. Indeed, even in the pre-trial stages there is, as we have seen, a complicated social process that occurs, which ushers into the picture the whole complex relationship with the lay client and solicitor and the professional milieu in which the barrister has to operate. This is why advocates, when questioned, emphasize consistently that they are not concerned with law, but with 'facts'. However, it is not the simple presentation of facts which is important, but the construction of them during the trial. Of course, advocates frequently decide before they enter the court what the facts will be, i.e., they get together with their barristerial opponent and actually agree upon what the case will be fought. So it is not only during the trial that this process of rhetoric/negotiation is carried through – it is in fact central to the entire barristerial world.

A simple example concerning the problem of facts might help. One of us witnessed a demonstration of a computer system which was, essentially, a blackboard with a built-in photocopier. It was designed for presenting evidence in court, allowing copies of anything on the board at any point in time to be prepared onto A4 sized paper and dispersed about the court. The demonstration was given by someone who frequently acted as an expert witness, who had to accept some scepticism from the mainly academic legal audience. It seemed too expensive a solution for that audience. Why, they asked the demonstrator, couldn't you simply prepare your maps of traffic accidents and such like before you entered the court? It was insightful to hear his reply of, 'But before you go into court, you don't know what the facts will be'. To the academic, the facts should be simple and non-controversial, but to the practitioner they have to be fought for and argued over.

We believe that the evidence we present in Part II demonstrates the nature of this rhetoric as persuasion in a complex world. Here, there are not the clear lines, excluded middles and certainty of logic. Every piece of legal knowledge has the potential for confusion – from identifying the problem in the brief, developing strategy and, if necessary, presenting the case in a full court hearing. That this happens in law is not surprising, for it also happens in logic too – every piece of logical knowledge had to come from the confusion of the logician's mind. To quote Ong once again:

> Formal logic, we know, did not grow out of a dispassionate or ironic [non-polemical] setting such as the concept of logic itself might suggest – what could be more objective, neutral, uninvolved than logic? Rather, it grew out of reflection on disputation, on verbal and intellectual contest, on the question 'How is it that what you say demolishes what I say?' Formal logic remains over the ages committed to diaretic [polemical] procedures, and it is no accident that formal logicians, past to present, have quite commonly proved to be disputatious people and not infrequently cantankerous (Ong, 1989: 21–2).

To return to storytelling, and to try to make it more real as a description of legal communication, we need to extend the paradigm which Bennett and Feldman present. Their view is too static a perspective, and is too concerned simply with the narrative element. There is more to legal knowledge than simply telling a good (i.e. a coherent and consistent) story: that something else is the rhetorical element of selecting issues and negotiating and battling for facts which might help one's own story – all within the milieu of professional life. This is all to do with the construction of 'information', either in the court or before a case is initiated, or more generally from the interrelationships between the participants in the legal process.[6] Furthermore, the information that is being constructed is, above all else, information that *works* within a given context and whose employment is closely determined by the pragmatic situation at hand. We need only think back to the example that we looked at earlier of the barrister who, with a client of limited means, scared off the other side by declaring at a preliminary stage that the law of Scotland should apply in the particular circumstances of the case (see p. 94). As Kuhn (1962: 170) says in the context of scientific debate, in the end the force of scientific argument is 'only that of persuasion where "there is no standard higher than the assent of the relevant community" but what better criterion could there be?' In the legal context, the ruling of the court, the successful persuasion of a tribunal to a particular outlook, is itself constitutive

of what is valid. Good legal information does not have to be 'true': it need
only work.

Emphasizing, as Bennett and Feldman do, the storytelling element at the
expense of the information element, skews our understanding of what comprises legal knowledge too much in one direction. They are both necessary
elements of the rhetorical constructional procedure which is the essence of
applying legal knowledge. We can define the application of legal knowledge,
in fact, as the bringing together of narrative strategies and information
construction. Hence, legal knowledge arises from a rhetorical and not a
logical process.

The rhetorical/negotiation factor can be used to highlight elements which
are not present in the simpler storytelling thesis. For example, it is obvious
from our interviews with barristers that the oral nature of the trial frequently
gives rise to scenes and interpretations which cannot come from the more
formal (but not necessarily non-narrative) use of paper advocacy. Observing
barristers in action, for example, gives the lie to the 'golden rule' that can be
found in most handbooks on advocacy and which was repeated by many
barristers – that one should never ask a question to which the barrister doesn't
know the answer. Though barristers all claim to be following this golden
rule, it can easily be seen in many cross-examinations that they cannot follow
it. An unexpected statement or a manner of answering a question by a witness
which might lead to a whole new line of questioning (to which the barrister
cannot know the answer) is marked by a silence of what seems several
minutes as that barrister collects his wits, tries to keep a cool head, and then
delves into the unknown. The manuals for the young barrister are explicit:
they tell him or her at this point how important it is not to so much as raise an
eyebrow in case the jury sees it! Notice that it does not have to be something
which is *said* which leaves these openings, for it can be the intangible,
non-verbalized signal which can only be seen or sensed and picked up
through oral testimony.

And our informants frequently told us that it was important to have a judge
who made some comment (either verbal or non-verbal) to show how the line
of reasoning was being taken. The last thing our barristers wanted was the
silent, static judge of the legal textbook. Without this feedback, their narratives would be cast, it seemed to them, into a void:

> You have to have people on the bench who can read barristers and
> witnesses just as barristers can read the [other] barristers and witnesses.
> They [the judges] are missing part of what is going on in court; they are
> no longer part of the process.

Legal theorists have too often ignored the element of the spoken nature of
introduced evidence, or the spoken nature of advocacy. It has, like rhetoric,
been seen to be mere flowery adornment, or the confusing of the real factors
of a case. Yet how a witness speaks, for example, is just as important as how
convincing is his story. And how a barrister reads a judge in a civil matter is
just as important as how he reads the strengths of the other litigant. There is a

large and growing body of literature on the nature of the spoken word which emphasizes the divergence between written and spoken information; it is perhaps timely that such perspectives should be brought to bear upon the current textual viewpoint of legal theorists.

One interesting aspect of spoken advocacy is that described as 'counter-attitudinal advocacy', where someone (not necessarily a barrister) advocates a position which they do not subscribe to. This is exemplified by a head of a department asking a subordinate to express the department 'line', i.e. to advocate in public beliefs which are not held privately. It has been found that this is usually an effective way to get the subordinate to change his or her own views to those which he or she publicly enunciates. To some measure, we must expect this rhetorical pressure to be a common characteristic of the barrister's life. The persuaders, in this type of situation, are actually the boss or the client who are using the subordinate or barrister as a mouthpiece (we assume that clients want barristers to believe in their case). The difference between traditional rhetorical advocacy and counter-attitudinal advocacy is, as Miller (1974: 283) suggests: 'Traditionally, the persuadee has been persuaded *by someone*; counterattitudinal advocacy rests on the assumption that if certain conditions exist, the persuadee will *persuade himself.*'

It is the fact that this counter-attitudinal advocacy occurs in *public* in *speech* where the advocate's own commitment to the process of advocacy seems to impact upon his or her own view of the subject. We see that the barrister is caught in a necessary position where his or her advocacy must be of this kind: his or her clients (both lay and solicitor) most usually determine what he or she advocates, and, no matter what his or her view of the best line of advocacy, his or her hands and tongue are tied. The 'Irish defence' is not open to him or her (see pp. 83–4). We can see here one possible reason why advocates aim at the detached role in their advocacy – why they suggest that too close a commitment to the client is not professional: speaking and arguing for a client can too easily lead to the client's own perspective been taken. Detachment from the client, we were told, allowed the best presentation of an argument. And since, it seemed to us, most barristers viewed their petty criminal clientele as guilty anyway, there seems to be a desire to find ways to circumvent this rhetorical process whereby they would find themselves changing beliefs about their clients.

There has been some work carried out into the use of language in the UK court system. For example, Atkinson and Drew's (1979) *Order in Court* uses ethnomethodological approaches to analyse the language and control issues in court. Sadly, it might be said, the too frequently found view of rhetoric as speechifying (rather than our view of it as a process of construction of argument and fact) seems to have made these researchers and others ignore the recent developments in the study of rhetoric. We believe that they would find insights from this parallel tradition which might enable them to understand more fully the courtroom drama. Certainly, rhetoric is now being seen in a more positive light than it has been since the demise of medieval education.

CONCLUSION: LEGAL KNOWLEDGE

Knowledge is usually thought of as an objective body, which we can hold and transmit and grasp. Thus we ask, 'How can we have knowledge of... ?' as though there could be a corpus of logical information which, once dis-covered, remains basically the same.[7] This view of knowledge is one which is to be found in the traditional view of law: legal knowledge is an objective, reasonably static body of information which consists of rules and principles.

This kind of concretized knowledge, it is traditionally believed, can be held in text – indeed, resides in text alone. The interpretation of this text is thus designed to extract the knowledge which is contained within; legal education gives the embryonic lawyer the necessary tools to access the corpus.

We do not agree with this view of knowledge at all. Our view is that *knowledge is a process*, not a corpus. We continually construct, handle and alter what it is that we know. We do this by means of social negotiation and verbal and non-verbal communication among the various communities we take part in. Even in everyday life, we are advocates for our views and we persuade or are persuaded by others. Knowledge, in this perspective, is not a concrete body of knowledge, but a host of conflicting beliefs and practices. So it is with legal knowledge: it is more strategic and negotiable than fixed and static. (It is processed and mediated by small groups of practitioners and judges within the rules and conventions of an established professional milieu and directed towards specific, practical goals rather than merely abstract or abstracted from definite ends in a real world.) Knowledge thus resides in *dialogue* and *dialectic*. As Ong has put it:

> The ultimate paradigm or model for dialectical relationships is not a flat contradiction of formal logic but something from the personal, human lifeworld, conversation itself, dialogue about a particular matter, in which each statement by one interlocutor needs qualification from the other interlocutor's statement in order to move towards a fuller truth. Dialogue entails a certain negativity, for there is always at least some subtle negative element in any articulated dialogic response. Even a 'yes' means 'Yes, I do agree, as you were *not* sure I did before I said yes – which is why you cast your positive question negatively, as "You do agree, *don't* you?"' This negative element is a response to the limitations of the original statement. And the response requires further qualifi-cation from the first interlocutor. There is opposition but no head-on collision, which stops dialogue. (Of course, sometimes dialogue has to be stopped, but that is another story.) (Ong, 1989: 32)

The legal process is just such a dialogic one. And like dialogue in real life (as if the court is not real life!), the various points could be continued forever. In some areas such as science, this dialogue and debate does continue for many years, but in the courtroom, timetables are brought to bear: truth is all very well, but the court system desires truth within given times. As Collins and Pinch (1982: 180) have suggested:

. . . judges and juries terminate debates according to a prescribed time-table, otherwise, one may be sure, the advocates themselves would rarely agree a verdict. In the case of science there is no agreed judge or jury or timetable.

Hence we can see why advocacy is of central importance to understanding law. A view which suggests knowledge as static and free from what we see as the essential dialogic process which keeps it alive and meaningful, is not concerned with advocacy. In our view, though, it is the advocates who are the medium for legal knowledge: they take it, process it, and act it out through the entire process of advocacy.

NOTES

1 See, for example, the increasing currency of a variety of rhetorical approaches (Perelman and Olbrechts-Tyteca, 1971; McLeod, 1985; White, 1985; Goodritch 1984; 1987; 1990).
2 It is interesting to note here how this barristerial view can be seen to have moved into the philosophy of law from the 1960s with Herbert Hart's (1961) *The Concept of Law*. Hart, before his rise to the Chair of Jurisprudence at Oxford as a repre-sentative of the now failed school of linguistic philosophy (see MacCormick, 1981), had been a barrister in London. His rather simplistic view of law was of a two-rule kind: one set of rules can be seen to have been dealing with substantive law and one kind dealing with procedure and practice. We can see that this attempt to radicalise jurisprudence was really only taking the barristerial view and formalizing it as a new view of the legal order. Incidentally, we can also see how social factors act upon the discipline of jurisprudence, Hart being made the most influential Pro-fessor of Jurisprudence (as the Oxford post is) purely because his philosophical face fitted, rather than from his past work in the discipline. As MacCormick suggests, 'Although Hart had not yet published extensively, he was a respected member of the new [ordinary language] school of post-war Oxford philosophers. Alone among them, he was a man of law as well as a man of philosophy. He was elected to the vacant Chair' (MacCormick, 1981: 2–3; see also Campbell, 1988).
3 Further discussion papers appear in Collins (1990).
4 See p. 150 for a discussion of how barristers feel a need to attempt to vary their presentation in the light of having to deliver the same old lines.
5 See Walter Fisher's (1987) attempt to provide a logic of good reason based on the narrative paradigm in his *Human Communication as Narrative*.
6 For an example of this, see Mann (1985), where he demonstrates the role of the lawyer in white-collar crime as negotiating what information will be made avail-able to the prosecuting authorities. No doubt stories are important in this task, but the major factor is the control and construction of information, not simply recon-structing reality for non-legal jurors.
7 Here is not the place to look at this historically, but we can see indications of the rise of this kind of mentality in Plato (Havelock, 1963).

9

CONCLUSION:
REALISM, LAWYERS
AND JUSTICE

INTRODUCTION

Our findings in this book can be seen to be a restatement and an extension of the legal philosophy of Jerome Frank, a leading member of the pre-Second World War, American Realist school. Of particular importance to our perspective, is that Frank was the most strident of the fact sceptics who argued against the perceived simplicity of legal facts. Frank's theory was thought out in a time prior to the rise of sociology and the sociology of science: he could not have known that the scientific edifice (and its claim to being able to prove the truthfulness of facts) would have cracked, and that many would now see science as beset by debate, squabble and opposing views of reality. It seems to us, though, that this newer view of science supports Frank's anti-positivist perspective. Since Jerome Frank is a writer on law who is frequently forgotten, or misquoted, a pencil portrait of his views is necessary to demonstrate how our views dovetail with his own.

Frank regretted the label 'realist' which was applied to himself as well as a number of other writers who stood outside the traditional view. Some of these other writers were Llewellyn, Oliphant, Hutcheson and Max Radin. Frank argued that all these who were grouped together could better be seen divided into two camps, which he described as *rule sceptics* and *fact sceptics*. The former group included Karl Llewellyn and their sceptical view of rules Frank (1963: x–xi) described as:

> The first group, of whom Llewellyn is perhaps the outstanding representative, I would call 'rule skeptics'. They aim at greater legal certainty. That is, they consider it socially desirable that lawyers should be able to predict to their clients the decisions in most lawsuits not yet commenced. They feel that, in too many instances, the layman cannot act with assurance as to how, if his acts become involved in a suit, the court will decide. As these skeptics see it, the trouble is that the formal

legal rules enunciated in court's opinions – sometimes called 'paper rules' – too often prove unreliable as guides in the prediction of decisions. The believe that they can discover, behind the 'paper rules', some 'real rules' descriptive of uniformities or regularities in actual judicial behavior, and that those 'real rules' will serve as more reliable prediction-instruments, yielding a large measure of workable predictability of the outcome of future suits. In this undertaking, the rule skeptics concentrate almost exclusively on upper-court opinions.

Put into the language of our preceding two chapters, we can see that Frank's rule sceptics are sceptical of textbook knowledge. However, they believe that by examining and looking to the practices of appeal courts, that they will be able to find the actual rules which are being applied. Frank, although he was an appeal court judge himself, was dismissive of this emphasis upon the upper courts – he described it as the *upper-court myth*. He did not agree that in order to understand the behaviour of the lower courts, the trial courts, one had to ignore them and look to the rule-making processes of the upper courts.

The second of Frank's realist groupings, in which he included himself, opposed the first group in emphasizing the lower courts and, also, suggesting both scepticism of rules and facts:

> The second group I would call 'fact skeptics'. They, too, engaging in 'rule skepticism', peer behind the 'paper rules'. Together with the rule skeptics, they have stimulated interest in factors, influencing upper-court decisions, of which, often, the opinions of those courts give no hint. But the fact skeptics go much further. Their primary interest is in the trial courts. No matter how precise or definite may be the formal legal rules, say these fact skeptics, no matter what the discoverable uniformities behind these formal rules, nevertheless it is impossible, and will always be impossible, because of the elusiveness of the facts on which decisions turn, to predict future decisions in most (not all) lawsuits, not yet begun or not yet tried. The fact skeptics, thinking that therefore the pursuit of greatly increased legal certainty is, for the most part, futile – and that its pursuit, indeed, may well work injustice – aim at increased judicial justice.

Frank's major texts, *The Courts on Trial* (1949) and *Law and the Modern Mind* (1963), were both primarily concerned with substantiating his view of the difficult nature of the fact-deciding process and how this problem with facts always impinged upon the understanding of rules. However, the basic legal myth, as Frank saw it, was that there was a need among lawyers as well as the general public (including, we might add, sociologists of law) for legal certainty, something which – as a sceptic – he could not support. He looked, in *Law and the Modern Mind*, for psychological reasons for the need for this certainty. Influenced by Freud and such thinkers he suggested that law, in part, took the role of a *father-authority* and that this was why the seeming 'pretenses' and 'professional hypocrisy' (1963: 10) was to be found. For, indeed, there was no pretence and professional hypocrisy, since lawyers and the public unconsciously failed to recognize 'the essentially plastic and mutable character of law'. We too see that there is a desire to believe in legal certainty. Our writings in *The Jurisprudence of Orthodoxy* (Leith and Ingram, 1988) emphasize that jurisprudence, in the 1960s and 1970s especially, was driven by a desire for a legal theory which emphasized safety and certainty and which derived from Herbert Hart. For example, of Hart's theory of excuses, one of us has written:

> Hart conjures up a situation where a law-abiding member of society is struck down, out of the blue, by some sort of incapacitating condition which removes the voluntary (intentional) nature of his conduct. This unfortunate pillar of society is then even more unlucky in as much as he then goes on to commit a crime. Is this a middle-class nightmare? We might be returning from the City on the 5.45 and suddenly turn from Dr Jekyll into Mr Hyde. Hart seems to be asking us to endorse a system of excuses because it means that someone who is unlucky enough to commit a crime unintentionally or involuntarily will not be punished for an action that is not the outcome of his free will, and that this is important because such knowledge is of vital importance in helping people predict and plan their lives. He is taking us here to John Betjeman country, Metroland, where we may legitimately expect to be 'Safe, in a world of trains and buttered toast. He suggests that chaos and uncertainty is the alternative to excuses' (Morison, 1988: 138).

While we thus agree that legal philosophers, as well as the public, do believe in the myth of legal certainty, we have to suggest that our barristers did not exhibit this in any developed form. We found no-one who argued that substantive legal rules were certain and sure in the manner of the 'textbook tradition'. However, there was a tendency to assume that the rules were relatively clear and everyone knew them or could find them. However, this was not clarity in the analytical, textbook manner of the legal academic. Instead, as we have suggested, there was a downplaying of the importance of substantive rules which mirrors the scepticism of Frank himself. Of course, we did not have sight of counsel's opinions, nor were we often present when advice was given to clients, so it might be that barristers do tend to present outsiders with a perspective of a more clear and concrete view of law than they tend to hold themselves (see Sir David Napley's comments on solicitors who do this in front of clients: Napley, 1983).

There was, in our interviews, a clear indication that a client's case, on paper and viewed through paper rules, was one thing but that this, when presented in court, could easily turn into a qualitatively different article. That is, barristers have a highly developed sense of the importance of the *trial court* – how a case will sound when presented orally, either in full trial or in front of a judge in, say, an interlocutory matter. As they constantly emphasized, rules

were not their main concern, but 'facts' were. Of course, as Frank suggests
and we look at below, the two are intimately connected: our barristers had to
keep an eye on the rules for potential appeals to higher courts if they felt that
moneys were available for such an appeal.

Frank's legal philosophy was trial court directed. He saw what happened in
the courtroom as central to the providing of justice. Thus his major text, *The
Courts on Trial*, looked to the trial courts to see how they affected law and
legal process. In this he emphasized the relationship of fact and rule with the
simple formula:

$$R \times F = D$$

where R stood for rule, F for fact and D for decision:

> ... according to the conventional theory, a decision is a product of an R
> and an F. If, as to any lawsuit, you know the R and the F, you should,
> then, know what the D will be.
>
> In a simple, stable society, most of the Rs are moderately well
> known. ... In our society, however, with the rapid changes brought
> about by modern life, many of the Rs have become unstable. Accord-
> ingly, in our times, legal uncertainty – uncertainty about future de-
> cisions and therefore about legal rights – is generally ascribed to the
> indefiniteness of the Rs. The increasing multiplicity of the rules, the
> conflicts between rules, and the flexibility of some of the rules, have
> arrested the attention of most legal thinkers. Those thinkers, perceiving
> the absence of rigidity in some rules, have assumed that the certainty or
> uncertainty of the Ds, in the $R \times F = D$ equation, stems principally
> from the certainty or uncertainty of the Rs (Frank, 1949b: 15).

Opposing this rule-boundness, Frank suggested that the real problem
about rule uncertainty actually arises from the F component of the equation.
Much of this comes, for example, from the difficulty that witnesses have in
remembering and accurately describing what they saw. Only recently has the
judicial system in the UK arrived at the same position as Frank in this matter,
and accepted that finding guilt from identification alone is often suspect. He
even posited that pre-trial consideration of 'facts' is a guessing process:

> ... usually, when men 'go to law', the facts are not admitted, and the
> testimony is oral and in conflict. ... It cannot be known in advance
> which cases will be 'contested'. To predict a decision in a suit not yet
> begun, about a dispute which has not yet occurred, requires, then, the
> most extensive guessing. For whenever there is a question of the
> credibility of witnesses – of the believability, the reliability, of their
> testimony – then, unavoidably, the trial judge or jury must make a
> guess about the facts. The lawyer, accordingly, must make a guess
> about those guesses. The uncertainty of many 'legal rights' corresponds
> to the correctness or incorrectness of such lawyer-guesses (Frank,
> 1963b: 16).

Certainly, in our interviews with barristers, we received a clear impression that before they go into court there was a definite tendency towards weighing up and guessing the likely strengths and weaknesses of their clients and opponent's arguments, as well as anticipating the particular nature of the judge and jury. This means that barristers have to be prepared to fight one case in several different ways. The court, as Frank suggested, was not a place to display the facts of a case, but to argue over them.

Just as our barristers were critical of the legal education which they had received at law schools as being too impractical and too divorced from their real activities, Frank suggested some alterations in the emphasis of legal education (see, in particular, Frank, 1949: ch. 16):

> I will be told – I have been told – that the law schools at most have but three short years to train lawyers, and that these years are already so crowded that there is no time to spend on the sort of first-hand material to which I am referring. I am not at all impressed by such talk. For in most university law schools the major part of the three years is spent in teaching a relatively simple technique – that of analyzing upper court opinions, 'distinquishing cases', constructing, modifying or critizing legal doctrines. Three years is much too long for that job. Intelligent men can learn that dialectical technique in about six months. . . . But in law schools, much of the three years is squandered, by bored students, in applying that technique over and over again – and never with reference to a live client or a real law suit . . . (Frank, 1949: 237).

Unfortunately, Frank's perspective has not got fully through to law schools. Clinical legal education (i.e. that dealing with 'real' problems) is still seen to be of much lesser import than the poring over substantive rules of law. At the same time when it seeks to do more than simply prepare students for practice, legal education fails to develop a fully dimensional view of its subject. For example, any changes in the legal curriculum which would allow legal education to keep pace with the speed of change in today's world (and the rapidly evolving role of the lawyer within it) seem as far away as ever. Indeed, in their introduction to *Law, Society and Change*, Livingstone and Morison (1990: 3) argue that:

> . . . at present legal education is not reponding adequately to this challenge. Currently too much of it remains backward-looking and excessively abstract. Emphasis continues to be placed, both in textbooks and courses on comprehending long established principles (and thus perhaps impliedly the virtues of stability). . . . Too many academics seem to regard an understanding of the contemporary world as an unwelcome hindrance to grasping legal rules and principles. . . . Many law students have long found courses which seek to drain their studies of any relation to the events in the world in which they live less than exciting. In a world that is constantly changing the failure to

develop a legal culture that stresses dealing with change rather than simply reproducing the past may be dangerous as well.

Frank's contemporary and fellow realist, the US jurist Felix Cohen (1935: 844), wrote:

> ... if the understanding of any decision involves us necessarily in prophecy (and thus in history), then the notion of law as something that exists completely and systematically at any given time is false. Law is a social process, a complex of human activities, and an adequate legal science must deal with human activity, with cause and effect, with the past and the future.

Currently, the education that many lawyers receive fails on two counts: it is neither an adequate preparation for practice nor an education in how society actually works.

An interesting part of Frank's writings deals with the tactics and strategies which lawyers use in their day-to-day adversarial role, which rather than directed at finding the truth, are too often directed at hiding the same. We were given several examples of these tactics as well as denials that they were ever used. However, it is clear that cross-examination by barristers is not made in the spirit of letting everything be told in court, and the truth will out. Our example of the cross-examination of the doctor illustrates our point (see p. 146). Evidence (that is information being brought to the attention of the court) should be tightly controlled. As Evans (1985: 135) puts it:

> That final question [given as an example of asking one too many questions] was dangerous. . . . It relinquished control of the witness and gave him full rein, effectively, to say whatever he wanted to say. Until then, you notice, the questions had complied beautifully with the 'one line of transcript' rule. They had been short and simple and had kept tight control over where the evidence was going. But suddenly all those commendable objectives were abandoned. The sergeant [as witness] was offered the chance, if he wanted to, of saying whatever he wanted to say.

All told, the difficulties in ascertaining facts, the changing nature of rules, and the problems with lawyers' tactics, made Frank aware of the fact that innocents were being sent to the electric chair and to long-term imprisonment. In *Not Guilty* (1957), Frank and Frank, gave a number of cases of such innocence and suggested that the court system had to come to terms with its potential for failure. Unfortunately, they felt that the power of the legal myth of certainty and logicity, would act against the necessity of making the court system realize that it could be guilty of finding innocence to be guilt. Note that Frank saw these judicial mistakes being made as a *necessary* outcome of the trial process, not simply that something had gone wrong with the court system. Writing at this time in the UK where persons found guilty of terrorist offences, later accepted as innocent, are being released after long sentences have been served, Frank's emphasis on the need for an understanding of the nature of myth and reality in criminal justice is surely just as important now as it was in the 1930s and 1940s when he did his writing and his judging.

The radicalism of Frank, which we can only now see beginning to re-emerge in various ways, never took particularly well in the soil of British jurisprudence. Generally, the realists were badly treated in the UK, their views being described as fashionably tied to the times in which it was carried out: 'jurisprudence for the jazz age'. British jurisprudence especially, was unkind to Frank and his kind of thinker, demonstrating its inability to free itself from the ideological constraints of a governing class. British jurisprudence has thus linked itself too closely with the textbook tradition in law, trying to find underlying explanations and moral justifications for law as it is (or rather, law as it has been seen to be). It has kept its hands clean by ignoring the murky reality of legal process.

EXTENDING FACT SCEPTICISM TO INFORMATION SCEPTICISM

The evidence which we presented in Part II and the analysis of that which we presented in the earlier chapters in Part III all, we argue, substantiate the general legal theory of Jerome Frank. Yet there are differences in emphasis. Frank was primarily concerned about courtroom behaviour and the difficulty of the evidential task there. Our work, more concerned with the role of barristers, emphasizes a wider aspect – that of the pre-trial construction of legal information, as well as its presentation to judge and jury.

It might almost be that, in extending Frank's two categories of scepticism with a third, we would describe our own views as *information sceptical* by which we include rules, facts and their mix and match together in legal information. Certainly, we could not argue that legal information is any more concrete than the facts and paper rules which Frank was concerned with.

But our research has only looked, centrally anyway, to one actor in the construction of legal information, the barrister. There are others. The solicitor, as we have suggested, has a strong means of control over the barrister in the construction and presentation of legal information. And the lay client, who we have hardly mentioned, must have his or her input into the information-producing system. If Frank was correct about the nature of the court system, and we are correct about the barristerial aspect, then we might surely expect that there are traditional myths about the lay client and the solicitor which should be examined in legal theory.

The kinds of cases which Frank was concerned with were relatively major criminal trials. We might extend this view by looking to the nature of the majority of the court cases which are held in the UK. These are not major trials; indeed, most of them – being for debts brought by electricity boards, local goverment, traffic offences, etc. – are not even fought. The clients of the barristers and solicitors in these sorts of cases show even more the mismatch between official legal information and actual legal information.

Take the driver charged with careless driving who feels that he should fight the case. He visits a solicitor who suggests that, if he fights and is found guilty, he might well receive a £300 fine by a judge determined to punish 'wasting the court's time'. But, if he accepts guilt, the fine might be £30. To the typical driver, accepting guilt is economically safer than pleading not guilty. There is no indication from either the solicitor or the lay client's reasoning that legal rules or facts are being considered here – what is being taken into account is that the legal process can be viewed as much as a psuedo-random number generator (where the chances of being found guilty are more than being found not guilty?) as a search for truth and justice. Yet, the official legal information (stamped onto the driver's licence) will suggest that a guilty plea indicates acceptance of guilt, rather than acceptance of the reality of court justice.

Frank believed, to an extent, that training and judicial goodwill would overcome many of the problems of presenting facts. Yet, it seems to us that there will always be problems in the construction of legal information which mitigate against any group of actors in the system being able to improve things so substantially that a real difference will be made. Part of this comes from the very nature of legal information as a two-dimensional artefact: the court does not know, in any real sense, the person or persons before it and can only act upon this limited two-dimensionality. For a fuller three-dimensional view, we would need to know witnesses, defendants and litigants personally (as was required in ancient Athens) so that we could match their testimony against our wider knowledge of their normal, everyday behaviours. We would also need to have unlimited time to refine and test our legal information and its construction. We do not have this, of course. Yet, the court is a place where the two dimensions of the witness's character which are on show, are often assumed to be three dimensions: the judge presumes that he or she is being presented with 'truth'. Henry Cecil, an English county court judge, had written of this problem of judges' comments on the unfortunates who appear before them:

> Now the judge may *think* that the witness, whose evidence he is rejecting, *was* deliberately intending to mislead him, but it isn't necessary for the purpose of the case for him to say so. He need only say that, having regard to the probabilities, he prefers the evidence of the other witness. But sometimes he will add – not very truthfully – some words of comfort as I have mentioned above. If he does this, he does it because he knows that it is always possible that his view is mistaken, however strongly he may have formed it. Why therefore blacken the witness's character unnecessarily? Most losing parties go away from the court slightly happier if they merely lose the case without also being called unmitigated liars (Cecil, 1970: 54).

The problem is that there is a tendency for the judge to believe that the legal information he was presented with was 'fact'. Why else could he feel the need to undermine and destroy the character of a litigant? This is not a minor problem: those who attend courts do not necessarily have pleasant experiences as their personalities are transformed from three dimensions to two.

Improvements in judicial behaviour are, naturally, to be sought. In our interviews with barristers, we were sometimes told that it really didn't make much difference who the advocacy was before, since the barristers felt that most judges did their best. Often, however, the less self-conscious barristers would regale us with stories of incompetent and pompous judges, stories which we were told were part of the everyday talk of the barristers' robing room and the bar messes – get togethers with much drinking and amusement where the doors are firmly closed on the outside world.

Such events do not appear in the textbooks of law, nor the substantive law courses in law schools. Yet, this (and much more besides) is all information which is part of the barrister's knowledge, and since being about the practice of law and being important for the barrister's own tactics and strategies, we must describe it as legal information. However, if we do accept it as this, it means the concept of legal information as the more traditional and limited one of evidence, witness statement, charge sheet, etc., must be extended by the sceptical viewpoint.

IS IT ALL THE FAULT OF THE LAWYERS?

The reader of this book might come away from it with a less than flattering view of all lawyers – barristers, solicitors and judges – especially if they hold the mythical view of the legal process as the never-ending striving after truth and justice. They might well have sympathy with the pioneers of the colonizing Dutch East Indies Company who, when contacting home for supplies and manpower, wrote 'Don't send lawyers'.

In the popular tradition of the USA in particular, the lawyer is seen as parasitical upon the litigant. It is the general view that lawyers are the problem with the law, rather than the law itself – if only, this viewpoint suggests, we could get rid of the lawyers, then the law would be made much clearer and easier to apply and understand. From the first days of Independence, this criticism of lawyers has been a remarkably consistent aspect of US thinking (see e.g. Cooke, 1981, for a discussion of the codification movement).

Some have argued that the situation could become the same in the UK, as lawyers become seen less and less as the solid basis for a well-ordered society, and become perceived as greedy, incompetent and/or whatnot. However, just as in the USA the legal profession has been criticized for hijacking and confusing the law, so it has been in the UK. Indeed, Jeremy Bentham's vitriolic attack upon common lawyers and the langauge of law gave impetus to the US codifiers. And readers of Charles Dickens will be well aware of his views on the legal profession. Even the political and legislative pressures upon the Bar (extant as we write) to change its behaviour and give up its monopoly position on certain rights of audience can be seen to be driven by a feeling that lawyers are having it too much their own way.

The question at the heart of this is, could we return to the Athenian ideal where we did (as much as possible) without lawyers and every man defended himself against charges and prosecuted others? That is, can law become clear enough and non-technical enough to be returned to the common person? It seems unlikely to us that this can occur. Studies of informal justice in action (see e.g. Henry, 1983) do not lead us to believe that it is returning to an idyllic legal system of the past. In fact, Henry has argued that informal justice of the type found in workplace courts is actually a serious contaminant of state law, which mitigates against successful changes in state law. And codification, as it exists in Continental Europe, does not seem to give benefits to the non-lawyer which its most enthusiastic proponents might claim.

Part of the problem seems to be that those who advocate simpler justice and codification of law, are just as entranced by the upper-court myth as any other. They forget that anyone presenting a case is taking part in a debate – an oral argument, where skills of advocacy are vital – where only one small part is formally and substantially legal. A whole host of other factors have to be taken into account – those factors which we have described as legal information and which require legal knowledge to apply. Thus, while many tribunal formats are brought in to allow non-legal presentation with simpler rules of procedure, they end up by being just as procedurally oriented as the full courts. What the tribunals actually mean by having informal rules of procedure is that each tribunal has set up its own rules of procedure which the litigant has, somehow, to discover in order to allow his or her case best to be presented.

Skills of advocacy are not spread uniformly throughout the population. Some would be able to argue their case effectively in an informal legal situation, but many others would not. Not only would they fail on the advocacy element, but they would probably fail on the strategic, knowledge-based elements of deciding how to present their case.

JUSTICE

There are two major schools in jurisprudence who take different, but not mutually exclusive, views of how best justice can be achieved. They are the *natural law* and the *positive law* schools. The first posits general and universal ideals and principles to which judges and lawyers should accord in order to ensure that justice is found; the second posits that by the strict following through of legal rules using a detached neo-scientific and logical perspective on law, justice is best reached by treating everyone according to the same rules. That these two views are not actually contradictory can be seen by Ronald Dworkin's (1986) attempt to have his cake and eat it, by conjoining the two and suggesting a rule-based approach with 'principles'.

It seems to us, though, that there could potentially be 'natural laws' if we mean general principles such as 'do not kill', 'don't steal', etc., but it is hard to see how a judge or barrister could operate on these: what is he, or she, to do with a soldier who kills, or a corporation which uses brutal commercial power to take over and asset strip a small family firm? On the other hand, we have already argued against the neo-scientific view of 'law as logic' which is held by the positivists. Thus, for our advocates, there is a problem in that legal philosophy doesn't seem to offer them a practical route to ensuring justice. So, what can the everyday barrister do about this?

In fact, our interviews did not become too involved in this aspect of the barrister's world, due to lack of time. What views we did get on justice, were offered as part of answers to other questions. For example, asking Scottish advocates what they thought of the Northern Ireland and English practice of plea-bargaining with the judge, to a man and woman, they were vehemently opposed to it. The Scottish advocates expressed real horror that such a practice could go on. We were stridently told that it was contrary to all principles of justice that a person's case was not heard fully in open court. Yet, in the other jurisdictions, it was held that justice might be better attained by proper and considered use of this plea-bargaining procedure.

Generally (but this is open to further study), we found that our barristers had a view that justice related to 'fairness', and the ability for the facts of a litigant or defendant's case to be heard and to be fully stated. It seemed obvious to them that not all who come before the court are accorded this fairness, but that within the constraints under which they worked, they tried their best to achieve this for their clients. However, as we have already stated, this sense of fairness for the client did not go so far as telling them of their solicitor's mistakes (see p. 51). And neither do the manuals for the barrister tell him or her to let the client or witness tell all.

CONCLUSION

We have attempted to take the study of law away from the purely textual and to orient it in a more oral and strategic line. This has given us a view of the relationship of textual law, legal information and the importance of rhetoric which are missing from other legal theories. Further, we feel that our interviews have lent credence to the writings of Jerome Frank, excepting that we offer a further level of scepticism which is marked by the pre-trial construction of legal information.

We cannot claim that our views or our researches are exhaustive. Far from it. But by taking the step which has been suggested by Abel, we feel that we are further legitimating the social nature of law. As Abel (1988: 3) wrote:

> One reason for writing [*The Legal Profession in England and Wales*] is my hope that its description of the social organization of the legal profession will enable and stimulate others to undertake the more difficult task of studying the content and form of their daily work activities.

In fact, we were not stimulated by Abel's interests – although we agree that they are important – rather, we were stimulated by the fact that so much was missing from the traditional sociological approaches to law and lawyers. We knew of the work which was being carried out in the sociology of knowledge, the study of the nature of information, and became aware of the study of rhetoric during our researches and felt that law as an area of study was unacquainted with these striking and important new perspectives. As we have already said, our colleagues from Queen's University who had part-time barristerial practices gave us many insights and perspective which we developed in our interviews and which we felt were being omitted from the study of law as a practical, rich and complex activity.

There are many other aspects which can be developed from our own work. Some are obvious and relatively traditional – extending our interviewing to solicitors and to clients and to judges. By a concentration upon the trial court process, we should have expected to find radically different views of law from that which have been obtained in the study of upper courts. And, of course, understanding the lower courts should make us appreciate more those studies of the upper courts which are epitomized by Paterson's *The Law Lords*. There are, of course, a large number of empirical research results into various aspects of the court process which have – as we have suggested – been partitioned off from substantive law by legal academics. Our work on legal information and advocacy should help to bring these more centre stage than they have previously been.

There are, though, areas which are not traditionally studied in law or the sociology of law which we feel can be seen as extensions of our present work. First and primary is a return to the study of forensic advocacy as an important element of the legal process, and how rhetoric links with oratory and poetics (White, 1985).

Second is the socio-historical study of law as advocacy, rather than law as the interpretation of texts. This is important because the oral, dialectic nature of law has seemingly been forgotten – histories of law emphasize the court structure and the written texts, never the way that law has been a necessary and consistent strand of oral or spoken tradition. This is not to say that the arrival of text (in tablet, manuscript and print forms) has not transformed the practice of law throughout these various stages, for it has, but that historians of law have too readily assumed that the textual interpretation of law in a tablet or manuscript culture is identical to that of a print culture. This is not so, and we cannot cast back our present insights on legal analysis and assume that the Dead Sea Scrolls are just another form of Local Government (Dog Control) Act. And we do not simply pass facts back and forth between each other in a never-changing, timeless environment. Rather, we debate and mould the very information which gives reality to our world. Thus barristers help mould and have moulded their legal information, and from this is constructed the barrister's world.

REFERENCES

Abel, R. L. (1988). *The Legal Profession in England and Wales.* Oxford: Blackwell.

Abel-Smith, B. and Stevens, R. (1967). *Lawyers and the Courts: A Sociological Study of the English Legal System 1750–1965.* London: Heinemann Educational.

Atkinson, J. M. and Drew, P. (1979). *Order in Court: The Organisation of Verbal Interaction in Judicial Settings.* London: Macmillan.

Austin, J. (1885). *Lectures in Jurisprudence,* London: John Murray.

Axelrod, R. (1984). *The Evolution of Co-Operation,* New York: Basic Books.

Baker, J. H. (1981) The English legal profession 1450–1550. In W. Prest (Ed.), *Lawyers in Early Modern Europe and America.* London: Croom Helm, pp. 16–41.

Baldwin, J. and McConville, M. (1981). *Courts, Prosecution and Conviction.* Oxford: Clarendon Press.

Bennett, W. L. and Feldman, M. S. (1981). *Reconstructing Reality in the Courtroom.* London: Tavistock.

Berger, P. L. and Kellner, H. (1981). *Sociology Reinterpreted: An Essay on Method and Vocation.* New York: Anchor Press/Doubleday.

Birkenhead, First Earl of (1926). *Famous Trials of History.* London: Hutchinson.

Birkett, Lord (1961). *Six Great Advocates.* Harmondsworth: Penguin.

Blake, S. (1989). *A Practical Approach to Legal Advice and Drafting,* 3rd edn. London: Blackstone.

Bonner, R. J. (1927). *Lawyers and Litigants in Ancient Athens: The Genesis of the Legal Profession.* Chicago, Ill.: University of Chicago Press.

Bonner, R. J. (1979). *Evidence in Athenian Courts.* New York: Arno Press.

Campbell, C. M. (1976). Lawyers and their public. In D. MacCormick (Ed.), *Lawyers in Their Social Setting.* Edinburgh: W. Green, pp. 195–214.

Campbell, C. M. (1988). The career of the concept. In P. Leith and P. Ingram (Eds), *The Jurisprudence of Orthodoxy: Queen's University Essays on H. L. A. Hart.* London: Routledge.

Cecil, H. (1970). *The English Judge.* London: Stevens.

Cohen, F. (1935). Transcendental nonsense and the functional approach. *Columbia Law Review,* **35**, 809–849.

Cohen, M. R. and Nagel, E. (1934). *An Introduction to Logic and Scientific Method.* London: Routledge and Kegan Paul.

Collins, H. M. (1990). *Artificial Experts: Social Knowledge and Intelligent Machines.* Cambridge, Mass.: MIT Press.

Collins, H. M. and Pinch T. J. (1982). *Frames of Meaning: The Social Construction of Extraordinary Science*. London: Routledge and Kegan Paul.

Cooke, C. M. (1981). *The American Codification Movement: A Study of Antebellum Legal Reform*. Westport, Conn.: Greenwood Press.

Cotterrell, R. (1989). *The Politics of Jurisprudence: A Critical Introduction to Legal Philosophy*. London: Butterworth.

Council of Legal Education (1989). *Advocacy and Interpersonal Skills*. London: Blackstone.

Du Cann, R. (1980). *The Art of the Advocate*. Harmondsworth: Penguin.

Dworkin, R. (1986). *Law's Empire*. London: Fontana.

Elster, J. (1989). *Solomonic Judgements: Studies in the Limitations of Rationality*. Cambridge: Cambridge University Press.

Erasmus, D. (1530). *De Civilitate Morum Puerlium* (On civility in children).

Evans, K. (1985). *Advocacy at the Bar: A Beginner's Guide*. London: Blackstone.

Feyerabend, P. K. (1978). *Against Method*. London: Verso.

Fish, S. (1989). *Doing What Comes Naturally*. Oxford: Oxford University Press.

Fisher, R. and Ury, W. (1983). *Getting to Yes: Negotiating Agreement Without Giving In*. London: Hutchinson.

Fisher, W. R. (1987). *Human Communication as Narration: Toward a Philosophy of Reason, Value and Action*. Columbia: University of South Carolina Press.

Fleck, L. (1979). *Genesis and Development of a Scientific Fact*. Chicago, Ill.: University of Chicago Press.

Flood, J. (1983). *Barristers' Clerks: The Law's Middlemen*. Manchester: Manchester University Press.

Foucault, M. (1976). *The Birth of the Clinic*. London: Tavistock.

Frank, J. (1949). *The Courts on Trial*. New York: Princeton University Press.

Frank, J. (1963). *Law and the Modern Mind*. Preface to sixth printing. Gloucester, Mass.: Anchor Books.

Frank, J. and Frank, B. (1957). *Not Guilty*. New York: Doubleday.

Galanter, M. (1974). Why the 'haves' come out ahead: Speculation on the limits of legal change. *Law and Society Review*, **9**, 95–114.

Gellner, E. (1985). *Relativism and the Social Sciences*. Cambridge: Cambridge University Press.

Genn, H. (1987). *Hard Bargaining: Out of Court Settlement in Personal Injury Actions*. Oxford: Clarendon Press.

Goffman, E. (1952). On cooling the mark out. *Journal of Personality and Social Psychology*, **25**, 451–63.

Goodritch, P. (1984). Rhetoric as jurisprudence: An introduction to the politics of legal language. *Oxford Journal of Legal Studies*, **4**, 88–122.

Goodritch, P. (1987). *Legal Discourse: Studies in Linguistics, Rhetoric and Legal Analysis*. London: Macmillan.

Goodritch, P. (1990). *Languages of Law: From Logics of Memory to Nomadic Masks*. London: Weidenfeld and Nicolson.

Gould, S. J. (1990). *Wonderful Life: The Burgess Shale and the Nature of History*. London: Hutchinson Rodins.

Haack, S. (1978). *Philosophy of Logics*. Cambridge: Cambridge University Press.

Hadas, M. (1954). *Ancilla to Classical Learning*. New York: Columbia University Press.

Hans, V. (1986). *Judging the Jury*. New York: Plenum Press.

Hart, H. L. A. (1961). *The Concept of Law*. Oxford: Clarendon Press.

Hastie, R., Penrold, S. D. and Pennington, N. (1983). *Inside the Jury*. Cambridge, Mass.: Harvard University Press.

Havelock, E. A. (1963). *Preface to Plato*. Cambridge, Mass.: Belknap Press.

Hazell, R. (Ed.) (1978). *The Bar on Trial*. London: Quartet Books.

Healy, M. (1939). *The Old Munster Circuit*. London: Michael Joseph.

Henry, S. (1983). *Private Justice: Towards Integrated Theorising in the Sociology of Law*. London: Routledge and Kegan Paul.

Huizinga, J. (1924). *The Waning of the Middle Ages*. London: Arnold.

Hutcheson, J. C. (1929). The judgement intuitive: The function of the hunch in judicial decisions. *Cornell Law Quarterly*, **14**, 274.

Hyam, M. (1990). *Advocacy Skills*. London: Blackstone.

Jackson, B. S. (1988). *Law, Fact and Narrative Coherence*. Roby: Deborah Charles Publications.

Johnston, V. and Shapland, J. (1990). *Developing Vocational Legal Training for the Bar*. Sheffield: Faculty of Law, University of Sheffield.

Kelsen, H. (1967). *The Pure Theory of Law* (translated by M. Knight). Berkeley: University of California Press.

Kennedy, G. (1963). *The Art of Persuasion in Greece*. Princeton, N.J.: Princeton University Press.

Kirk, G. (1976). *Homer and the Oral Tradition*. Cambridge: Cambridge University Press.

Kline, M. (1980). *Mathematics: The Loss of Certainty*. New York: Oxford University Press.

Kuhn, T. S. (1962). *The Structure of Scientific Revolutions*. Chicago, Ill.: University of Chicago Press.

Lakatos, I. (1976). *Proofs and Refutations: The Logic of Mathematical Discovery*. Cambridge: Cambridge University Press.

Lanham, R. (1976). *The Motives of Eloquence: Literary Rhetoric in the Renaissance*. New Haven, Conn.: Yale University Press.

Latham, D. (1990). The modern bar. In J. Grosvenor (Ed.), *The Ivanhoe/Blackstone Guide to the Legal Profession 1990*. Oxford: Ivanhoe Press, pp. 11–14.

Leith, P. (1989). Review of B. S. Jackson's, *Law, Fact and Narrative Coherence*. *Northern Ireland Legal Quarterly*, **40** (4).

Leith, P. (1990). *Formalism in AI and Computer Science*. Chichester: Ellis Horwood.

Leith, P. (1991). *The Computerised Lawyer*. London: Springer-Verlag.

Leith, P. and Ingram, P. (Eds) (1988). *The Jurisprudence of Orthodoxy: Queen's University Essays on H. L. A. Hart*. London: Routledge.

Livingstone, S. (1988). Of the core and penumbra: H. L. A. Hart & American Realism. In P. Leith and P. Ingram (Eds), *The Jurisprudence of Orthodoxy: Queen's University Essays on H. L. A. Hart*. London: Routledge.

Livingstone, S. and Morison, J. (Eds) (1990). *Law, Society and Change*. Aldershot: Darmouth.

Lloyd, M. (1986). *Legal Databases in Europe: User Attitudes and Supplier Strategies*. Amsterdam: North-Holland.

Luban, D. (1985). Bargaining and compromise: Recent work in negotiation and informal justice. *Philosophy and Public Affairs*, **14**, 397–416.

MacCormick, D. N. (1978). *Legal Theory and Legal Reasoning*. Oxford: Clarendon Press.

MacCormick, D. N. (1981). *H. L. A. Hart*. London: Edward Arnold.

Mackie, K. J. (1989). *Lawyers in Business and The Law Business*. London: Macmillan.

McLeod, B. (1985). Rules and rhetoric. *Osgoode Hall Law Journal*, **23**, 305–29.

Madnick, S. E. and Donovan, J. J. (1974). *Operating Systems*. Tokyo: McGraw-Hill/Kogakusha.

Mann, K. (1985). *Defending White Collar Crime: A Portrait of Attorneys at Work*. New Haven, Conn.: Yale University Press.

Marjoribanks, E. R. (1932). *The Life of Lord Carson*. London: Victor Gollancz.

Marx, K. (1970). *A Contribution to the Critique of Political Economy*. Moscow: Progress Publishers.

Massery, L. (1978). *Psychology and Persuasion in the Courtroom*. Washington and Reno, Nev.: Association of Trial Lawyers of America.

Megarry, R. (1962). *Lawyer and Litigant in England*. London: Stevens.

Merton, R. K. (1968). *Social Theory and Social Structure*. London: Collier and Macmillan.

Miller, G. R. (1974). Toward a rhetoric of counterattitudinal advocacy. In W. R. Fisher (Ed.), *Rhetoric: A Tradition in Transition*. Michigan: Michigan State University Press, pp. 279–99.

Morison, J. (1988). Hart's excuses: Problems with a compromise theory of punishment. In P. Leith and P. Ingram (Eds), *The Jurisprudence of Orthodoxy: Queen's University Essays on H. L. A. Hart*. London: Routledge, pp. 117–46.

Morley, I. (1986). Negotiating and bargaining. In O. Hargie (Ed.), *A Handbook of Communication Skill*. London: Croom Helm.

Murdoch, A. (1981). The advocates, the law and the nation in early modern Scotland. In W. Prest (Ed.), *Lawyers in Early Modern Europe and America*. London: Croom Helm.

Napley, D. (1983). *The Technique of Persuasion*. London: Sweet and Maxwell.

Ong, W. J. (1958). *Ramus, Method, and the Decay of Dialogue: From the Art of Discourse to the Art of Reason*. Harvard, Mass.: Harvard University Press.

Ong, W. J. (1977). *Interfaces of the Word: Studies in the Evolution of Consciousness and Culture*. Ithaca, N.Y.: Cornell University Press.

Ong, W. J. (1981). *The Presence of the Word: Some Prolegomena for Cultural and Religious History*. Minneapolis: University of Minnesota Press.

Ong, W. J. (1989). *Fighting for Life: Contest, Sexuality and Consciousness*. Amherst, Mass.: University of Massachusetts Press.

Parris, J. (1961). *Under My Wig*. London: Arthur Barker.

Parry, M. (1971). *The Making of Homeric Verse: The Collected Essays of Milman Parry*. Oxford: Clarendon Press.

Paterson, A. (1982). *The Law Lords*. London: Macmillan.

Perelman, Ch. and Olbrechts-Tyteca, L. (1971). *The New Rhetoric*. Notre Dame, Ind.: University of Notre Dame Press.

Phillips, D. L. (1977). *Wittgenstein and Scientific Knowledge: A Sociological Perspective*. London: Macmillan.

P'ng, I. (1983). Strategic behaviours in suit, settlement and trial. *Bell Journal of Economics*, **14**, 539–50.

Posner, R. (1988). *Law and Literature: A Misunderstood Relation*. Cambridge, Mass.: Harvard University Press.

Pound, R. (1910). Law in books and law in action. *American Law Review*, **44**, 12–36.

Quintilian, (1921). *Institutes of Oratory* (translated by H. E. Butler). London: Loeb Classical Library.

Raiffa, A. (1982). *The Art and Science of Negotiation*. Cambridge, Mass.: Harvard University Press.

Reisman, D. (1951). Toward an anthropological science of law and the legal profession. *American Journal of Sociology*, **57**, 121.

Rose, W. (1990). *Pleadings without Tears: A Guide to Legal Drafting*. London: Blackstone.

Rosenthal, D. (1974). *Lawyer and Client: Who's in Charge?* New York: Russell Sage.

Ross, H. (1970). *Settled Out of Court: The Social Process of Insurance Claims Adjustment*. Chicago, Ill.: Aldine.

Sanders, A., Bridges, L., Mulvaney, A. and Crozier, G. (1989). *Advice and Assistance at Police Stations and the 24 Hour Duty Solicitors Scheme*. London: The Lord Chancellor's Department.

Semple Piggot, M. and Ramsay, R. (1990). The selection of law courses. In J. Grosvenor (Ed.), *The Ivanhoe/Blackstone Guide to the Legal Profession in 1990*. Oxford: Ivanhoe Press, pp. 29–38.

Sherr, A. (1986). Lawyers and clients: The first meeting. *Modern Law Review*, **49**, 323–57.

Shklar, J. (1986). *Legalism: Law, Morals and Political Trials*. Cambridge, Mass.: Harvard University Press.

Siemer, D. (1984). *Tangible Evidence: How to Use Exhibits at Trial*. San Diego, Calif.: Harcourt Brace Jovanovich.

Stone, I. F. (1988). *The Trial of Socrates*. Boston, Mass.: Little, Brown and Co.

Stone, M. (1988). *Cross-examination in Criminal Trials*. London: Butterworth.

Stryker, L. (1954). *The Art of Advocacy*. Washington: Zenger.

Sugarman, D. (1986). The making of the textbook tradition. In W. Twining (Ed.), *Legal Theory and Common Law*. Oxford: Basil Blackwell, pp. 34–63.

Tacitus, C. (1970). A dialogue on oratory in *Tacitus, Vol. I*. Cambridge, Mass.: Harvard University Press, pp. 239–40.

Tammelo, I. (1969). *Outlines of Modern Legal Logic*. Weisbaden: Franz Steiner-Verlag.

Turner, R. (1974). *Ethnomethodology*. Harmondsworth: Penguin.

Vickers, B. (1988). *In Defence of Rhetoric*. Oxford: Clarendon Press.

Walter, B. (1988). *The Jury Summation as Speech Genre: An Ethnographic Study of What It Means to Those Who Use It*. Amsterdam: John Benjamins.

White, J. B. (1985). *Heracles' Bow: Essays on Rhetoric and Poetics of the Law*. Madison: University of Wisconsin.

Wilson, A. (1990). *Legal Studies*. **10**, 2, 2–227.

Wilson, F. P. (1941). Shakespeare and the diction of common life. In *Proceedings of the British Academy*, **27**, 167–97.

Wilson, N. (1965). *The Sociology of a Profession: The Faculty of Advocates*. Unpublished PhD thesis, Edinburgh University.

Woodward, B. and Armstrong, S. (1981). *The Brethren: Inside the Supreme Court*. New York: Avon Books.

Zander, M. (1968). *Lawyers and the Public Interest*. London: Weidenfeld and Nicolson.

Zander, M. (1978). *Legal Services for the Community*. London: Temple Smith.

INDEX